"Plate thinks with and not only about Benjamin, constellating a scintillating aesthetics of the senses, of their material public and their 'working art.' With its kabbalistic oscillation of 'dispersion' and 'assemblage', Benjamin's concept of allegory is itself allegorized by Plate. The map of literary, poststructructuralist and feminist theories of language is itself worth the cost of the book, which will be (darkly) illumining not just for readers of Benjamin but for all who read religion and its creations bodily."

—Catherine Keller, Professor of Constructive Theology, Drew University and author of *Face of the Deep: A Theology of Becoming*

"Though there is a substantial body of criticism that would disagree, Professor Plate's engaging book reminds us that Benjamin did not so much abandon aesthetics, or simply relegate it to authoritarian politics, but redeemed it with the help of its Greek sources in perception and sensation. Plate persuasively argues that, like Messianic religion, which Benjamin translated into its material (and even revolutionary) social bases, the aesthetic returns in Benjamin's writing to the realm of the senses, where it reveals its connection to both religious practice and a utopian sensus communis."

—Vincent P. Pecora, University of California, Los Angeles

D0217707

Some Recent Titles from the *Perspectives on Gender* Series

Series Editor: Myra Marx Ferree, University of Wisconsin, Madison

Black Feminist Thought: Knowledge, Consciousness, and the Politics of Empowerment
Patricia Hill Collins

Feminisms and the Women's Movement: Dynamics of Change in Social Movement Ideology and Activism
Barbara Ryan

Black Women and White Women in the Professions: Analysis of Job Segregation by Race and Gender, 1960-1980
Natalie J. Sokoloff

Gender Consciousness and Politics
Sue Tolleson Rinehart

Mothering: Ideology, Experience, and Agency
Evelyn Nakano Glenn, Grace Chang, and Linda Rennie Forcey, Editors

For Richer, For Poorer: Mothers Confront Divorce
Demie Kurz

Integrative Feminisms: Building Global Visions, 1960s-1990s
Angela Miles

Rock-a-by Baby: Feminism, Self-Help, and Postpartum Depression
Verta Taylor

School-Smart and Mother-Wise: Working-Class Women's Identity and Schooling
Wendy Luttrell

Community Activism and Feminist Politics: Organizing Across Race, Class, and Gender
Nancy A. Naples, Editor

Grassroots Warriors: Activist Mothering, Community Work, and the War on Poverty
Nancy A. Naples

Complex Inequality: Gender, Class, and Race in the New Economy
Leslie McCall

Maid in the U.S.A.: 10th Anniversary Edition
Mary Romero

Home-Grown Hate: Gender and Organized Racism
Abby L. Ferber, Editor

Stepping Out of Line: Becoming and Being Feminist
Cheryl Hercus

WALTER BENJAMIN, RELIGION, AND AESTHETICS

Rethinking Religion Through the Arts

S. Brent Plate

Routledge
New York • London

Published in 2005 by
Routledge
270 Madison Avenue
New York, NY 10006
www.routledge-ny.com

Published in Great Britain by
Routledge
2 Park Square
Milton Park, Abingdon
Oxon OX14 4RN U.K.
www.routledge.co.uk

Routledge is an imprint of the Taylor & Francis Group.
Printed in the United Stated of America on acid-free paper.

10 9 8 7 6 5 4 3 2 1

Library of Congress Cataloguing-in-Publication Data
    Plate, S. Brent, 1966–.
        Walter Benjamin, religion and aesthetics: rethinking religion
            through the arts / S. Brent Plate
            p. cm.
        Includes bibliographical references.
        ISBN 0-415-96991-3 (alk. paper) — ISBN 0-415-96992-1 (alk. paper)
        1. Benjamin, Walter, 1892–1940. 2. Aesthetics—Religious aspects.
    3. Arts and religion.   I. Title.
    B3209.B584P53 2004
    111' 85 ' 092—dc22   2004014131

Contents

Prescript:
The Religious Uses of Benjamin

I could begin by introducing Walter Benjamin (1892–1940) with all the standard fare—that he is notoriously difficult to understand, that the latter half of the twentieth century saw an enormous proliferation in scholarship on him, that his death still remains shrouded in mystery—but I'll encourage the reader to go elsewhere for that.[1] Besides, I'm still not sure that this book is *about* Benjamin. I might wish to claim that this book was "inspired" by my readings of Benjamin in the way many films are "based on true stories," even when we realize the movie is far from true. Benjamin is indeed my most important interlocutor, but in the following book he remains just that, a conversation partner. Some of my readings of Benjamin's writings verge on the unorthodox, but then again there are few serious readers of Benjamin who seem willing to suggest that they have worked out definitions of terms like "aura," "allegory," or "history," especially since his own definitions keep slipping throughout his writings. He *is* notoriously complex, and he seldom followed the rules of intellectual engagement. Which is precisely why he is so attractive a figure, and which leads me to speculate that my unorthodoxy may in fact be Benjaminian orthodoxy. In any case, I will proceed as such.

This book is really about aesthetics and religion, and how Benjamin can offer renewed perspectives on the interrelation between them. There are already many good book-length studies of Benjamin available in English, many of which are listed in the bibliography, and I have learned a great deal from my predecessors. I do not wish to add another volume to the growing list of "Benjamin studies," however; readers looking for a comprehensive overview of Benjamin will not find it here. Many important dimensions of Benjamin's corpus are missing from my account, including a sustained engagement with Benjamin's philosophical precursors and contemporaries, and a concern with placing Benjamin strictly in his own early-twentieth-century European environment. Instead, I am concerned to uncover fragments of his writings and reactivate critical seeds embedded in his work that offer new channels for rethinking some of the structures of religion in relation to the arts. Which is to say that I am utilizing his now historical writings to shed light on the present and am not so concerned with the past per se, including Benjamin's own life. On this I follow Susan Buck-Morss's thoughts about reading Benjamin's *Arcades Project*: "[O]ur attitude should not be for reverence for Benjamin that would immortalize his words as the product of a great author no longer here, but reverence for the very mortal and precarious reality that forms our own 'present,' through which Benjamin's work is now telescoped."[2] I suggest that this is being more true to Benjamin's mode of thinking than any historical biography could be.

I am interested in Benjamin because he offers imaginative flights of the intellect, writing his struggles out somewhere between utopian visions and the material conditions of his day, and he would want his readers to do the same. For the interests of this book, Benjamin offers imaginative forays into "religious aesthetics," or what may be read backward to be an "aesthetic religion," which is not to conflate the two terms, but to examine how one uneasily demarcated field of enquiry influences, resists, and remakes the other. I have wanted to write this book because Benjamin offers alternative ways of thinking about aesthetics from a religious standpoint, and religion from an aesthetic standpoint. I believe I am not alone in my desire to see a religious aesthetics that does not take as its starting and ending point, Beauty, Truth, or God. The writings of, for example, Hans Urs von Balthasar, Alejandro García-Rivera, Frank Burch Brown, and Jeremy Begbie are all interesting works, and I believe there is much to be gleaned from these authors.[3] Yet, my wager is that there are others like myself who work from the untenable position that religious aesthetics can be materially grounded, and yet leave open some space for what can only be called the mystical. Terry Eagleton precisely labeled Benjamin the "Marxist Rabbi," as accurate a phrase as can be applied to him, and questions about whether he was more one than the other have been debated for half a century now.[4] One of his closest friends and deepest admirers was the scholar of Jewish mysticism, Gershom Scholem, who says of Benjamin's mysticism that it "was a far cry from the experience of God," for "Benjamin knew that mystical experience is many-layered, and it was precisely this many-layeredness that played so great a role in his thinking and in his productivity."[5] As with his late-in-life colleague, Georges Bataille, Benjamin maintained something of an atheological bent, and may thus contribute to what Mark C. Taylor once termed an "a/theoesthetics."[6]

Rereading Benjamin from a religious studies standpoint, as I am doing here, I hope to cast a different light on several of his theoretical ideas, meanwhile seeing a handful of religious studies concepts from a new perspective. Benjamin is utilized and read in academic contexts as diverse as sociology, anthropology, history, art history, urban studies, visual culture studies, film studies, philosophy, and literature; yet only a handful of publications appear on Benjamin from a religious studies perspective. He is certainly mentioned in passing often enough, but in comparison to his reception in other disciplines in the humanities and social sciences, Benjamin has yet to make much impact on the field.[7] Many commentators mention his theological interests, which Benjamin himself made explicit statements about, but rarely have scholars taken the time to suggest how more generally religious dimensions intersect with his ideas, or even what was meant by his "theology."

Part of the reason for this is precisely his ambiguous relationship to religion. While his mother came from a Reform tradition and his father from an Orthodox one,[8] they were nonetheless a family whom the Zionists of their time would have called "Christmas Jews," because of their overassimilation into the predominantly Christian culture of Germany.[9] But clearly Benjamin's greatest religious influence came from his lifelong friendship with Scholem, who was best known for his work on the Kabbalah. Scholem emigrated to Jerusalem in 1923 and constantly tried to get Benjamin to join him, just as he also consistently encouraged Benjamin to take up Hebrew. Benjamin always refused both the emigration and the Hebrew, usually stating something along the lines of his wanting to understand the European condition before he could attempt to understand the Jewish condition. He is not being an assimilationist here; rather, he saw Judaism as providing many of the tools with which to reshape the sociopolitical face of Europe. He states, "Judaism is to me in no sense an end in itself, but the most distinguished bearer and representative of the spiritual."[10] His concerns were more to do with religious life on earth—which is also to say religion is ultimately political and social—than with anything transcendental. While many scholars of Benjamin have argued otherwise, I believe his metaphysics were quite consistently subservient to his physics.

Furthermore, early in his life he believed that religion would rise again in Europe and offer a positive social structure, but that this religion would come from "the writing class." "Writers want to be honest," he claimed, "they want to express their enthusiasm for art, their 'love of the distant,' in Nietzsche's phrase but society rejects them: they are themselves driven to eliminate, in a process of pathological self-destruction, everything that is all-too-human yet necessary for life."[11] In the end, Benjamin sees art to be a liberating force, but what he means by art is a far cry from the standard definitions. Art, like religion and literature, was a powerful social force for Benjamin because of the oscillation hinted at here between creation and destruction, notions we will have ample time to revisit. Benjamin believed in a peculiar form of "aesthetic religion," which he thought would bring about change in the world. Later in his life, in exile in Paris when he met up with Bataille and others in the College of Sociology, he would toy with their commitments, and those of other surrealists, to bring the sacred into everyday, modern life. Yet, for Benjamin, like Bataille, the sacred was orientated within sociopolitical structures.

This present book is not a study of Benjamin's overt religious comments, as interesting as that would be. Rather, this book is a project of sifting through Benjamin's writings, looking for tools with which to articulate a religious aesthetics and an aesthetic religion. That Benjamin was or wasn't Jewish is not my concern. (Likewise, that Benjamin was or wasn't a good Marxist is also not my concern.) That this can actually be raised as a question about Benjamin is what intrigues me. This study wavers between theories of religion, theories of art, and an argument for the relations between religion and the arts. While Benjamin had closest affinities with (mystical and messianic) Judaism, and wrote amid a predominantly Christian (primarily Lutheran and, while in exile in Paris, Roman Catholic) culture, this book does not stay squarely within one religious tradition. Rather it takes a step back and theorizes on religious structures (chiefly those of the modern West) with the goal of recreating the link between aesthetics and religion. Such a recreation also entails destruction, and Benjamin provides some intriguing notions with which to create and destroy.

What may be noticed already is an insistence on interdisciplinarity, and a reliance on both the humanities *and* the social sciences in formulating theories of religion. The following chapters attempt to interpret *and* explain, and attempt to perform what Daniel Gold has argued as an "interpretive writing" on religion.[12] Benjamin, I offer, is a captivating figure from which to think through religion from both the humanities and social sciences, especially since scholars from both fields have utilized his works for their own studies, and since Benjamin would follow Marx's dictum about how philosophers have only interpreted the world but the point is to change it. I am unapologetically a theorist of religion and apologetically an interdisciplinary theorist, and here I enlist Benjamin to provide a path to tread through the forest of religion. But there are many forks along the way.

Finally, to stress again, I'm not sure this book is *about* Benjamin, but rather where Benjamin might take us in the twenty-first century, which is as close to Benjamin's thought as we may come.

Acknowledgments

Like most books, I imagine, this one had a number of incarnations. Some of the initial ideas found here were incubated during the writing of my dissertation at Emory University's Institute of the Liberal Arts in the late 1990s. As I was writing on contemporary video art as postmodern ritual, I continued to go back to Walter Benjamin's ideas. Much has changed in my thinking since then, but the dissertation provided me some first forays into the fragmented writings of Benjamin. So, in the first instance, I must thank my committee for insights into my speculations on the arts, religion, and Walter Benjamin. Specifically, I would like to thank Robert Paul, Rebecca Chopp, Robin Blaetz, William Doty, and Robert Detweiler. Also, vital early feedback was provided by Tel Mac, whose verbal acuity and psychological perspicuity fostered the seedlings of thought given here.

In the manuscript's later forms, I have received integral linguistic feedback from Timothy K. Beal, Tod Linafelt, Roland Boer, and Darren (Dazza) J. N. Middleton. Damian Treffs at Routledge helped see this through from the beginning, and his support has been great. Emotional support of varying types and degrees was fostered by Douglas Gay, Chas Gay, Christopher Boesel, David R. Nienhuis, and some much needed socio-legal advice from Simon Halliday. Ultimately, it must be quickly noted, I bear the final responsibility for the readings given here.

In the end, as always, is Edna Melisa, *quien es siempre aquí y allí y entre para mí.*

Abbreviations of Works Cited

AP   Walter Benjamin, *The Arcades Project*. Translated by Howard Eiland and Kevin McLaughlin. Cambridge, MA: Belknap Press of Harvard University Press, 1999.

OGTD   Walter Benjamin, *The Origin of German Tragic Drama*. Translated by John Osborne. London: Verso, 1977.

SW I   Walter Benjamin, *Selected Writings, Volume 1, 1913–1926*. Edited by Marcus Bullock and Michael W. Jennings. Cambridge, MA: Belknap Press of Harvard University Press, 1996.

SW II   Walter Benjamin, *Selected Writings, Volume 2, 1927–1934*. Edited by Michael W. Jennings, Howard Eiland, and Gary Smith. Cambridge, MA: Belknap Press of Harvard University Press, 1999.

SW III   Walter Benjamin, *Selected Writings, Volume 3, 1935–1938*. Edited by Howard Eiland and Michael W. Jennings. Cambridge, MA: Belknap Press of Harvard University Press, 2002.

SW IV   Walter Benjamin, *Selected Writings, Volume 4, 1938–1940*. Edited by Howard Eiland and Michael W. Jennings. Cambridge, MA: Belknap Press of Harvard University Press, 2003.

List of Illustrations

Introduction
Creative Aesthetics Creating Religion

> Man is nothing but a bundle of sensations.
>
> *Protagoras*

In the essay "Franz Kafka," Walter Benjamin narrates Kafka's life by weaving together Kafka's own parables and allegories with older Talmudic stories. In the midst of this, Benjamin suggests how "modern man lives in his own body," and yet, "the body slips away from him, is hostile toward him. It may happen that a man wakes up one day and finds himself transformed into vermin" (*SW II*, 806). The Kafkaesque image, reminiscent of *Metamorphosis,* intimates how bourgeois society is an-aesthetized by habit and by the egocentric desire for its own comfort. Like Kafka, Benjamin struggled against a modern society in which humans live in estrangement from their own bodies. As such, his battle against complacency is ultimately an *aesthetic* struggle.

But what does this mean, an "aesthetic struggle"? Isn't aesthetics a complacent field of interest itself? Isn't aesthetics obsessed with beauty (natural and artificial), high culture, fine arts, collectors' tastes, and other bourgeois interests? The answer, of course, is yes and no. Yes, this is certainly the predominant understanding of aesthetics today, both in and out of the academy: When one hears the word "aesthetics," one tends to think of art and beauty (or of plastic surgery and beauty parlors). But this is not a complete answer, for there are other ways to understand aesthetics, and these other options occupy my interests in this book.

A more productive way to understand aesthetics is to start with the term's etymology. Stemming from the Greek *aisthesis*, aesthetics has to do with "sense perception." Its focus is on how we perceive (and, simultaneously, create) our worlds through vision, taste, smell, touch, and hearing, among other possible senses.[1] Sensations emerge when stimuli from the world around us are received through bodily sense organs such as the ears, skin, eyes, and nose. These sensations are then interpreted and made meaningful by a conscious brain that is guided by learned and biologically inherited structures of the mind, most notably memory. (Properly speaking it is sensation *plus* interpretive activity that make up what we call *perception*, though these two are often conflated.) Sense perception varies owing to geographical and chronological circumstances, and according to age, race, class, gender, sex, and religion; it is crucial to identity formation, both individually and socially, based on how we sense and are sensed by others; it is a primary component of our interactions with religious myths, rituals, symbols, and memories; and it is the fundamental nexus for understanding both religion and art, and particularly the passage between the two. With sense receptors as the crux of the matter, perception also links the inner world to the outer world, the body to the physical stuff around us, the body to the mind, and bodies to other bodies; ultimately, the activities of perception are responsible for the formation of community and society. This, then, is the aesthetic point of my opening paragraph when I proposed that Benjamin writes against the anaesthesia of bourgeois society, the alienation of modern humans from their own bodies. To connect with one's own body, and one's own world, is an aesthetic activity.

Following from Benjamin's suggestive writings, this book attempts to rescue aesthetics as an originary point for the study of religion. Fundamental to this project is the contention that sense perception is a central locus for the reception, creation, and reproduction of our religious worlds. By looking at aesthetics through its materialist guise of sense perception, we find ourselves scrutinizing the construction of our religious worlds in a way more primary than the second-order reflection that is standard in much of religious studies with its examinations of sacred texts and theological doctrine. Religious historian David Chidester argues in his study of the religious discourse surrounding the senses of seeing and hearing: "To adapt (and modify) a familiar aphorism from Paul Ricoeur, perception—particularly the perceptual modes of seeing and hearing—gives rise to symbols, and symbols give rise to thought."[2] By understanding the ways humans sensually interact with the world around them we understand the ways humans create symbols, myths, rituals, and, indeed, entire religious worlds. Thus, aesthetics offers itself as a mode for analyzing and comparing religions. Comparative religionist William Paden states, "religions do not all inhabit the same world, but actually posit, structure, and dwell within a universe that is their own,"[3] and he goes on to regard the sensory dimension to these worlds, "all living things select and sense 'the way things are' through their own organs and modes of activity. They constellate the environment in terms of their own needs, sensory system, and values. They see—or smell or feel—what they need to, and everything else may as well not exist."[4] The senses organize and structure our world, dividing it up into proper perceptible forms that allow us to move and breathe and have our being.

This is not to claim sense perception as the *arche*, or foundation, of religion, but it is one fertile field from which to begin. Indeed, to take into account the material basis of aesthetics leads us to recognize its historical contingencies, becoming a groundless ground for comparative studies that counteracts a universal conception of religion. In the first volume of the *Journal of Religion*, in 1921, early psychologist of religion Edwin Diller Starbuck suggests: "Since there is more than one way of interpreting the outer world of experience, the ultimate reason for it may be that there is more than one sort of objective reality."[5] Starbuck is not setting perception within a historical framework here, but he realizes, as with William James, the varieties of sensual experience and their relation to the construction of religious worlds.

Nonetheless, this does not imply that the "experiential dimension" is at the base of religious studies either, especially since what usually goes under that heading—the numinous, the holy/wholly Other, feelings of dependence, the mystical—are conspicuously nonmaterialistic experiences. At times it is striking how antisensual religionists' descriptions of experience actually are, as if to have a religious experience, one barely even needed a body, or if the body is present it is rapidly overcome by transcendental forces that remain invisible, spiritual, intellectual.[6] When discussing religious experience, philosophers of religion mention the senses primarily from an epistemological standpoint, asking whether we can trust the senses to give us true knowledge of the world. This becomes something of a zero-sum game, as they ignore the many historical contingencies of the human sensorium and ultimately set the reasoning mind as foundation for experience.

I am not interested here in contributing to an epistemology of sensual experience, but rather to the religiocultural constructions of perception, and in the ways we experience the world on a material basis. Our perception of the physical world is not a perfect transmission of the world itself (if there actually *is* an objective, singular "real world"), yet the discrepancies between inner and outer worlds cannot be understood simply through biological or theological means. Debates over the status of experience in philosophy and religion have wavered between the subjective and objective basis of reality, yet in this book I am grounding aesthetic experience in another place: in a dialectic between material culture and the human creative activities of religious practice. As such, aesthetic experience cannot be bracketed out as an autonomous realm of human religious existence because it always exists in a dialogical relation with language, cognitive capacities, religious practices, political ideologies, technological developments, and economic conditions.

Experience is a critical category for Benjamin—some would say *the* critical category—who articulates a dialectical relation between two types of experience already found in the Germanic philosophical tradition: *Erfahrung* and *Erlebnis*. *Erfahrung* is the tradition-bound experience that unfolds over time; it is "inseparable from the representation of a continuity, a sequence" (*AP*, 802). *Erlebnis* is the immediate, isolated experience of the individual. Empirical and neo-Kantian schools of thought favored the former because it stresses outer sensory stimuli and conceptual reflection on objective experience, thereby creating a coherent narrative out of experience. The latter is understood to be more intuitive, stressing an inner subjective experience that was esteemed by the romantic-infused thought of Goethe, Wilhem Dilthey, and others. Benjamin was not content with either —the former being too rationalistic and pragmatically impossible to render in a modern age full of shock, the latter being too immediate and individualistic—and so instead he sets up a dialectic between the two varieties of experience, attempting to overcome the subject-object distinction. For whatever else the complexities of Benjamin's dialectics of experience demarcate, I emphasize up front that such a view of experience never escapes the material, historical conditions of the human sensorium. Benjamin strongly argued the historical nature of perception and experience, and he became famous (however posthumously) for asserting as much, particularly in reference to the ideologies of power and technology's role in altering perception. These alterations ultimately alter society itself.

Along the lines of the aesthetic construction of social reality, many philosophical and anthropological studies are currently and have already taken place, and the senses are an important touchstone for a number of them. From philosophical standpoints, sense perception is understood for its epistemological valence, for example, in Govardhan P. Bhatt's study of medieval Vedic philosopher Kumarila in *The Basic Ways of Knowing*, while Jane Geaney has more recently looked at the epistemology of the senses in early Chinese thought. In each case, the structure of sense perception is shown to be somewhat distinct from the modern Western configuration.[7] Meanwhile, a growing number of cultural anthropologists have been exploring the ways in which the construction of culture and identity is bound to the construction of the sensory realm, including Kathryn Linn Geurts's *Culture and the Senses,* and Robert Desjarlais's *Sensory Biographies.* Geurts's study of the Ewe in West Africa suggests they have a sixth sense, that of balance, which informs their modes of being in the world. Desjarlais's study compares biographies of a Nepalese man and woman, noting the importance of the senses in their comprehension of the world and of themselves, as well as how they are distinct—the male informant emphasized vision, the female informant emphasized hearing.[8]

There are many facets to consider in the construction of religious worlds, and an emphasis on the senses helps highlight the multiplicity of these worlds because it shows the ways in which they are culturally diverse. Sensual understanding opens up comparative modes of relating myths, symbols, rituals, and experience across cultures, meanwhile grounding comparative work on a materialist basis. Historian of culture Constance Classen has written several works along these lines, comparing, for example, the cosmologies of the South Pacific Ongee and their emphasis on the olfactory with the Tzotzil of Mexico and their focus on the sensation of heat.[9] By illuminating various approaches to the aesthetic construction of reality, Classen demonstrates how those of us in the modern West have tended to think of sense perception as *reception*, as a passive quality that "takes in" what is given in the world. Other ways of construing the world display a more active quality, and indeed contemporary studies on the workings of the brain display exactly this kind of active work: The senses organize our worlds; they are proactive, not passive.[10] Modern science has made it evident that the eyes do not actually emit rays of energy, as ancients from Plato to Patanjali believed,[11] yet that does not excuse us from the active manner of sensing the world that the ancients and others have promoted. Sensing the world is not a passive but an active process, as we act and exist among the smells and sights and sounds of social life, selecting, arranging, and forgetting various of these impulses, and thereby shaping our world. This does not make us sovereign, but rather, active participants in the material world of sense.

Art

In the first chapter of this book, which more fully outlines the realm of aesthetics, I will show that although a recovery of the sensual dimension of aesthetics is important, I do not intend to neglect what has become the more common connotation of aesthetics as a theory of art. Instead of articulating the idea of aesthetic experience via epistemology, theology, or even anthropology, I will herein follow Benjamin and situate the terms of this experience primarily in the artistic realm. For it is in the experience with art (or at least with certain types of art that promote a heterogeneous, collective, nonindividualistic experience) that Benjamin believes the two varieties of experience noted earlier can be productively brought together. In the modern age, we are subject to stimuli that are shocking, and we end up alienated from each other, unable to share communally as in the old days of oral storytelling. The modern age is marked by the rise of the novel, created by and for the single individual, and possible only through the mass reproduction of books: "The birthplace of the novel is the individual in his isolation" (*SW III*, 146). To this, Benjamin contrasts a number of collectively oriented, modern artistic endeavors, from Bertolt Brecht's theater work to surrealist performances, and especially, the work of cinema.

My emphasis on the arts and their relation to religion brings me close to the recent thoughts of archaeologist Colin Renfrew:

> [T]he visual arts of today offer a liberation for the student of the past who is seeking to understand the processes that have made us what we are now. Over the past century or so the visual arts have transformed themselves from their preoccupation with beauty and the representation of the world into something much more radical. Today, I would claim, the visual arts have transformed themselves into what might be described as a vast, uncoordinated yet somehow enormously effective research program that looks critically at what we are and how we know what we are—at the foundations of knowledge and perception, and of the structures that modern societies have chosen to construct upon those foundations.[12]

Renfrew's interest in the arts and their ability to tell us something about "what we are and how we know what we are" is not unlike Benjamin's interests in the here and now, as opposed to "art history," whose emphasis is on what went before. For Benjamin, as for the present book, the focus is on the present, not the past and discovering ourselves along the way.

So although my book benefits from the work of anthropologists and epistemologists, it is also and primarily a work situated between the study of religion and theories of art, inasmuch as it sees the critical importance of artistic creation in the making and shaping of religion. I am convinced that the study of the arts provides a privileged perspective from which to investigate religious practices, and that a key way to recognize and appreciate the aesthetic dimension of religion is to explore the ways, shapes, and forms of artistic practices, as well as to understand the reception of art by sensate humans. One cannot adequately examine symbols, myths, or rituals unless one has a comprehension of the role of, for example, genre, metaphor, metonymy, iconology, performance, or aesthetic reception.

Thus, an aesthetic theory of religion must take into account the relation between the sensual-bodily basis of aesthetics and the artistic basis. To be sure, under the gaze of Benjamin, art begins to look a lot different than the way we commonly imagine it, particularly as it is submerged within everyday life, yet his perspectives challenge commonplace ideas about art, while at the same time his writings provide new tools for an aesthetic approach to religion.

Art allows a window onto the past, as Renfrew's remarks suggest, but it also has an orientation toward religion's future, which is not to say that we are advancing scientific knowledge to a better point for prediction. Art, or perhaps more properly "artistic activity," functions in religious and cultural worlds because it is *inventive*, and thus transformative of the very tradition from which it grows. An invention, as literary theorist Derek Attridge suggests,

> may be a new device or program, but the act of invention is a mental feat that makes possible both the manufacture of the new entity and, perhaps more important, new instances of inventiveness. Inventiveness in the cultural field, too, connotes not only the creation of a new artifact but also a way of deploying materials that can be both imitated and inventively developed, parodied, challenged. These further forms of inventiveness cannot be predicted from the invention that makes them possible—if they could, they would not be inventive.[13]

Attridge's inventiveness can best be related to religion, and especially ritual, through the famous parable by Kafka: "Leopards break into the temple and drink to the dregs what is in the sacrificial pitchers; this is repeated over and over again; finally it can be calculated in advance, and it becomes a part of the ceremony."[14] Probably the first thing noticed here is that this is not exactly what we call "art," particularly since the leopards do not act consensually: Animals, by most accounts, are not artists. However, Kafka's parable offers an instance of inventiveness that brings us closer to what Benjamin saw in the relations between art, religion, and social life. That is, such invention points toward a creative activity that does not depend on myths of artists as micro-gods creating *ex nihilo*. Instead, invention happens somewhat by chance, within a logic veering toward chaos as much as cosmos.

Since religious practices are inventive practices that create new artifacts and stories out of the old, often for their own survival, an examination of religious traditions must involve a perspective that retains a flexible approach able to account for the creative dimensions of myths, rituals, and symbols, even as they verge on the chaotic and complex. Many theorists of religion continue to provide "anatomies" of the sacred, and they draw on an increasingly outmoded scientific mode of experimentation, whereby the structure studied is understood to be an immutable, unmoving object (some contemporary forays into the cognitive science of religion are only the latest examples). A growing number of contemporary religious scholars are beginning to account for the alterations of myths, rituals, and symbols when the old structure gives way to something new: a community's dominant hero myth adapts to the presence of a related but previously unheard of story; a food offering is amended by a new recipe; the latest technological developments create tools that allow for a revised way to paint one's body or to represent deities in a highly reproducible medium. With a view toward inventive ritual, ritual theorist Ronald Grimes contends how "without constant reinvention, we court disorientation. Without rites that engage our imaginations, communities, and bodies, we lose touch with the rhythms of the human life course."[15] Ritual and myth name performances that, while utilizing some formal guidelines, nonetheless adapt to new situations, and morph to meet the demands of local communities and new eras. It is, I suggest, the artistic dimension of religious practice that allows for both the survival and transformation of religious traditions, and religious studies as a whole must understand something about the imaginative and creative arts before it can analyze the other systems of religious belief and practice.

Benjamin argues against art's autonomy; yet, there nonetheless remains a critical function for an art of invention, for something that shakes up the given order of things and propels religion into the future. As Jacques Derrida plays on the homology of invention (*l'invention*) and its orientation toward the future (*l'avenir*), he interrogates the ways "the word 'invention' is going through a rebirth, on a ground of anguished exhaustion but also out of a desire to reinvent invention itself . . . we dream of reinventing invention on the far side of the programmed matrices. For is a programmed invention still an invention? Is it an event through which the future (*l'avenir*) comes to us?"[16] The leopards in Kafka's parable are *not* programmed, but become programmatic, so what is invention? Is there anything beyond the programmed? Derrida's queries here, which can be usefully applied to religious practices such as myths and rituals, get us thinking about some of the aesthetic issues that Benjamin raises: At what point does a ritual become routine? How far can a ritual be reinvented, made new, and still carry tradition with it? When does tradition become burdensome rather than liberating? And although Benjamin does not ask questions in such a religious studies oriented way, his writings open up ways of rethinking the potency of myth and ritual, especially as they carry the potential for sociopolitical change.

Benjamin and Aesthetics

With aesthetics-as-sense-perception in the foreground (further outlined in Chapter 1), in the remaining chapters I sift through Benjamin's writings, seeking the useful, oftentimes fragmented, remains for what I will cursorily call *an aesthetic theory of religion*. In particular, Benjamin's concepts of art and allegory are inventive aesthetic forces that undo traditionally stabilizing religious functions such as myth, symbol, memory, narrative, creation, and redemption. Via Benjamin's writings, I contend that religion, and more importantly, religious *practice*, is about process and movement; it is about creativity more than creation, mythologizing more than myth, memory making more than memory, consecration and deconsecration more than the sacred. Benjamin's writings seek to disrupt the perceived coherence and guaranteed redemptions of these latter terms, emphasizing instead the processes of religion, oftentimes via avant-garde artistic practices. And although Benjamin's emphases on disruption and destruction might seem at first to be antireligious, I will suggest that religious aesthetics must take into account the interlocking forces of creation and destruction—a dialectic perhaps more unfamiliar to Western religions than to South Asian religions.

As commonly understood, Benjamin barely fits the title of "aesthetician"; his *Habilitationschrift*, eventually published as *Ursprung des deutschen Trauerspiels* ("Origin of German Tragic Drama"), was rejected by the Department of Aesthetics at the University of Frankfurt; and today histories and anthologies of aesthetics seldom mention him. Indeed, he may even be appropriately labeled an "antiaesthete," for as I show in Chapter 2, he is interested in, among other things, baroque allegories. These allegories are artistic forms that emphasize fragments and ruins and thus have no regard for a whole, meanwhile Benjamin finds in their decay a focal point for his project: they are "beyond beauty." Most later aestheticians, primarily in the German romantic tradition, ignored baroque allegories because these fragments and confused artworks could barely be taken up into the realm of the beautiful, much less the divine. If aesthetic inquiry is interested in beauty and wholeness, then Benjamin is the proverbial square peg in a round hole. Alternatively, as I note in Chapter 3, he is also skeptical of traditional aesthetic ideas (and ideals) such as "creativity and genius, eternal value and mystery" (*SW II*, 101)

Herein I shift the common conception of aesthetics itself, making more space for Benjamin's writings within a materialist, sensual understanding of the world. I see the idea of aesthetics as a "constellation," to use one of Benjamin's illuminating metaphors. A constellation is a group of stars, each at a particular point in time and space, which are interpreted by viewers as a distinct group. At first they may appear to be indistinguishable from all the other stars, yet when an interpreting community distinguishes a pattern among certain of the stars, they become meaningful and are transformed into symbols that are understood to have some bearing on a person's life and fate—or, on a more pragmatic level, they are used for navigational purposes, helping sailors find their way. In a constellation, as Benjamin puts it, "Every idea is a sun and is related to other ideas just as suns are related to each other. The harmonious relationship between such essences is what constitutes truth" (*OGTD*, 37). Each idea is a star, emitting its own light, but finding cosmic significance only in its relation to other bright, thematic stars. In their orientation to each other, meanings can begin to be deciphered by observing their relationship. There is no one thing that aesthetics *is*, but particularly because of the liminal status of the bodily senses and their ability to make connections between things, aesthetics enables just such a relation between the "stars."

The constellation herein will be named aesthetics, and among the stars are those called art, allegory, symbol, myth, memory, words, images, bodies, technology, community, and several other terms that will illumine the following chapters. One might note that several of these are religious studies terms, and indeed they are. Nonetheless, it is oftentimes necessary not to look directly at a star in the night sky, for it seems to disappear, caught in our retinal blind spot. Instead, the viewer must look just to the side of the star, and perceive it only indirectly. This is what Benjamin's writings offer: a chance to look indirectly at established religious studies terms, seeing them out of the corner of the eye, indirectly, and only in relation to several other stars—in other words, nothing less than a new perspective on the cosmos, one that is, in accordance with avant-garde artistic practices, slightly askew. This arrangement is nonetheless always subject to *dis-aster* (literally, a "dispersal of the stars"). Since a stellar constellation has no center and is considered an "arbitrary formation of stars *perceived* as a figure or design,"[17] "truth" itself is never singular, but created out of relations. The truth of aesthetics can be understood only through the interrelations of its constituent suns.

Constellations are further dependent on an interpreter or, better, an interpreting community, who "reads" a group of stars *as* a group, distinct from other stars. The interpreters, nevertheless, cannot possess the truth; they can only aid in pointing toward it. In a wonderful phrase Benjamin expresses as much: "Truth, bodied forth in the dance of represented ideas, resists being projected, by whatever means, into the realm of knowledge. Knowledge is possession" (*OGTD*, 29). Truth cannot be possessed—only knowledge can —but truth is instead "bodied forth in the dance of represented ideas."

While Benjamin's metaphoric language is understood, the active, corporeal nature of truth must be acknowledged. Just as there is no final distinction between the dancer and the dance, there can be no final discernible truth apart from the dance of represented ideas. Truth is historical and contingent.

Finally, extending Benjamin's constellation metaphor, I would suggest that, as a dialectical thinker, oftentimes the stars within his constellations are "binary" or "twin" stars: two stars that revolve around each other and are often perceived as a single mass. Benjamin tends not to deal in binary oppositions so much as he seeks out two closely related themes, genres, or ideas, and shows their differences. Usually this difference entails a distorting or destructive force on one theme/genre/idea exerted by the other. This is a critique from within, by which he would adapt the style and tone of another artist, philosopher, or writer, and twist their meanings for his use. This is the way he famously "brushes history against the grain" (*SW IV*, 392).[18] Since binary stars are often perceived as a single mass, their appearances can be deceiving, and Benjamin's criticism works in much the same ways. Some of the key binary stars discussed in the following include: tragedy and tragic drama, symbol and allegory, metaphor and metonymy, collection (*Sammlung*) and dispersal (*Zerstreuung*), as well as the two-sided nature of experience (*Erfahrung* and *Erlebnis*), and the two functions of memory (*Gedächtnis* and *Erinnerung*). In each case, the one distorts the other, not as its opposite but as its confused, and confusing, "twin."

Outline of the Book

In Benjaminian fashion, in Chapter 1, I sort through a history of modern aesthetics, rescuing several important themes and dimensions that have been too often overlooked or buried in contemporary philosophy and religious studies. As already begun here in the introduction, I will continue to plea for a materially and sensually based aesthetics. Central to this reconfigured aesthetics are theories of creation, both cosmologically and artistically speaking. Benjamin's theories of creation are the flip side to his crucial theories of destruction, and a rethinking of this dialectic offers news ways to think about both the arts and the cosmos, and especially about the ideologies that necessarily accompany created worlds.

In Chapter 2, I develop his theory of allegory, establishing several of its themes as a basis for a theory of art, especially as laid out in his work on the German baroque *Trauerspiel*. I translate this obscure dramatic genre as a "Lament-play," hoping to reassert what I believe to be Benjamin's religious interests in allegory, and linking it to the Jewish genre of *lamentation*.

Benjamin's aesthetic emphasis is on the dispersing, disrupting forces that perpetually take totalities apart, among them the totalizing myths and symbols of philosophy and religion. As such, allegory, because it deals in ruins, takes as its focus the fragmented images from a past life and sets them in a modern environment: "Allegory should be shown as the antidote to myth" (*SW IV*, 179). By utilizing Benjamin's concepts of aesthetics, allegory, and art, I hope to point toward a plural structuring of culture that is open to multiple religions along with multiplicities of ethnicity, gender, and sexuality that have already been put into current cultural discourse.

In the third chapter, I look at Benjamin's understanding of the function of art in his famous essay, "The Work of Art in the Age of Its Technological Reproducibility." Here, I shift the emphasis of the title to highlight the *work* of art, suggesting art's functionality rather than its objectivity. Art is not a thing, but has a work to do; art *works* within a culture, affecting perceptions of the world, and causing humans to reorient their understanding of the construction of the cosmos.[19] As the conception of art is exploded beyond the bounds of the modern museum, infiltrating all aspects of everyday life, the work of art impacts ritual and memory-making activities, which is why Benjamin is so interested in the avant-garde practices of Dada and surrealism, as well as the work of cinema. Benjamin clearly overstates the utopian potential of film in his essay, but his interests in it continue to be instructive. And central to his arguments here is the role of technology and its ability to reconfigure the human sensorium, a point picked up on later by media theorists such as Marshall McLuhan and Walter Ong.

In the final chapter, I continue to work through Benjamin's aesthetics as a way to reimagine ritualized formations of community and their relation to memory and architecture. Benjamin's final years were spent in exile in Paris, where he made the acquaintance of the surrealist philosopher/ pornographic writer/librarian Georges Bataille and participated in the College of Sociology. Here I bring Benjamin's interest in the sociopolitical activities of art into the realm of memory, ritual, and communal formation. This community is a "community of sense," which is not to say there is such thing as "common sense" or a *sensus communis;* rather the term is more accurately summed up, in the later work of Maurice Blanchot as *the unavowable community*, or by Jean-Luc Nancy as *the inoperative community*. I will thus end with such a confluence, connecting aesthetics to architecture, memory, and community.

As a study that is situated between religion and art, I work to open up channels between the two registers that have heretofore remained closed. An astonishing amount of religious studies' approaches to the arts remain bound to romantic ideas of art: focused on the media of painting and sometimes sculpture, created by a single artist seemingly *ex nihilo*, and designed to inspire an experience of transcendence in the depths of the viewer's soul. Benjamin's writings, in contrast, look at the overlooked arts of baroque drama, modern film, and urban planning, and focus attention on the multiplicity of creators forming art out of fragments of past history, which are then received in the present by a community of people who, rather than reaffirming themselves, enact their inner visions in the streets. This is not about sociopolitical art per se, but about how sociopolitical life affects *all* art, which in turn alters sociopolitical-religious life.

1
Aesthetics (I):
From the Body to the Mind and Back

About the time Benjamin was working on his postgraduate studies, developing his aesthetic theories, the Dadaists were in full swing, smashing the sacred status of the object of art. Although many of the Dada artists channeled their enraged energies against the institution of art itself, working betwixt and between contemporary art theories and larger social myths and ideologies, the German Hannah Höch (1889–1978) stands out among them—a woman in a still patriarchal art world, wrestling with gender specificities in an age of mechanical reproduction. In her photomontages Höch displays the body, chiefly the female body, within miniature tableaus that are allegories of society, drawing attention to the male gaze (long before it became de rigueur in theory) and, as with Kafka, to the alienated nature of human life in the modern industrial world. Though Benjamin never refers to Höch, she was working in Berlin at the same time as Benjamin, and her creative modes introduce us to Benjaminian aesthetics, and thus she is worth a brief discussion in this regard.[1]

Utilizing strategies of appropriation and juxtaposition, Höch employs visual fragments culled from photographic reproductions of art, ethnographic artifacts, and popular culture images (newspapers and magazines), mixing and merging them in new forms and thereby creating new meanings. She thus lends credence to avant-gardist Maya Deren's claim: "All invention and creation consists primarily of a new relationship between known parts."[2] By mixing high and mass art, conflating diverse cultures and epochs, and amalgamating everyday life and sociopolitical ideologies, Höch ushers in a style of aesthetic creation that dispenses with the image of the solitary genius forming art "out of

15

nothing." In its stead she offers the historically motivated understanding that we cannot, in fact, break free from the past but must rather constantly deal with the images and fragments of previous conditions, environments, and situations. Viewing her aesthetic strategies through a Benjaminian lens, we see that the past is not a unified entity to be seen as an intact whole or a well-written narrative; for to see the past within the present, it is necessary to fragment it and have it offer itself up as isolated images, which can be perpetually rearranged and resituated within the present. Only in this way is history, in Benjamin's view, able to be reactualized in the present, and only in this way does it refrain from the overwhelming ideology of myth. By fragmenting images of various worlds, Höch puts together a new image, a pieced-together creation in which the lines of juxtaposition continue to show through. There is no beautiful, unified whole, no seamless blending of past and present, same and other, here and there; the world is merely frozen into an image of juxtaposition.

Working in this vein, from 1924 until 1934 Höch created a photomontage series that she called "From an Ethnographic Museum" in which she reimagines images of otherness in modern life, often juxtaposing the "primitive" and the "woman" as objects of a visual gaze. Among this series is the 1925 piece *Denkmal I: Aus einem ethnographischen Museum* (Monument I: From an Ethnographic Museum), which portrays a female figure fashioned from cutouts of magazines and wearing an African mask. She is a modern European woman and an African simultaneously (See Figure 1.1). The figure is placed on a platform (as with most of the pieces in the series), thereby stressing the objectifying way of seeing that is endemic to the modern, deritualized museum; "woman," like the "primitive," is put on a pedestal and offered as a commodified image to be consumed by, alternatively, the male, the Western ethnographer, and the museum viewer. Later commentators did not find Höch to be critical enough of the exoticizing tendencies of early ethnography in its approaches to African and Asian material culture, yet her point was to draw attention to the female body's objectified status in Weimar Germany. Maud Lavin's book-length study of Höch develops the artist's sociopolitical interests via her aesthetic strategies:

> What might be perceived as Höch's humanistic linking of the subjecthood of Western and tribal peoples through montaging body parts (or often ethnographic artifact fragments representing body parts) is made ironic through her use of allegorical displacement. In structure as well as in tone, her exploration of self through a representation of the Other is explicitly ironic. Because of the fluid operations of reading a montage, however—the Blochian flowering of allegory—such a distanced irony is not a static or ever-present element of reception . . . . Oscillation is therefore important in Höch's montages—prompting a disjunctive

Figure 1.1 Hannah Höch, *Denkmal I: Aus einem ethnographischen Museum* (Monument I: From an Ethnographic Museum), 1925. ©2004 Artists Rights Society (ARS), New York/VG Bild-Kunst, Bonn.

shift between one allegorical reading and another, allowing different types of identification and distance.[3]

Höch, like all artists, sets out to recreate the world, to defamiliarize and re-familiarize objects, allowing us to look again at our worldview, yet she does so in a way that does not create an image that is possessable, or with a fixed and final meaning.

Höch's alternative title for this series was *die Sammlung* (the collection; a critical term for Benjamin to which I will return at many points), evoking the colonialist activity of "collecting" images and objects of the other. Colonization arises coterminously with the creation of modern museums of art and anthropology, both which arise alongside scientific observation and the scientific study of religion. The desire to collect, and therefore possess, is parallel to the desire to gaze and behold the other, and the impulse behind modern art and aesthetics is barely different from the masculinist, colonialist, scientific world-view: Modern science and modern aesthetics both view the other as distinct and autonomous, and only in this way can it be collected, possessed, and gazed upon by a self-reliant subject in a position of power. Höch's ironic reappraisal of the colonialist situation disperses such collections, just as she offers up a collection that is made from fragments.

Inventing Religion

Through the allegorical fragment, Höch's art, on one level, visualizes Benjamin's aesthetic strategies, playing in the space between distance and proximity, between the part and the whole, as the images stress the pieced-together nature of social reality. She thus stands at the beginning of this chapter and book as a way into the field of Benjamin's aesthetics. Furthermore, Höch's art emblematizes the kind of creative activity that I will suggest Benjamin contributes to the study of religions.

Jonathan Z. Smith's argument in his 1982 article, "In Comparison a Magic Dwells," is that comparative religious studies have continued to retain a certain "magic" that sees too much resemblance among religious structures across cultures and thus tends to be unscientific. He ends up suggests an interesting distinction for comparing religions: "Borrowing Edmundo O'Gorman's historiographic distinction between discovery as the finding of something one has set out to look for and invention as the subsequent realization of novelty one has not intended to find, we must label comparison an invention."[4] As already suggested in my introduction, invention is a rich creative notion that works beyond the intentions of the single creator and cannot maintain control over its subject. It is oriented toward a future that has not yet arrived and may never do so. Invention remains on the side of creativity, not objective science. In response to the objective, scientific endeavors of religious studies, a collection of essays on the topic was published entitled *A Magic Still Dwells*, in which editors Kimberley C. Patton and Benjamin C. Ray note the importance of Smith's article, even as they acknowledge that there are revisions to be made: "We reclaim the term 'magic' to endorse and to extend his claim that comparison is an indeterminate scholarly procedure that is best undertaken as an intellectually creative enterprise, not as a science but as an art—an imaginative and critical act of mediation and redescription in the service of knowledge."[5]

Relatedly, and not far from Benjamin's own production as an author, Wendy Doniger suggests, "The comparatist, like the surrealist, selects pieces of *objets trouvés*; the comparatist is not a painter but a collagist, indeed a bricolagist (or a *bricoleur*), just like the mythmakers themselves."[6] Religious worlds are made up of borrowed fragments and pasted together in ever-new ways; myths are updated and transmediated, rituals reinvented, symbols morphed. Correlatively, to do religious studies one must become something of an artist, or as Daniel Gold puts it, "if part of what many writers on religion do is to communicate their visions of human truths, then they have something in common with artists."[7] Many artists, mythmakers, and religionists, however, often attempt to cover over the fact that their work is made up of borrowed fragments and instead they point to a seamless, wholly pure, and beautiful worldview. To the contrary, the aesthetics asserted herein do not allow the seams, the cuts, the fragments, the borrowings, to disappear. Religion is unfoundable, an impure activity full of sutures and pasted cutups. Benjamin's religious aesthetics work in between the attraction of art and the distance of scientific objectivity, between fascination for the object and a critical detachment from it, between collecting and the collection (*Sammlung*): "the life of a collector manifests a dialectical tension between the poles of disorder and order" (*SW II*, 487).

Aesthetic Apprehensions

> [O]nce words come to dominate and occupy flesh and matter, which were previously innocent, all we have left is to dream of the paradisiacal times in which the body was free and could run and enjoy sensations at leisure. If a revolt is to come, it will have to come from the five senses!

> Michel Serres[8]

To introduce Benjamin, religion, and aesthetics more fully, we must step back and rethink the definition of aesthetics itself. As my introduction notes, this book works from the etymological basis of aesthetics as sense perception, and it considers the ways in which materialist-oriented aesthetics might offer a new perspective from which to rethink religious studies. To rescue aesthetics via the senses, a few comments about the institutionalized field of study are necessary. Since most libraries' stacks are already replete with histories of aesthetics—I briefly consider a few fragments of aesthetic history that are worth rethinking and will play out in relation to Benjamin's writings.[9]

It is commonly understood that Alexander Gottlieb Baumgarten founded the modern study of aesthetics in the mid-eighteenth century. Like all inventors, he did not "discover" something as yet unseen, but rather demarcated a particular section of the world, and gave it a name. Beginning with his dissertation in 1735 (published in English as *Reflections on Poetry*) and expanded upon in his 1750 *Aesthetica* (which remains untranslated into English), he cordoned off the field of sense perception and revived the Greek term *aisthesis* (sensory perception) as its name. Aesthetics was to be a new science dealing with the knowledge that is gained through the bodily senses. It would be a complement to the field of logic, the two together forming a more comprehensive theory of knowledge. Logic supplies us with "things known" (conceptual), while aesthetics supplies us with "things perceived" (perceptual). In Baumgarten's initial positing of the field of aesthetics, there is no mention of "beauty." And although it may seem a bold move in the realm of eighteenth-century philosophy to include such corporeal interests, Baumgarten is nonetheless clear that aesthetics trucks with the "inferior faculty" of perception, while logic deals with the "superior faculty" of the rational mind.[10] Following Baumgarten's ultimate subduing of the sensual body to the rational mind, the sensual roots of aesthetics are largely forgotten today.

Baumgarten's ideas led Terry Eagleton to state, "[a]esthetics is born as a discourse of the body."[11] Yet the discipline of aesthetics has been displaced into inquiries about style, art, beauty, and taste (i.e., the "taste" achieved by the mind not the tongue—even the terms used turn into disembodied metaphors). Baumgarten called these latter things *aesthetica artificialis*, as opposed to the sensually oriented *aesthetica naturalis*. So, whereas the "natural" scope of aesthetics is to examine the relation between "the material and the immaterial: between things and thoughts, sensations and ideas,"[12] it has "artificially" involved itself in abstract theories about art and beauty. In their natural state, "The senses maintain an uncivilized and uncivilizable trace," contends one of Benjamin's most astute interpreters, Susan Buck-Morss, in ways that resonate with Serres and Eagleton, "a core of resistance to cultural domestication. This is because their immediate purpose is to serve instinctual needs—for warmth, nourishment, safety, sociability—in short, they remain a part of the biological apparatus, indispensable to the self-preservation of both the individual and the social group."[13] Such natural aesthetics are so close to our existence as *Homo sapiens* that we often overlook them, yet Buck Morss's comments here suggest ways in which we might continue to tap into aesthetics as a powerful force for invention, for rethinking who we are as humans, and rethinking the status of religion.

Because its etymological roots and Baumgarten's initial notions of it were materially based, philosophy's pursuit of "truth" and theology's pursuit of things "spiritual" have consistently had to push this corporeal, non- or prelinguistic category to the sidelines. Western philosophy and theology have pursued a truth that is transcendent and/or spiritual, and thus opposed to (or at least very skeptical of) the material. So in spite of some prominent philosophers attending to aesthetic matters, the field has fairly consistently been a marginalized subfield of philosophy, and even more of theology and religious studies. When not pushed to the sidelines, the study of aesthetics has developed ways to open material sensation to, as Eagleton puts it, "the colonization of reason;" aesthetics is "a kind of prosthesis to reason, extending a reified Enlightenment rationality into vital regions which are otherwise beyond its reach."[14] Reason, in its logocentric guise, guarantees borders and structures, promises unity, and puts the reasoner in control and possession.

In order for the mind to exert control over its objects of study, Western, dualistic modes of thought must maintain clear distinctions. Although mind-body dualism is a key contributing factor to the denigration of aesthetics, the most significant heritage is that which is at the heart of many religious traditions the world over: the interlinked dualities of the inside and outside, and the pure and impure.[15] Because the bodily sense organs are physiologically situated at the cusp of the inside and the outside of the body—ears, nose, mouth, eyes, skin—the realm of aesthetics must be appropriated by the mind and retained "inside"—that is, subservient to the logic of reason—or is excised from the realm of thought and deemed unimportant for truth. Along with the anus and genitals, the five senses occupy a corporeal borderland, and this border is endlessly contested.[16]

Immanuel Kant is of course a key figure here, delineating various types of knowledge through his three critiques and attempting to account for knowledge that is separate from any experience. Yet as Buck-Morss sums up his relation to the senses: "Kant's transcendental subject purges himself of the senses which endanger autonomy not only because they unavoidably entangle him in the world, but, specifically, because they make him passive ('languid' [*schmelzend*] is Kant's word) instead of active ('vigorous' [*wacker*]), susceptible, like 'oriental voluptuaries,' to sympathy and tears."[17] Even if the sublime is experienced through the senses, Kant is clear that the judging, independent human ultimately overcomes this experience and stands over and against the awesome powers of nature. Such understandings have dogged philosophy ever since the Enlightenment, and the exclusion or appropriation of sensual perception by the critical faculties of the mind constantly marginalizes aesthetics. The perceptual is again and again swallowed up by the conceptual, and as the body itself has been expunged from Western thought, so are aesthetics excised.

Postmodern philosophy deconstructs the boundaries between inside and outside, subjectivity and objectivity, though has actually theorized very little on what goes on *in between* the inner and the outer worlds, in the realm of the senses. On one hand, postmodern thought is greatly concerned with liminality and borders, but even when the body has become a central focus for philosophy the senses' specificities are generally ignored. So the body is disciplined, sexed, and historicized, but the body of contemporary theoretical discourse all too often remains a homogeneous mass, and sensual differentiation is seldom found. The writings of Luce Irigaray are perhaps the key exception.

From Baumgarten's day forward, the subject of aesthetics has been open to debate and has changed foci over time, even as the bodily senses are subjugated to a minor role in all the varieties of aesthetics. Although theories of beauty are still in evidence,[18] more recent aesthetic theory has displaced the focus on beauty and instead considers aesthetics to be a "philosophy of art." The confusion over what goes under the name *aesthetics* can be seen by glancing through the stacks at a research library and finding the shelf housing books about aesthetics: One may see a book with the title *A Theory of Beauty* sitting next to *An Introduction to Aesthetics*. A row down, *Feeling and Reason in the Arts* neighbors *Philosophy of Art*. Highlighting the diversity of semantics, Noël Carroll, writing in the latter, admits that in a broad sense, "'aesthetics' and the 'philosophy of art' are interchangeable. Choosing one over the other is a matter of indifference."[19] So the question remains: What does aesthetics actually deal with: art? beauty? reason? feeling?

Not only is the focus of aesthetics slightly unclear, its status in modern intellectual history also remains vague. Some claim aesthetics to be prevalent in modern philosophy, while others say it is marginal. The differences seem in part to be bound up with who is looking and what they are looking for. In the lead article to the recent collection *Visual Culture and the Holocaust*, Liliane Weissberg casts a skeptical eye over what she sees as recent academic interest in aesthetics.[20] The resurgence in aesthetics that Weissberg objects to functions under the conception that aesthetics have to do with beauty, and it is juxtaposed to the politics of identity that have been so prominent in the academy for the last two or three decades. This juxtaposition leads Ian Hunter to begin an article entitled "Aesthetics and Cultural Studies," by claiming: "The cultural studies movement conceives of itself as a critique of aesthetics."[21] In other words, as conceived in the current intellectual milieu, aesthetics and ethics are split. Since aesthetics are presumed to be concerned with beauty and judgments about art, and based in individual subjectivity, they have little to do with our relations to others. If aesthetics and ethics are related, it is merely based on a fuzzy, romantic notion that people who contemplate beauty will be more inclined to be ethical people. (Just don't tell the viewers of Leni Riefenstal's beautiful *Triumph of the Will*.)

Although not fitting the bill of an aesthetician, Benjamin is a crucial figure here, for he retains a materialistic understanding of aesthetics by maintaining their connection to sensual perception, while also displaying the interactive relation between art and everyday life, leading to a "new, dynamic, dialectical aesthetics" (*SW II*, 294). Indeed, after noting the interchangeability of "aesthetics" and "philosophy of art," Noël Carroll observes the differences more closely, saying: "The philosophy of art is object-oriented; aesthetics is reception-oriented."[22] In this sense Benjamin is very much an aesthetician, concerned as he is with the lived, receptive, meanwhile mediated, experience of the world. Benjamin is concerned with both "natural aesthetics" and "artificial aesthetics," with the contingent, material interactions of social life, and with the role of something we can only continue to call "art" within that social structure. At the same time, rather than defining the boundaries of art, as we will see in chapter 3, he destroys any autonomous realm within which art might reside. Thus, I argue that Benjamin's aesthetics ignore the philosophy of art's boundary-setting activities (again, the desire to maintain distinctions between the inside and outside) and dwell in the broader sensual experience of everyday life: walking in the city, going to the movies, smoking hash, and unpacking one's library, as well as looking at paintings such as Benjamin's much-valued possession, Paul Klee's *Angelus Novus*. Because Benjamin's writings destroyed the line separating high and low art, and because he is interested in everyday social life and the creative activities found therein, he has become a foundational figure for more contemporary studies of visual and material culture.[23]

Aesthetics and Ideology

The history of modern aesthetics is not merely an intellectual history, as Eagleton's work makes clear, but it is also bound up with ideology, not least of which is the ideology of gender. The autonomous rational subject is, as many feminist theorists have argued in recent years, a masculine subject and the denigration of the bodily basis of aesthetics can also be seen as a denigration of the feminine. (Höch, we will recall, was already aware of the liminal status of the female body in Weimar Germany.) In their essentialist guises, masculinity is associated with reason, while femininity is associated with the corporeal feelings and passions. The sense organs are also divided according to gender; the sense organ of sight and secondarily hearing are associated with the masculine, while the "lower" senses of touch and smell are feminine. In Hegel's aesthetic schema, furthermore, the eyes and ears are "spiritual" while the mouth and nose are "animal:" "the sensuous aspect of art only refers to the two *theoretical* senses of *sight* and *hearing*, while smell, taste, and feeling remain excluded from being sources of artistic enjoyment."[24] (It is little coincidence that vision and hearing are distant senses—we can see objects one meter, one mile, or a million miles away—while touch and smell are proximate senses.) To suggest that a recovery of aesthetics' sensual basis is also a recovery of the "feminine" is not incorrect, though such an idea leans toward essentialist versions of gender that Benjamin both would affirm and dispute. I would not suggest that this book is a gender-oriented study, but aesthetics is always tied up with gender ideologies (as well as other ideologies) and, therefore, feminist theorists will appear in the following pages. The desire here is to break new ground for religious studies, to pluralize the possibilities, and to explore the plenum of the human sensorium.

From Michael Serres, in the previous epigraph, we have hints at how the marginalized heritage of aesthetics correlatively allows it (both as a discipline of study and more specifically as that which pertains to the body and its senses) to be a place from which to disrupt the seemingly seamless structure of the rational autonomous subject, which is deeply related to the seemingly seamless ideology of sociopolitical power. Ideologies not only present a worldview, but simultaneously act to cover over their own artifice and present themselves as powerful and immediate—that is, "without mediation." In other words, the ideological worldview appears to its subjects as perfectly natural, organic, and unified. We might say ideology is *aesthetica artificialis* masquerading as *aesthetica naturalis:* It pretends it is beautiful and wholistic while it is as much an artifice as the painting on the wall. However, there is no escaping ideology. Hélène Cixous considers that, "For me ideology is a kind of vast membrane enveloping everything. We have to know that this skin exists even if it encloses us like a net or like closed eyelids."[25] Ideology closes us off, disconnects us, anaesthetizes us.

Yet there are methods for becoming aware of the ideological skin's existence, of smelling and touching the skin, of opening the eyelids. Or, as Cixous continues, "we have to know that, to change the world, we must constantly try to scratch and tear it. We can never rip the whole thing off, but we must never let it stick or stop being suspicious of it. It grows back and you start again."[26] Benjamin's writings, like Höch's montages, emphasize the material basis of culture, social interaction, and the always mediated nature of reality. In so doing Benjamin pries open the seams that have been sutured together with a hidden stitch and kept closed through powerful ideologies, including those that are manifested as myths. Unified narratives are unraveled; autonomous objects of art, complete unto themselves, are fragmented; political systems that appear to offer harmony in an otherwise alienated life are shattered. This critical activity demands both an understanding of our sense perception's constructedness, as well as a theory of art that is able to examine cultural creations. Benjamin's writing aids this pursuit.

At this point I am tempted to go the full route and argue for a recovery of a notion of aesthetics as sense perception, to overturn the progress of modern aesthetics and get back to the body. But there is no return. There is ultimately no way to get behind the cultural, artificial accumulations placed on aesthetics and recover the senses in some sort of pure state. Just as sense perception underlies art and beauty, so are the senses acculturated and educated through ideas of art, beauty, and taste that are passed on through generations and within cultures. Thus, it is critical to maintain both aspects of aesthetics, the natural side (dealing with the physical world and the sensual body) and the artificial side (dealing with art and the conceptual mind), and to see how they work together and against each other. In reference to Baumgarten and the split between the perceptual and the conceptual, Nicholas Davey suggests how Baumgarten's schema reminds us that "confusion is of the essence not because aesthetic experience is a tiresome muddle but because it is a productive bringing together, a confusion of thought and perception which enables us to *see* the idea embodied in a work and to *see* the work as an instance of that idea."[27] The field of aesthetics exists on the margins of philosophy and theology, nagging thinking to be aware of its material components, and offering a standpoint (however shifting) for ideological critique. Likewise, the bodily senses exist on the borders of the body, opening the embodied self up to something other than itself: smells, sights, and sounds of the world. In these experiences the subject perceives the world beyond his or her own body and is simultaneously connected to this world. Sense perception exists as a point of connection, a hinge, conjoining inside and outside. The aesthetic occurs at borders, at limits, allowing continual contamination and connection in both directions. Moreover, the subject is itself constituted through these sensual experiences.

The relation between the self and other is always primarily an aesthetic relation and, to borrow Emmanuel Levinas's language, this relation is therefore also ethical. Levinas's ethics are summed up in the confrontation with the "face of the other," a confrontation that is aesthetic: We see and touch the other.[28] If, as Levinas claims, ethics is first philosophy, preceding even ontology, then we could easily back up a step and suggest that aesthetics must precede even ethics, which in some ways is what Irigaray achieves in her critique of Levinas.[29] Otherness simply does not exist without the aesthetic realm, for relationships are made real only through sense perception. Even so, this argument of ontological primacy quickly grows tiresome, though I do wish to argue for the intimate and necessary connections between aesthetics and ethics. In the materialist schema of aesthetics I am attempting to describe here, the self is imbricated with the other, the internal and external worlds cross, and aesthetics cannot be disentangled from ethics. For Benjamin, aesthetics are enacted within a social realm, between others. This is especially true in reference to allegory, which in its literal meaning is the "speech of the other" (from the Greek: *allos*, "other" + *agoreuein*, "to speak publicly"). The aesthetical-ethical relation will also be an important dimension in the final chapter in relation to community and "common sense."

Re-Creation: Divinely Dividing (and Creatively Destroying)

Theories of creativity are also buried among the various definitions of aesthetics. If aesthetics deals in the work of perception, it also has something to say about the way the world is perceived by a creative artist, who then takes that world and represents or re-creates it in a distinct form that is offered to the senses of others. And here is where these notions of aesthetics meet again the concerns of religion, and also why it is perhaps not even interesting to fully separate out aesthetics from any creative activity that might be called art. Even neurobiologists and physiologists return to the importance of art when examining the senses.[30] Although art may be a modern, Western idea (many languages do not have an equivalent term to what European languages mean by the word), it nonetheless dwells within the realm of human creative activity, making it a useful concept for religious studies; for by providing theories of creation—along with sense perception and a philosophy of art—aesthetics may also tell us something about cosmologies and cosmogonies.

Constance Classen's intriguing study *The Color of Angels* suggests how premodern cosmologies operated in accordance with a range of bodily senses. Although the modern industrialized world has been overtaken by vision, to the neglect of the other senses, Classen's study uncovers a past in which there was more interplay among all the senses. This interplay was bound up with the cosmological structure of the universe, from Aristotle's linking of the senses with the four elements (sight with water, hearing with air, smell with fire, and taste and touch with earth) to Hildegard of Bingen's five-part division of the world in accordance with the five senses to Jacob Boehme's mystical suggestions that various sensory qualities (sweetness, sourness, heat) acted together at the creation of the universe. Even in Augustine's NeoPlatonism we find the five senses showing up repeatedly in the pivotal tenth book of the *Confessions*, especially when he answers his memorable question to God: "What do I love when I love Thee?" Augustine reveals he is not loving anything that is ultimately material and sensible, but rather he is loving "*a kind of* light, and melody, and fragrance, and meat, and embracement when I love my God, the light, melody, fragrance, meat, embracement of my inner man" (*Confessions*, X.6). For Augustine there is an "inner sense" that perceives God, just as there is for many contemporary theologians, yet even this is a knowledge structured *like* the bodily senses. There is a particular structure to the world, and since it is assumed to be a knowable world (and a knowable God), the structure must be parallel to the structure of the self—the microcosmos mimics the macrocosmos. Each part of the body has its proper place, and its proper activity, and is understood to be in the proper proportion to the whole. The aim of human activity corresponds to the need for harmonizing the corporeal components.[31]

The modern world—brought about through the triumph of rationality and visuality, and through their most influential offspring, the printed text—has cut us off from the plenitude of the full sensorium and thus also from a grander cosmological understanding. "It is as if," Classen suggests, "in order to bring the world in line with our current sensory priorities, the cosmos has been technologically recreated as a visual spectacle."[32] My study of Benjamin's aesthetics does not necessarily argue against vision and reason; rather, it hopes to once again recreate the world's sensual makeup, taking us away from instrumentalist reason and vision, to see the artifice of our worldview, to relink *aesthetica naturalis* with *aesthetica artificialis*.

To think through cosmologies and cosmogonies via aesthetics, we must also think through the nature of creative activity, and in particular to get away from the modern artistic notion of an individual working in private, creating solely from the inspiring images in his own head. If we try to locate the beginning, as it were, we discover there is no beginning, no creation *ex nihilo*, as many tra-ditional (patriarchal) Christian theologians would have it. There is always something before the beginning. Looking in the Hebrew Bible we find undif-ferentiated matter, *tohu wabohu* (the "formlessness and void" of Genesis 1.2), at the heart of creation. This phrase is not found elsewhere in the Hebrew Bible and it ambiguously refers to a chaotic realm over which God's spirit soars. God's creative actions, then, are not to speak things into existence out of nonexistence, but to mark divisions in this originary chaotic matter. Land is separated from sea, heavens from the earth; humans are distinguished from an-imals, and eventually man and woman are separated from out of the original, genderless *Adam*. Creation is separation and divinity divides. If there is no dif-ference or distinction, then there can be no interrelations on which the cosmos is based. The cosmic order comes about through formation of the chaos, put-ting the disarray into array.[33]

Divine dividings are also found at the origin of the biblical God's social con-tract on earth. At the beginning of the establishment of Israel, God "cuts" a covenant with Abram (Genesis 15.7–18). The covenantal creation occurs when God tells Abram the absurd news that he and Sar'ai will have a child (and many decendents). Then, God and Abram work a ritual together. Abram takes some animals and cuts them in half, laying the two sides open and apart from each other. After a strange sleep and dream sequence, the divisions of the animals are again emphasized when a "smoking fire pot," and a "flaming torch" pass through the divided animals. What is especially significant is that God "cuts" a covenant. The Hebrew *karath* is the term here, the same term used elsewhere with the signification: "cut down," "cut off," or "destroy." In other words, it is a term of division and destruction. Yet the covenant is the opposite of division; it is that which marks a connection between two or more parties. A covenant unites. A covenant cuts. A covenant cuts both ways. An animal is sacrificed by cutting, and through this cutting others are brought together. Creation and de-struction seem to be inseparable.

Although there are many other ways of thinking about the origins of the cosmos, we do find a parallel destructive creativity taking part in cosmogonies across the globe, such as the primal creative activity of taking apart the bodies of gods as seen in the Vedic story of Purusha, or the tale of Tiamat from the *Enuma Elish*. And the myth of a divided cosmos out of chaos is also found in modern phenomenological terms (drawing on ancient Greek ones), particu-larly with Edmund Husserl's concept of the *hyle* (Gk., matter): an undifferen-tiated preconscious *material*, something that may be "sensed" but not "perceived." Phenomenology then finds its own cosmogony in the conscious subject who acts upon the undivided world through observation, separating it out according to judgment. And here we come across what is perhaps the grandest myth of modernity: the myth of the individual human subject, the transcendental ego, complete unto himself, and able to generate unique artistic products. Even so, in creation story after creation story: in the beginning was the body.

Benjamin's Beginnings and Endings

Based on the preceding, I want to draw attention to two points that serve as a backdrop to Benjamin's theories of creation, art, and mythology. The first is that there is no single creative genius creating "out of nothing," for as I will describe in chapter 3 in reference to the "Work of Art" essay, "creativity and genius, eternal value and mystery" are outmoded concepts. Creation always occurs within a historical setting, with a set of given materials, circumstances, ideologies, and technologies. Second, all creation entails destruction, or as Benjamin says overtly, "'Construction' presupposes 'Destruction'" (*AP*, 470). The theme of destruction is a bedrock of Benjamin's philosophical-theological-aesthetic impulse. He shares the theme of creative destruction with Freud—seen in the "death drive" and its movement toward homeostasis—and the Dadaists and surrealists—with their destruction of limits between art and life, public and private. For Benjamin, destruction lies at the heart of creation, and to get to truth, the boundaries imposed at creation must be taken apart. Shiva-or Dionysus-like, the cosmos is perpetually destroyed and recreated in an ongoing dance. Although the cosmos is formed through separations, those very divisions are impermanent and could always be restructured. Benjamin's short 1931 piece "The Destructive Character" tells about this other side of creation:

> The destructive character knows only one watchword: make room. And only one activity: clearing away. His need for fresh air and open space is stronger than any hatred. Really, only the insight into how radically the world is simplified when tested for its worthiness for destruction leads to such an Apollonian image of the destroyer. This is the great bond embracing and unifying all that exists. The destructive character sees nothing permanent. But for this very reason he sees ways everywhere. Where others encounter walls or mountains, there, too, he sees a way. But because he sees a way everywhere, he has to clear things from it everywhere. . . . What exists he reduces to rubble—not for the sake of the rubble, but for that of the way leading through it. (*SW II*, 541)

This is a form of creative activity different from that typically conceived in Western philosophy and theology. Creation, on Benjamin's account, does not come simply through putting things together, but in clearing away, in taking things apart, resituating walls, moving mountains, and then rearranging the terrain in order to lead through it. To move toward redemption and/or revolution (an ambiguity that exists throughout Benjamin's writings) is to destroy the artificial limits that have been built up through history and myth. Like Hannah Höch, Benjamin cuts up preexistent creations that were believed to have been whole, reshuffles the pieces, and pastes them together in a new way. As a dialectical thinker, he sees aesthetic creation as a two-part process, being as interested in how meanings get created as in how meanings are destroyed; thus his ruminations on ruins, his attraction to the literary fragment and cinematic montage as destroyers of narrative continuity, and his exposition on photography's destruction of the aura of a work of art, are just a few initial examples of creative activities that simultaneously destroy. He believed in the adage that sometimes things heading over a cliff may need a little push. He was a critic who not only sought out the underlying meaning of things, but also sought to destroy older meanings. Destruction occurs "for that of the way leading through it," and where we wind up is always the present.

In light of the creative-destructive dialectic, one of the more noteworthy myths that influenced Benjamin is that found in Kabbalistic literature. Here I believe Benjamin stumbled on a radical alternative cosmogony to that of the modern West and found several ideas that paralleled his own religiopolitical concerns. His relations to Kabbalah have been questioned, and it is unclear how much he actually knew about what was still a relatively obscure topic in the early twentieth century. Of course Gershom Scholem was one of Benjamin's closest friends throughout his life, and upon his emigration to Palestine in 1923 Scholem proceeded to investigate the history of Kabbalah and almost single-handedly introduced scholarship surrounding Jewish mystical thought to the twentieth century. The Benjamin-Scholem correspondence reveals a number of exchanges related to Kabbalah, and several commentators on Benjamin have noted various ways in which Benjamin drew on Kabbalistic thought.[34] But more importantly, there are several points in Benjamin's writings where the parallels to Kabbalistic themes seem quite clear. Thus, I argue throughout this book that Kabbalistic thought resonated with Benjamin, especially in relation to cosmogony, creativity, and destruction. By no means was he an expert in the literature, but to dismiss its influence simply because he did not know Hebrew, or never pursued a rigorous line of research into its history, is surely to misunderstand the research practices of Benjamin the allegorist, the one rooting around in the ruins of history looking for useful fragments to take up into a new collection.

In relation to Benjamin's destructive-creation, a key telling of the creation in Kabbalah is taken from the influential works of Rabbi Isaac Luria, whose cosmogonical account is described in three movements: *tzimtzum* (withdrawal, reduction), *shevira* (fragmentation, breakage), and *tikkun* (mending, repair). In the beginning, the primordial infinite abstraction of God, *Ein-Sof*, contracts or reduces itself (*tzimtzum*) to permit the creation of the world to take place. If God is all encompassing, then the world would need its own room to exist; otherwise, the world would be simply equivalent to God. The existence of the world can then emerge within the space that God opens up. (The Hebrew word usually translated as "world" is *olam*, which originally connoted a space of disappearance, emptiness; in other words, "the world is absence."[35]) Through the action of *tzimtzum*, then, the wholeness of God is given up, sacrificed, "for *Ein-Sof* does not begin Its process of creation by 'giving' something, but rather by taking something away."[36] Or, "In the beginning there was the void. . . . "[37]

After this process of reduction, the *Ein-Sof* begins to fill in the void left by Its withdrawal and shapes this absented space via light, attempting to fill a number of various forms (or "vessels") that will constitute the created world. In Luria's system, these vessels are none other than the ten *sephirot* (emanations) of God, which denote God's various attributes (wisdom, intelligence, love, etc.) but are also connected with a number of other structural orders within the divine and material worlds, including the microcosmic-macrocosmic relation of the human body to the created universe: "For as a man's body consists of members and parts of various ranks all acting and reacting upon each other so as to form one organism, so does the world at large consist of a hierarchy of created things, which when they properly act and react upon each other together form literally one organic body."[38] To understand the human body is to understand the universe and the attributes of God, and vice versa. These 10 *sephirot* interconnect and represent the underlying order to the cosmos. (See Figure 1.2.)

The divine light that was meant to fill the forms is too much for the created forms, and the vessels break and fragment into many pieces. The divine light is thus dispersed, with some of it returning to its divine source, but some of it falling and scattering in the material world. Here the word "disaster" takes on its deeper significance and also connects up with Benjamin's metaphor of the constellation, as well as connecting to the fragment, the ruin, and the destruction of the aura, as will be seen in later chapters. Shimon Shokek describes the *shevirat ha-kelim* (breaking of the vessels) in terms deeply congruent with Benjamin's own cosmological vision:

> The picture of the broken world is a morbid symbol for the total ruin of all; it is a somber myth about the descent and the downfall of a spiritual world that falls into the material abyss. It is the myth of annihilation and pain; the myth of cosmogonial crisis and of cosmological failure; it symbolized the exile of the Jewish people, the exile of the physical cosmos, and the exile of the Divine Presence, know in Hebrew as *Galut ha Shekhinah*.[39]

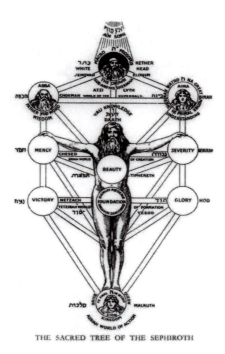

THE SACRED TREE OF THE SEPHIROTH

Figure 1.2 Microcosmic-macrocosmic relation of the tree of the *sephirot*

The implication here is that cosmological disaster parallels political disaster. In the sixteenth century, as Luria conceived of the divine sparks breaking apart, the Jewish people were living in exile from the land of Israel, but the Jews had also recently been expelled from the Iberian Peninsula where they had flourished for so long. This was the end of the Golden Age of Spanish Jewry, when Maimonides wrote his philosophical musings, when Solomon Ibn Gabirol wrote his poetry, and when Muslims, Christians, and Jews cocreated and coexisted (at least, for the most part) in *convivencia*. The Spanish *reconquista*, finalized in 1492, put an end to all that as a Spanish national identity was established, based on the unification of Iberian peninsular provinces under a single monarchy, the consolidation of a common language (Castilian), and a common religion (Roman Catholicism). Even so, all acts of identity formation also entail an opposite action: For some elements of identity to be included, other elements must be excluded. In this case, the establishment of the linguistic-religious-political confederation of Spain is simultaneously marked by the expulsion of Muslims and Jews from the Iberian Peninsula. And hence Luria's cosmology (like all myths of creation and destruction) also revealed historical-political realities of the present day. The exile of God mimics the exile of God's people, with the persistent hope for eventual unity.

After the fragmentation, the exile, comes the third and final activity, and that is the orientation toward the future, the healing and putting together of this fragmented world: *tikkun olam* (mending the world). The mythic cycle comes to completion, but it is only through the work of humans, on Luria's account, that *tikkun* can occur, and thus "Man and God are associated in Creation;"[40] both humans and God enter into creative, aesthetic history. Likewise, "redemption" is bound up with "repair" and is tied to the work of humans who keep the *mitzvoth* and hence bring about the Messiah's coming. Marc-Alain Ouaknin interprets this final stage in Luria's cosmology as a political and humanistic gesture: "[T]he Messiah is not he who produces redemption, but only the manifestation of his success. One can no longer await the Messiah; one must create him. As a symbol of the completion of the *tikkun*, the Messiah loses his personal value, and we can understand why he is of so little importance in the Lurianic Kabbalah."[41]

Ouaknin's interpretation is a profound articulation of Benjamin's fundamental struggle and points toward his view of messianic history. In Benjamin's view, the "keeping of the *mitzvoth*" is essentially translated into artistic practice, attached to political activism. In spite of his own Jewish background and references to Kabbalistic themes interspersed in his writings, he is not an observant Jew, but a critical observer of culture, and not a theistic believer in the Messiah, but a sociopolitically oriented writer of words that point toward the ruinous material conditions of modern life. Employing various creative theories—Dadaist, Freudian, Brechtian, Kabbalistic, baroque dramatic, among others—Benjamin attempts to work out the repair of the world *in the world*. The messiah comes when the world is made whole and the messiah, rather than being a singular redeemer, I suggest in the final chapter, is found in the creation of the aesthetic community, the *sensus communis*.

What I have continued to find again and again in Benjamin's aesthetic writings is a dialectic between two terms that can be intimately related to the Kabbalistic cosmology of *shevira* (fragmentation) and *tikkun* (mending). In Benjamin's German these activities become the twin stars of *die Zerstreuung* (dispersal, distraction, dissemination) and *die Sammlung* (collection, assemblage; it can also denote a library, and even contemplation; *sich sammeln* is the one who concentrates, or gathering together of the individual self). The following chapters will display how the baroque *Trauerspiel*, the technologically reproduced work of art, and the sensual, remembering community all actively function within and between these two polarities. But rather than suggesting that Benjamin sees a kind of mysticism at the heart of cultural change, I claim that Benjamin is instead doing what he does best: observing the arts, cultures, religious myths and rituals, and finding fragments that he can cut up and re-create in a new production—a leg here, an arm there, a face beyond. The body at the heart of creation is recollected under Benjamin the allegorist's pen. This is not the Eliadean periodic renewal of the world or the myth of eternal return, for, like Benjamin's famous angel of history, the allegorist faces the past while being thrown into the future, and the focus is always on the here and now. Significantly, in the end the dialectic between dispersal and collection is not re-solved for Benjamin and messianic completion never comes to a close.

Benjamin picked up on Luria's relations between cosmological myth and material history, and owing to this interrelation Benjamin's accounting of cre-ation is critically crucial to an aesthetic theory of religion, particularly in as much as it circumvents the notion that there is one singular origin that might be fully recollected. Thus, Benjamin becomes a critical figure in regard to the scholarly desire to find the origins of religion. Tomoko Masuzawa, utilizing the work of Benjamin, posits a number of questions that deconstruct this concern for origins, this "absolute beginning": "Does a typical myth represent and re-actualize a pristine moment which is itself outside of time? Or, to put the mat-ter most generally and pointedly, do repetition and representation presuppose an absolute origin and the concomitant logic of origination? Could repetition and representation be conceived, or performed, in some other way?"[42] The question of an origin to myth and religion has continued to entice religionists, yet perhaps this is asking the wrong question, and perhaps, as Masuzawa sug-gests, we might be able to conceive of its repetition in some other way. From another perspective, Hélène Cixous suggests that "The origin is a masculine myth: I always want to know where I come from. The question 'Where do chil-dren come from?' is basically a masculine, much more than a feminine, ques-tion."[43] Myths of origin, of positing some pristine "out of time" moment at the beginning, amounts to a desire for control, for power, to authenticate any and every work of creation as the result of a singular, self-collected individual (God or man).

All too often, as commonly conceived in Eurocentric philosophies, creation is a one-way process. It is about creating out of nothing, from the biblical God to the myth of the romantic genius working alone—all of it comes down to a singular event that might, with the best of research, be made present again. What is consistently forgotten are the divisions, the cuttings that accompany every creative activity. Benjamin introduces us to a grander view of the creative process. Myths, symbols, and narratives are powerful forces in human culture, but they become dangerous precisely when they only get at one side of creation, and when they make us believe that the whole is assembled, or reassembled. For Benjamin, these "wholes" (and there are many) are always subject to dispersal, and it is his creative work to be a destructive character. Creation occurs, chaos is cosmicized, yet the coherence of the cosmos is only an illusion and there is no going back to a pristine origin. As Höch displays an always fragmented unity, bodies that are destroyed and reconfigured, so Benjamin suggests how our world is a world of history, full of death, decay, and fragmentation. We fool ourselves believing otherwise in our myths of the past. In response to our pacifying myths that lead to complacency and anaesthesia, Benjamin seeks to eliminate myths of creation and to display the dividing lines of creation, thereby exposing the illusion of our myths, the fault lines on which creation is built.

Seeing Fragments in Collections

While Hannah Höch re-created the world through her cutups during Benjamin's day, more contemporary recreations can be seen in the work of Anselm Kiefer. Kiefer continues to create in a manner akin to Benjamin's cosmological visions, though in a post-Holocaust Germany. His massive mixed-media paintings and installations probe Germany's past, noting the binds between mythology, ideology, and history, particularly as they came together in Nazism. As with Benjamin's writings, Kiefer's works dismember and remember myths in physical forms so that they may be reactualized in our current cultural consciousness. The key difference is that Benjamin wrote before the Holocaust, and Kiefer remains fixated on the Holocaust as a very real "breaking point" of history, especially German history.

One of the mythologies to which Kiefer has consistently turned is that of Kabbalah, and his 1990 installation, *Breaking of the Vessels* (See Figure 1.3), offers a captivating emblem for the creation-destruction dialectic found in Jewish mysticism and in Benjamin's writings. Faced with a mammoth bookshelf of lead books, with shards of glass embedded between the pages and scattered on the floor, the viewer seems to have just missed some catastrophe that caused the glass to fall. While the viewer questions the breaking, she or he is simultaneously impelled to approach the shelved books and leaf through the pages. They would appear to contain some secret writing. The broken glass on the floor nonetheless serves as a barrier, leaving the books inaccessible. If this is a library or collection of books (in German we could call this *die Sammlung*), it is nonetheless a scattered (*Zerstreuung*) library, and ultimately illegible.

Surrounding and amid the bookshelves are lead nameplates indicating the ten *sephirot* of the Kabbalistic system, connected together, at least in some instances, by wire. Kiefer places these nameplates exactly where they appear in relation to each other on the diagrammed tree of the *sephirot* (refer to Figure 1.2). In the Kabbalistic system, the interrelation of the *sephirot* indicates the structure of creation, the ordered law of nature, and "Divinity in action appears as the dynamic unity of the *sephirot*."[44] Although each attribute of God is important, equally critical is the connectedness between them. But with the breaking of the vessels the world becomes disjointed, fallen. In a radical theological

Figure 1.3 Anselm Kiefer, *Breaking of the Vessels*, 1990. ©The Saint Louis Museum of Art. Funds given by Mr. and Mrs. George Schlapp, Mrs. Francis A. Mesker, The Henry L. and Natalie Edison Freund Charitable Trust, The Arthur and Helen Baer Charitable Foundation, Sam and Marilyn Fox, Mrs. Eleanor J. Moore, Mr. and Mrs. John Wooten Moore, Donna and William Nussbaum, Mr and Mrs. James E. Schneithorst, Jain and Richard Shaikewitz, Mark Twain Bankshares, Inc., Mr. and Mrs. Gary Wolff, Mr. and Mrs. Lester P. Akerman, Jr. the Honorable and Mrs. Thomas Eagleton, Alison and John Ferring, Mrs. Gail K. Fischmann, Mr. and Mrs. Gyo Obata, Jane and Warren Shapleigh, Lee and Barbara Wagman, Anabeth Calkins and John Weil, Museum Shop Fund, the Contemporary Art Society, and Museum Purchase; Dr. and Mrs. Harold J. Joseph, estate of Alice P. Francis, Fine Arts Associates, J. Lionberger Davis, Mr. and Mrs. Samuel B. Edison, Mr. and Mrs. Morton D. May, estate of Louis H. Franciscus, and anonymous donor, Miss Ellas M. Boedecker, by exchange.

idea, divinity itself is here put in exile as it fragments and falls to earth, where it is captured and enclosed within *qlipot* (husks or shells). Divinity remains (divinity's remains) among us creatures of the world, but because of the *qlipot* surrounding its fragments, the divine is not immediately accessible, and the work of humans is to free the divine sparks and work toward *tikkun*. Kiefer's installation is cosmogonical, depicting the origins of the world, while it further suggests that the world is like a library, there to be read, if only we could. Indeed, *sepher* is the Hebrew for "book," and there is the hint that reading the world as text is an activity to help mend the world putting the *sephirot* in harmony. Even so, we are kept from the hidden truths, the divine sparks, by the fragments of glass, forming something of a *qlipa* around the library.

Although the cosmological dimensions are clear, the principal connection that Kiefer makes is that between the mythological and the historical, for as the installation invokes the beginning of the world as we know it—a fallen world containing fragments of divinity—it also triggers the more immediate circumstances of further exile and the attempted elimination of the Jews during Hitler's reign. Art historian Lisa Saltzman points out that Kiefer's *Breaking the Vessels* is "at once deeply Kabbalistic in its thematizing of mystical creation and destruction and deeply historical in its insistent reference to the events of Kristallnacht."[45] The shattered glass is reminiscent of the mystical breaking of the vessels, and the historical breaking of the actual glass of Jewish stores and homes in Germany in 1938. Just as Luria conflated cosmology and political reality, so does Kiefer, challenging us to perform perhaps the greatest activity in the process of *tikkun olam*: a re-membering that connects myth and history. Unless myth and history are put together, the world is incomplete, left in fragments.

The problem with the mythology of the modern world is that through the industrializing and technologizing of our bodies, we are separated from our own material realities. Modern life substitutes its own mechanical (or now, "informational") body for our senses, and we end up not even knowing we are living in ruins. The phantasmagoric mass-mediated myths of modern life prod us into believing that the world is whole, running as it should be. What is needed then are aesthetic shocks to wake us up to the reality of our lives. This is not shock for shock's-sake, which seems to be where much of twentieth-century art took us, but shock to realize where the natural and artificial aesthetics diverge. Benjamin saw cultural and historical forces such as Freudian psychoanalysis, baroque allegory, Dadaism, surrealism, Brechtian theater, Soviet montage, Baudelaire's poetry, and Lurianic Kabbalah as shaking the foundations, bringing us to our senses, and displaying the fragments we live among, and thus waking us up to the ethical obligations of *tikkun*.

By taking apart the world, Benjamin's writings allow us to rummage through the ruins in order to put pieces back together. In Benjamin's texts we see a cosmogonical and eschatological structure again and again, beginning with a fragmentation that leads to the possibilities of reassemblage. Yet at a certain point Benjamin the Kabbalist confronts Benjamin the avant-gardist, and it is never clear whether his re-creations, his attempts at *tikkun olam*, are attempts at restoring the world in some manner that God originally intended, or whether the "God-given" lines are transgressed and what we end up with is an ever new construction of the cosmos based on the work of the masses.[46] What is central to Benjamin is not the past but the present, political life here and now (*Hier und Jetzt*). By dynamiting the past and offering up the shrapnel as images, Benjamin mines what was forgotten in the past, to reveal and thereby potentially redeem the lost other. And it is through allegory that this unearthing begins.

2
Allegorical Aesthetics

Every poem is a misinterpretation of a parent poem. A poem is not an overcoming of anxiety, but is that anxiety. Poets' misinterpretations or poems are more drastic than critics' misinterpretations or criticism, but this is only a difference in degree and not at all in kind. There are no interpretations but only misinterpretations, and so all criticism is prose poetry.

Harold Bloom[1]

In an episode from the 1990s hit television series *Seinfeld,* character George Costanza accidentally squirts grapefruit juice into his eye, causing him to involuntarily twitch his eye for the next couple of days. People with whom he speaks interpret his "twitch" as a "wink," and thus, he essentially undermines all that he is saying. While he speaks one way and means one thing, he is betrayed by his own eye, which others take to be a signal that what he is saying is not quite true. His body constantly thwarts his messages. The "wink" turns his speech into something other.

Perhaps the writers of *Seinfeld* read their anthropology, as Clifford Geertz (drawing on the work of Gilbert Ryle) discusses the difference between a wink and a twitch. In a "thin" phenomenological description, the two actions are the same; their appearance is identical. But anthropologists must give a "thick" description; they must try to decipher actions, and then tell of the intention behind the action. In the difference between a wink and a twitch, meanings are drastically altered.[2] The people George Costanza encountered may have been bad ethnographers by confusing the wink with the twitch, yet they nonetheless functioned as allegorists—which is not to say that allegorists are simply bad anthropologists.

George's companions allegorize George's speech, making him speak otherwise by driving a fissure between what is said and what is intended: To speak allegorically is to speak otherwise, in public, for allegory is other speech (Greek: *allos*, "other" + *agoreuein*, "to speak publicly"). One may protest that George was an unwitting allegorist, but therein lies a key to understanding allegory, especially Benjamin's version. As typically conceived, there is an author who writes allegories, who says one thing and means another; but there is also the necessity of a reader, an interpreter who reads on two or more levels. The *Seinfeld* sequence puts the emphasis, as Benjamin does, on the interpreter; for indeed, "ultimately, allegory occurs only under the critical gaze,"[3] and its meaning is uncovered only in public. The role of the critic will be a particularly pertinent element of allegory for Benjamin, and this is directly tied to the way in which allegory, like the symbol, is a public and cultural mode of communication.

For Geertz and other anthropologists, cultures are made up of systems of symbols. In the symbol there is a necessary, if conventional, link between what an object, image, or speech *says*, and what it *means*; the symbol's appearance is fundamentally tied to its meaning. Allegory functions in a related way—each has a split between appearance and meaning—but mutates the conventions of the symbol. An allegory, to give a provocative initial definition, is thus *a mutating symbol*. Literary theorist Angus Fletcher discusses such a rôle of allegory:

> In the simplest terms, allegory says one thing and means another. It destroys the normal expectation we have about language, that our words "mean what they say." When we predicate quality x of person Y, Y really is what our predication says he is (or we assume so); but allegory would turn Y into something other (*allos*) than what the open and direct statement tells the reader. Pushed to an extreme, this ironic usage would subvert language itself, turning everything into an Orwellian newspeak. In this sense we see how allegory is properly considered a mode: it is a fundamental process of encoding our speech.[4]

George Costanza's "wink" is therefore allegorical, turning his speech into something other, encoding his language, which is read and interpreted by his interlocutors.

As with most of his concepts, Benjamin's notion of allegory is made up of a constellation of other concepts, and a single term becomes embedded among other terms, sometimes completely disguising the original term itself. Allegory is one such term, but then again, disguise and distortion are in the nature of allegory. This chapter identifies and describes the allegorical constellation as found in Benjamin's writings. The thematic "stars" discussed include the relation between allegory and symbol, tragedy and lamentation, metaphor and metonymy, word and image, as well as natural history, memory, the ruin, myth, and redemption. His most developed theory of allegory is articulated in the third and final chapter of *Ursprung des deutschen Trauerspiels*. The intents of my analysis here are not to provide a thorough or systematic reading of this dense and obscure book, but to move directly to the notion of allegory as given in Benjamin's chapter, "Allegory and *Trauerspiel*," and developing that through a number of more contemporary twentieth-century thinkers. In particular, I wish to trace the roles that a conception of allegory might play for religious aesthetics, or what we might otherwise here call "allegorical aesthetics."

A Text of Lamentation

In the *Trauerspiel* book Benjamin examines dramas of the baroque period: German plays that were influenced by Lutheranism and Spanish Counter-Reformation plays. While stemming from theologically countered positions, the two types are united in Benjamin's study in their "secularization" and allegorization of the previous medieval mystery play. While the Spanish plays—particularly those of Calderón (1600–1681/3) and Lope de Vega (1562–1635)—are artistically superior in Benjamin's estimation, it is finally the German dramas—those of Daniel Caspers von Lohenstein (1635–1683), Johann Christian Hallmann (1640–1704), and Andreas Gryphius (1616–1664)—that produce the effect of lament so crucial to Benjamin's rehistoricizing accounts of the *Trauerspiel*. The results of Benjamin's analysis are nothing less than a critical reexamination of the origins of modernity. Benjamin's investigation seeks out lost fragments in the pre-history of the modern world, uncovering themes that had been left to ruin in its own progressive mytho-logic. In his rescuing of allegory, Benjamin affirms its mutating function, weaving this mutation into the mythological past as related to the present, and thus allowing the unified story of modernist progress to unravel.

In many ways, Benjamin's *Trauerspiel* study is a culmination of much of his early work, and portions of it appeared in print in the 10-plus years prior to its completion. It is dedicated as follows, to his wife at the time, Dora Pollak: "Conceived 1916. Written 1925." Originally written as his failed *Habilitationsschrift*, it was published in 1928, received little attention, and essentially disappeared after 1931 with the rise of National Socialism in Germany. As his *Habilitationsschrift*, it got him nowhere, being too incomprehensible to his readers in the university (including a reader in the department of Aesthetics) and not fitting the rigid demands of the German university system. This failure effectively barred him from any academic career, and he spent the remainder of his life eking out a living through translation work, journalistic pieces, and some editing. Copies of the failed dissertation remained with a few friends (including Theodor Adorno, Gershom Scholem, Hannah Arendt, and Siegfried

Kracauer), and it was eventually made public again with the publication of his selected works in 1955, under the editorship of Theodor and Gretel Adorno. The first English translation was completed in 1977. In part, the dissertation-turned-book was castigated because it was so strange, the product of a critic who liked to mix genres, a practice for which the institution of the German university had little tolerance. The book was a collection of some arcane research, mixed with an underlying theological and quasi-mystical approach to language, and an added personal touch, causing George Steiner in the introduction of the English-language edition to call it an "uncomfortable hybrid." In many ways, Benjamin simply did not fit the mold of the German university system, especially in the Germany of the 1920s and 1930s.

Before turning to Benjamin's concept of allegory, I briefly consider a few matters of contextualizing the final chapter on allegory within the larger book. First, it is important to note a problem with the English translation of the book's title. The translation of *Trauerspiel* as "tragic drama" is misleading, as many have pointed out, leading most contemporary English-speaking scholars to translate it as "mourning-play." To the English reader, "tragic drama" sounds too much like the genre of "tragedy," to which *Trauerspiel* is related, although it is a distinct genre for Benjamin, and he spends the hundred-page second chapter (fully one-half of the entire book) playing out the differences between the two. He is also keen to elevate the *Trauerspiel* as a legitimate genre in its own right, rescuing it from the disfavor of most critics who had seen it as a "failed tragedy" (and, along with it, the mode of allegory). Various theories of tragedy influenced his thought at this point—significantly Nietzsche's *Birth of Tragedy*, and Franz Rosenzweig's *Star of Redemption*, published in 1921, while Benjamin was writing the *Trauerspiel* book—but the distance he maintained from the genre of tragedy was crucial, for it shows his concern with a historical-materialist aesthetic even in this early period of his writing.

In this early period, Benjamin had yet to fully engage with the Marxist-political orientation endemic to his subsequent work.[5] Toward the end of his research for the *Trauerspiel* book, he was introduced to a theater actor and director named Asja Lacis, who in turn helped introduce Benjamin to Marxism and, eventually, Bertolt Brecht. Around the same time he became enamored with Georg Lukác's *History and Class Consciousness*. If his Marxist leanings were burgeoning at this point, they were not yet well developed.

Nonetheless, there is an interest in an aesthetics grounded in historical-materialistic concerns, and he is particularly keen to avoid the ideologies of myth. In this regard, the distinction Benjamin makes between tragedy and *Trauerspiel* is significant, and although there is not enough space to fully come to terms with this distinction, and we are ultimately concerned with the theory of allegory, I will relate George Steiner's nicely synthesized introductory definitions of these two genres, provided in his introduction to the English translation. On the one hand,

> Tragedy is grounded in myth. It acts out a rite of heroic sacrifice. In its fulfillment of this sacrificial-transcendent design, tragedy endows the hero with the realization that he is ethically in advance of the Gods, that his sufferance of good and evil, of fortune and desolation, has projected him into a category beyond the comprehension of the essentially "innocent" though materially omnipotent deities. . . . This realization compels the tragic hero to silence. (*OGTD*, 16)

Benjamin does not dislike tragedy as such; rather, he is against certain "naïve" and "vain" views that "present the tragic as something universally human" (*OGTD*, 101). Tragedy upsets the old mythic order, which Benjamin appreciates, but it institutes yet another new order in the place of the old: "Benjamin's emphasis is not on the new *order* but on the explosive and subversive force against the old mythical order."[6] Thus he emphasizes *Trauerspiel*, as it is grounded in the particularities of history, not myth, and this groundedness, as Steiner sums it up,

> Generates both content and style. Feeling himself dragged toward the abyss of damnation, a damnation registered in a profoundly carnal sense, the Baroque dramatist, allegorist, historiographer, and the personages he animates, cling fervently to the world. The *Trauerspiel* is counter-transcendental; it celebrates the immanence of existence even where this existence is passed in torment. It is emphatically "mundane," earth-bound, corporeal. It is not the tragic hero who occupies the center of the stage, but the Janus-faced composite of tyrant and martyr, of the Sovereign who incarnates the mystery of absolute will and of its victim (so often himself). (*OGTD*, 16)

Benjamin theorizes that the *Trauerspiel* marked a decisive break with the theatrical tradition of the past, particularly as the tradition was influenced by mythical Greek tragedy. While earlier medieval mystery plays and Renaissance dramas were situated within a cosmically ordered world, the *Trauerspiel* interested Benjamin because it delved into the profane and even chaotic realm of a fallen, corporeal world. And in its setting within the carnal world, *Trauerspiel* offers a place to rethink the site of the aesthetic—that liminal passageway between the inner and the outer worlds—bound to the vicissitudes of history.

The further difference between tragedy and the *Trauerspiel* is a distance Benjamin wishes to strike with a Heideggerian view of history, particularly that established in Heidegger's early works and leading up to *Being and Time*, published one year before Benjamin's book was published. Howard Caygill suggests that for Heidegger the *Dasein* of the authentic subject can gather past, present, and future together, "*even in the moment of death*."[7] There is always room for a subjective will to come together on this view and make a final mean-ingful decision, just as the mythic hero of tragedy ends with destruction but also a new order. Benjamin's version of the *Trauerspiel*, contrarily, retains no possibility for final meaningful decision, there is "simply indecision and acci-dent in the face of catastrophe."[8] Death is not a denouement of the actions lead-ing up to that point, a final and glorious *coming together* of action; rather, death in the mourning-play simply occurs *by accident*, there is no final subjec-tive completion. "The Baroque knows no eschatology; and for that very reason it possesses no mechanism by which all earthly things are gathered in together and exalted before being consigned to their end" (*OGTD*, 66). The interrelated notions of "accident" and a lack of an overarching eschatology are critical ele-ments in the mode of allegory.

Even with these distinctions, Benjamin refrains from a too-strict delin-eation of genres and offers the possibility that Shakespeare's *Hamlet*, classically understood as a tragedy, could be construed as a *Trauerspiel*.[9] This is part of the allegorical impulse, to uproot elements from their native understanding, to transpose them, and to shine new light on them from another perspective. Tragedy and *Trauerspiel* are related, but what is revealed in such an examina-tion is that the second term distorts or mutates the first one. If *Hamlet* can be considered a *Trauerspiel*, a history of criticism of Shakespeare is in some ways rewritten.

Having noted these distinctions, and having noted recent scholars' transla-tions of *Trauerspiel* as "mourning-play," I wish to alter the translation once more for my purposes herein. "Mourning," according to most modern English dictionaries, entails the use of conventional signs to express sadness in response to a tragedy. This would include rituals such as wearing black or covering one's body with sackcloth and ashes. These are symbols and as such have intrinsic, conventional relations to that with which they are connected. Furthermore, there is a shared code to these actions: The same ritual is acted out by different people at different times.

Shifting this slightly, in the following I will be implementing the English translation of *Trauerspiel* as "lament-play." Benjamin used the traditional title of *Trauerspiel*, which would indeed be more accurately translated as "mourning-play." Nonetheless, "lament-play" is within the semantic range of *Trauerspiel* and actually moves us closer in English to what I believe Benjamin was after. As Benjamin sought to rescue *Trauerspiel* from tragedy, and allegory from symbol, my translation seeks to rescue lamentation from mourning.

There are two reasons for my translation: the first is a religious one, the sec-ond is an aesthetic one. By using lament, I intend to draw attention to Benjamin's own interest in the relation between the *Trauerspiel* and certain tra-ditions of Judaism. In a letter to his friend Gershom Scholem, in the midst of his reflections on the language of the *Trauerspiel* in 1918, Benjamin realized that his concerns "must be asked on the basis of the Hebrew lament."[10] Perhaps this is because, as biblical scholar Claus Westermann states, rather than serving to explain or admonish, "the real significance of [biblical] laments resides in the way they allow the suffering of the afflicted to find expression."[11] Another biblical scholar, Tod Linafelt, sees lament as a "literature of survival," and explains that "In the bible lament is always more than just mourning (i.e., a dirge or elegy) and is an address to God to change the present circumstances. So it must be theoretically persuasive and hence good literature."[12] In the context of the Hebrew Bible a lamentation entails an interaction with God, an interaction that may be as much a protest as a prayer. Indeed, the character of God is conspicuously absent from the biblical book of Lamentations.

Which is worth noting, since Benjamin himself makes an interesting fluctuation in his writings between "protest" and "prayer." In the early 1920s, he wrote a short article addressing the socioeconomic problems Germany was experiencing at the time. When he first wrote the piece, he included the line that the person suffering from hardship should "so discipline himself that his suffering becomes no longer the downhill road of *hate*, but the rising path of *prayer*." The piece wasn't published until five years later, by which time Benjamin had changed his mind on a number of things. So, the published version offers an intriguing rewrite: the person suffering should "so discipline himself that his suffering becomes no longer the downhill road of *grief*, but the rising path of *protest*."[13] Hate turns to grief, and prayer turns to protest. This anecdote tells of Benjamin's intellectual transformation, and also offers a rethinking about the importance of lamentation as both a religious and political genre. Lamentation provides a way to bring prayer and protest together.[14]

Besides the religious connection, I use the term "lament" rather than mourning for aesthetic reasons, since a lamentation is often expressed in poetry and/or song and, as Linafelt suggests, it must be "good literature." In sketches on the language of the *Trauerspiel*, Benjamin suggests the importance of music: "In the mourning [lament] play, sounds are laid out symphonically, and this constitutes the musical principle of its language"(*SW I*, 60).[15] Mourning may be an emotional expression of grief and sadness, but lament takes the raw expressions and puts them into an artistic form. In this way, the lament is not a solitary activity. The songs of despair must be heard and, in the midst of grieving, there is nonetheless the work to be done of putting the chaos of emotions into an ordered form, of connecting the inner experience with the outer world.

Given both the aesthetic and religious reasons, I will suggest that a lament (or lamentation) is akin to the function of Benjamin's allegory. Thus, in the following I will use *lament*, though readers should be aware of other connections and disconnections with mourning and tragedy.

Allegory and/or Symbol

This chapter began with some preliminary distinctions between the allegory and the symbol, and I suggested that allegory was a mutating symbol. This difference underlies much of Benjamin's study on the German lament-plays and the final chapter of the *Trauerspiel* book begins with this difference. Through the influence of the romantics, according to Benjamin, the symbol was "abused" and led to a "comforting effect on the practice of investigation into the arts" (*OGTD*, 160). "Comfort" is not a positive term for Benjamin, striking too bourgeois a chord and causing the transformation of humans into vermin. The symbol, theologocentrically speaking, "insists on the indivisible unity of form and content" and "as a symbolic construct, the beautiful is supposed to merge with the divine in an unbroken whole" (ibid.). Further, this harmonious unity is finally affected within the interiority of the individual; the symbol is reliant on individual subjectivity.[16]

Up through the Renaissance, Western thought utilized the figures of allegory and symbol in a way that made them practically indistinguishable, and the terms were used more or less interchangeably. The romantics, however, found a difference, and the difference led them to exorcise allegory in favor of the richness of the symbolic.[17] A symbol, in its strictest denotation, deals with the representation of an "idea," but it is a representation that is not distinguished from the idea. Rather, the full meaning of the symbol has to do with the *connection* between the material thing (word, image, or other) and the metaphysical idea to which the thing refers. The symbol is thus constituted of two parts. The result of this unifying connection is that, as the mind comes to a comprehension of what is being symbolized, the material thing itself disappears into the greater idea *beyond* the thing. Heidegger mimics this romantic thinking in "The Origin of the Work of Art": "In the work of art something other is brought together with the thing that is made. To bring together is, in Greek, *symballein*. The work is a symbol."[18] Heidegger goes on to show, contra the romantics, the impossibility of finding a single metaphysical source from which physical art might spring, instead highlighting the multiplicity of art in a manner akin to Benjamin. What is important here is to note the way the symbol works toward unity. A symbol is enacted when the work of art *qua* object connects to the deeper idea or spirit beyond it, and that connection is singular.

Benjamin is interested in allegory because of its mutating character, its assertion of the precariousness of any relation between form and content. As Rainer Rochlitz comments, allegory is itself "a symbolic form in the most general sense, allegory reveals the fragility of the symbol, its always provisional and momentary victory over 'the arbitrariness of the sign.'"[19] The allegory looks like a symbol, but opens the material sign/signification relation to further possible meanings, especially those due to the perception of the interpreter(s). There is a vital relation between form and content, but the fleeting, subversive nature of the allegory is what Benjamin is after. Rehashing the suggestions made by romantics such as Goethe—who first distinguished and consequently dismissed the allegory—and Schopenhauer, Benjamin seeks to rescue and rethink allegory as a potent *mode* of criticism. He takes the romantic negative descriptions of allegory and reproduces it, making it productive again for the present.

Regarding the importance of symbols for cultural and religious studies via the aesthetics of sense perception, David Chidester notes: "To adapt (and modify) a familiar aphorism from Paul Ricoeur, perception—particularly the perceptual modes of seeing and hearing—gives rise to symbols, and symbols give rise to thought."[20] And anthropologist of symbols Mary LeCron Foster puts it bluntly: "As a 'thing,' a symbol has material reality and is experienced through the senses."[21] What an allegorical aesthetics then does to these formulae is to put the symbol in motion, to distort it by showing the social structuring of sense perception, and how a change in sociocultural factors alters perception, which then alters the symbols that give rise to thought. Owing to the influence of structural anthropology, symbols are often understood in their syntagmatic form—they are deeply embedded in culture, and their conventional understanding is not immutable, yet very stable—while Benjamin's allegory instead points toward the historical fluidity of perception and symbolizing processes.

Quoting extensively from a classic nineteenth-century text on symbols, Friedrich Creuzer's *Symbolik und Mythologie der Alten Völker* of 1819, Benjamin retains Creuzer's separation of allegory and symbol: "The [allegorical] signifies merely a general concept, or an idea which is different from itself; the [symbolic] is the very incarnation and embodiment of the idea. In the [symbolic] a process of substitution takes place. . . . In the [allegorical] the concept itself has descended into our physical world, and we see it itself directly in the image" (*OGTD*, 164–65). While Creuzer and others of his time take this difference as a reason to praise the symbol and denigrate the allegory, Benjamin revisits the romantic hierarchy and rescues the lesser term.

Whereas the symbol aims at a single meaning, directly related to one idea, allegory is open to a multiplicity of meanings because of its earthbound and constantly visible existence. The material dimension of the symbol is disregarded once the meaning has been grasped, but allegory asserts its own physical nature. Note in the following how the symbol would pretend to bypass its physicality and become "hidden," while allegory retains the dialectical energy that disallows its physical disappearance:

> The measure of time for the experience of the symbol is the mystical instant in which the symbol assumes the meaning into its hidden and, if one might say so, wooded interior. On the other hand, allegory is not free from a corresponding dialectic, and the contemplative calm with

which it immerses itself into the depths which separate visual being from meaning, has none of the disinterested self-sufficiency which is present in the apparently related intention of the sign [i.e., "symbol"]. (165–66)

This difference begins to suggest Benjamin's material (even his metaphors are earthly) emphasis. It is the visual image of the allegory that is crucial, because it is here and now in this world, retaining the dialectical impulse between material object and immaterial meaning. The symbol, on the other hand, always points to a transcendental ideal, existing out of time, in the "mystical instant," leading to an esoteric knowledge held in the "wooded interior." The symbol dissolves the dialectical relation between object and meaning while the allegory keeps it open; thus the allegory is a precursor to Benjamin's well-known "dialectical image." The symbol's self-sufficiency and internalization bar connections to other possible meanings, but such a wooded interior invokes the allegorist in Benjamin, another guise for his "destructive character" who knows "only one activity: clearing away" (*SW II*, 541–42). In this way the allegorist reveals what is kept within the hidden forest.

Allegory, Symbol, and Sign in Twentieth-Century Criticism

To shine further light on the relations between symbols and allegories, we must digress through other renditions of the terms in twentieth-century criticism.[22] In spite of a recent reviving of allegory through Paul de Man, Harold Bloom, and other "postmodernists" (often referring back to Benjamin's work), allegory, especially in religious circles, has maintained a negative image owing in part to earlier Christian interpreters' supersessionist readings of the "Old" Testament through the "New." (I will return to this at the end of this chapter.) The effects of these definitions are therefore not just a play of semantics but, like all language games, are bound up within hermeneutical ideologies.

Ferdinand de Saussure understood the gravity of the unifying nature of symbols, and this knowledge stands at the heart of his linguistic theory. Although he is best known for his posthumously published *Course in General Linguistics,* in which he lays out the nature of the linguistic sign, what is often overlooked is the way he opted for the "sign" rather than the "symbol" precisely because of the unifying tendencies of the latter. Saussure is significant because he is acknowledged as the first to fully argue that there is no natural or intrinsic correspondence between signifier and signified in the sign; rather, "*the linguistic sign is arbitrary.*"[23] (This does not mean, however, that it is wholly relative, since "the individual [speaker] does not have the power to change a sign in any way once it has become established in the linguistic community."[24]) Because the sign is arbitrary—because the relation between signified and signifier is not intrinsic or natural—Saussure disregards the conventional term *symbol*, for "one characteristic of the symbol is that it is never wholly arbitrary; it is not empty, for there is the rudiment of a natural bond between the signifier and the signified. The symbol of justice, a pair of scales, could not be replaced by just any other symbol, such as a chariot."[25] Replacing the natural bond of the signifier and signified within the symbol, Saussure founds his linguistics on the arbitrariness of the *sign*, which provides more space to play.

In an early work, "From Symbol to Sign" (written in 1966–1967), Julia Kristeva follows Saussure's distinction between the symbol and the sign and expands the difference. Quoting from C. S. Peirce, she notes that the symbol "refers to the object that it denotes by virtue of a *law*, usually an association of general ideas."[26] As such, "the signified object is *represented* by the signifying unit through a restrictive function-relation," and is therefore "monovalent."[27] Historicizing the symbol, Kristeva argues that a shift occurred in European culture at the end of the Middle Ages (especially the thirteenth through the fifteenth centuries on her account) in which the ambiguity found in the *sign* began to replace the universal transcendent orientation of the symbol. Kristeva notes:

> Once the relation between the signifying unit and the idea had been weakened, the signifying unit became more and more "material" until it forgot its "origins." Thus, up until 1350, it is the *Word*, in the guise of Jesus Christ, which creates the world. After this date, we see the appearance of "an old man who measures the earth with a compass and throws the sun and the stars into the heavens." The Word, that is, "the interpretant" (if one wishes to use modern terminology), becomes blurred and its replicas more visual and substantive, linked together in a horizontal chain firmly situated in this world. This is why it is no longer the Word (Christ as idea) that *retains the meaning*; instead it is the combination of "markings" (images of the old man, the sky, the stars) that *produce* it.[28]

This quotation displays the theological orientation of the symbol, rooting meaning in a transcendent realm, which allows but a singular meaning. With the rise of the sign, there is no longer a solitary and stable *Logos* that provides meaning, but rather the combinatory activity of material, graphic "markings." The movement from symbol to sign, according to Kristeva, eventually allows for the rise of the novel in Europe and is responsible for generating the literary and artistic tradition. Central to this shift is a usurpation of metaphor by metonymy. To be multiple, the sign must bring forth a vital "horizontal" function, as opposed to the symbol's primarily "vertical" function, and to this reorientation we now turn.

Metaphor, Metonymy, and Transformational Poetics

Traditionally, one of the distinguishing ways to relate the idea of allegory is to consider it to be a particular combination of metaphor and metonymy. Indeed, these twin tropes offer another perspective on Benjamin's notions of allegory, and it is worth hashing out some of the details of these terms here. Joel Fineman synthesizes many precedent ideas from Quintilian to Roman Jakobson, to suggest that allegory is concerned with "the poetical projection of the metaphoric axis onto the metonymic, whereas metaphor is understood as the synchronic system of differences that constitutes the order of language (*langue*), and metonymy the diachronic principle of combination and connection by means of which structure is actualized in time in speech (*parole*)."[29] The metaphoric is oriented vertically, creating a hierarchical order, while the metonymic unfolds horizontally through time.

The printed word allegorizes allegory itself, and the interrelation of the metaphor and metonym must be reviewed through the lens of technology. The centrality of technology, the relation of words and images, and orality and literacy will all be dealt with later in this chapter and the next, but up front it must be noted that a key historical shift paralleling the move from "symbol to sign" observed by Kristeva is a move from orality to literacy, and the time period she discusses is also the time of the rise of large-scale manuscript production in Europe, eventually leading to the development of the printing press. In the preceding quotation from Kristeva, we already note how the metonymic dimension is hinted at through "graphic markings." Therefore, bound to the modern movement toward the metonymical is the concomitant movement toward literacy. So in discussing the metaphoric and metonymic, we must remain aware of the differences between the oral and the written.

In spite of the sign's doing away with universals, Kristeva points out that the sign yet retains the symbol's "dualist, hierarchical and hierarchizing" functions. The difference would be that the sign simply refers to "entities of lesser dimensions that are more *concretized* than the symbol," and as such "does not refer to a single unique reality, but *evokes* a collection of associated images and ideas."[30] Meaning is not banished, simply diversified. Here, we begin to get a sense of the importance of multiplicity over against singularity, multivalence over against monovalence; and this is intimately bound to the metonymic dimension. Kristeva's sign becomes strikingly similar to Benjamin's allegory:

> Within their horizontal function, the units of the sign's semiotic practice are articulated as a *metonymic chain of deflection [écarts]* that signifies a *progressive creation of metaphors*. Opposing terms, which are always exclusive, are caught up in a system of multiple and always possible deflections ("surprises" in narrative structures) giving the illusion of an

open structure that is impossible to terminate, and which has an *arbitrary* ending.[31]

These deflections, these "surprises," are precisely what interest Benjamin about the allegorical mode of the Baroque lament-play, and they are what connects the dialectical relation of the two types of experience: *Erfahrung* provides the narrativized, ordered structure, while *Erlebnis* is that element of "surprise" that upsets the order and deflects the overall meaning. While symbols retain a narrative whole, an allegory disrupts the totalizing tendencies as it allows an open and arbitrary structure, susceptible to multiple future interpretations. These disruptions are metonymical in structure, and a further look at the interrelation between metaphor and metonymy will assist us in an examination of Benjamin's allegory.

Roman Jakobson is the name in literary studies now perhaps more or less synonymous with these bifurcated tropes. To give initial, working definitions for these terms: metonymy has to do with contiguity (from Latin *com*, with + *tangere*, touch) and implies a predicative series, or "chain," of terms, each coexisting together. These terms are placed side-by-side—thus "touching" each other—and form phrases and meaningful sentences. The metaphorical is based on a similarity between a word and its invisible, often transcendental, meaning (based on the structure of language itself), and through this similarity the absented meaning is brought to light. In a metonymical structure, several terms may coexist, while in the metaphorical structure only one exists at any given time.

Jakobson, who started from Saussure's structural linguistic theories of *syntagmatic* and *associative* linguistic performance (language's horizontal and vertical axes, respectively), was struck by the condition in brain-damaged people called aphasia (lit. "without speech"—denotes a loss of the power to understand and use speech) and the two major aphasia disorders, the "contiguity disorder" and the "similarity disorder." These disorders, and Jakobson's understanding of linguistic theory through them, is significant because here we learn about language precisely where it breaks down and falls apart, an idea not foreign to Benjamin. For patients with a contiguity disorder, the ability to put together a meaningful sentence becomes difficult: the grammatical order becomes chaotic, prepositions and conjunctions tend to drop out, and there is often only the ability to name a single thing/idea, thus solely relying on the metaphorical dimension of language. Those with similarity disorder have problems using the correct terms at the correct times, so a "knife" might be called an "apple parer," or a "pencil sharpener," and although not incorrect (those terms name alternative uses of a knife), the similarity aphastic has problems understanding the context in which a particular word should be used—

one does not go to battle with a "pencil-sharpener"—and relies on the metonymic aspect of language. Jakobson saw that these twin disorders were related to metonymy and metaphor. The "normal" speech-user operates with both these levels intact, and is able to comprehend and use metaphor and metonymy to various degrees in everyday speech.

In Saussure's linguistic theory, messages are constructed by combining both the vertical (associative, or paradigmatic) and horizontal (syntagmatic) elements of language. Saussure puts it thus: "In the syntagm a term acquires its value only because it stands in opposition to everything that precedes or follows it, or to both." The syntagm is placed in an order within discourse's necessary linearity (you can't speak two things at once) and results in a "chain of speaking." In contrast, the vertical/associative aspect of language occurs "outside discourse," where "words acquire relations of a different kind. Those that have something in common are associated in the memory, resulting in groups marked by diverse relations." Associative relations are chosen in the mind as "part of the inner storehouse that makes up the language of each speaker." Saussure further relates the relation between the syntagmatic and the associative to a difference of presence and absence: "The syntagmatic relation is *in praesentia*. It is based on two or more terms that occur in an effective series. Against this, the associative relation unites terms *in absentia* in a potential mnemonic series."[32] Language thus works within a play of presence and absence, horizontality and verticality.

Jakobson rewrites the paradigmatic (vertical) and syntagmatic (horizontal) into metaphor and metonymy, and he understands them together to be fundamental functions of "normal" human language. But he is not simply a linguist; he is also a formalist interested in the function of poetic language. The two-part process of language functions in a specific way when it comes to poetry: "The poetic function projects the principle of equivalence from the axis of selection into the axis of combination."[33] Poetry is like pulling metaphors off a shelf and lining them up in a metonymical chain. Jakobson is interested in a certain rescue operation of metonymy, in which he sees the possibility for poetics. Thus, "similarity superimposed on contiguity imparts to poetry its thoroughgoing symbolic, multiplex, polysemantic essence. [. . .] In poetry, where similarity is superinduced upon contiguity, any metonymy is slightly metaphorical and any metaphor has a metonymical limit."[34] In poetry the two components are overlaid, and their oppositional status begins to slide together and hence ceases to be clearly distinguishable. Although Jakobson is, in fact, interested in poetry *qua* poetry, he is also interested in the poeticalness involved in all language, and of its radical potential to alter all discourse: "poeticalness is not a supplementation of discourse with rhetorical adornment but a total re-evaluation of the discourse and of all its components whatsoever."[35]

In the short section on metonymy and metaphor that ends the 1956 *Fundamentals of Language*, Jakobson and his colleague Morris Halle set up the problem of aphasia, connect it to the twin poles of metonymy and metaphor, and then give several examples of how this relation is played out in various places. In the midst of an analysis of Benjamin, the examples given by Jakobson and Halle offer a way of connecting the present conversation with Benjamin's media studies. The linguists note how filmmakers such as D. W. Griffith, Charlie Chaplin, and Sergei Eisenstein (some of Benjamin's favorites) were able to use metaphoric and metonymic devices in cinema ("metaphoric montage," "metonymic set-ups") as ways to break "with the tradition of the theater."[36]

Like several other thinkers, Jakobson and Halle also state that the relations between metaphor and metonymy are coordinated with the Freudian primary processes of condensation and displacement, respectively. Through these forms, dreams and parapraxes become allegories that can be interpreted, and deep desires stemming from the seeking of pleasure are disguised and revealed, temporarily breaking through the sublimating devices of the reality principle. Kaja Silverman summarizes the psychoanalytic activities thus: "Displacement involves the transfer of psychic intensity from an unacceptable element to an acceptable one, while condensation effects the formation of a new signifier from a cluster of previous signifying materials."[37] Benjamin does not explicitly discuss psychoanalysis in his work on allegory, but it is not a great leap to co-ordinate metaphor and metonymy with condensation and displacement which are all then rewritten in Benjamin's terms as *Sammlung* (collection) and *Zerstreuung* (dispersal) as he unveils the prehistory of modernity. Allegory, afterall, has to do with speaking in public, and is therefore akin to the interpretive work of psychoanalysis.

Returning to the literary form of allegory, Jakobson and Halle display the use of metaphor and metonymy within romantic and realist literatures:

> The primacy of the metaphoric process in the literary schools of romanticism and symbolism has been repeatedly acknowledged, but it is still insufficiently realized that it is the predominance of metonymy which underlies and actually predetermines the so-called "realistic" trend, which belongs to an intermediary stage between the decline of romanticism and the rise of symbolism and is opposed to both. Following the path of contiguous relationships, the realist author metonymically digresses from the plot to the atmosphere and from the characters to the setting in space and time. He is fond of synecdochic details.[38]

Metaphor is commonly associated with vertical elements, thereby establishing a kinship with an aesthetics of transcendence in which the materiality of the signifier is stepped over in the pursuit of the immaterial Idea, creating a whole and complete image. However, as Jakobson and Halle imply here, such a unity can only exist through a denial of the metonym, the repressed that eventually returns.

Although the lament-plays are not exactly realism, the observations of Jakobson and Halle are useful for understanding the structure of the baroque dramas. Metonymy, we detect in the preceding quotation, deals in the small stuff, the details, situated in a material setting of atmosphere, space, and time. As metonymy is taken up and used in the allegorical mode, allegory pays attention to material details even to the point of the fragmentation of the whole. The unified picture is sacrificed to its features, and the parts are always more then their sum, leading this expressive dimension of allegory to an encounter with the sublime: "with every idea the moment of expression coincides with a veritable eruption of images, which gives rise to a chaotic mass of metaphors. This is how the sublime is presented in this style" (*OGTD*, 173). The sublime is a mass of meaning, an overwhelming boundless sense of signification. This is the point at which the metaphoric slides most fully into the metonymic, and metaphors are arranged alongside each other, rendering impossible a choice of substitution. Sublimity occurs through the horizontal dimension, rather than being linked to some transcendence.

As the sublime, chaotic mass of metonymical metaphors increases, the multivalency of the allegorical sign is posited, and a limitless work is suggested. So Karl Giehlow noted in 1915 that "the many obscurities in the connection between meaning and sign . . . did not deter, they rather encouraged the exploitation of ever remoter characteristics of the representative object as symbols" (quoted in *OGTD*, 174). The freedom given to allegorical interpretation reaches a vertiginous accumulation and begins to lead to the inevitable conclusion that "[a]ny person, any object, any relationship, can mean absolutely anything else" (175). Allegory says one thing and means another, but the search for this other meaning has a veritably unlimited potential. Metonymic reflection is without end. Susan Buck-Morss states that "Allegorists, like alchemists, hold dominion over an infinite transformation of meanings, in contrast to the one, true word of God."[39] Against the final culmination of self-reflection that marks the late romantics and the early Heidegger, or the logocentric aesthetics of most of the Western philosophical and theological traditions, metonymic reflection has no grounding, and no eschatological unity.

Postmodernism, Gender, and Allegory

Just as Benjamin was writing a prehistory of the modern period and found these qualities in the baroque, there is a strong continuity of history whereby the metonymic still threatens to overtake the metaphoric in the postmodern age. The postmodern condition is nothing new, but merely another twist in history. Jean Baudrillard claims that metonymy has triumphed as he extends my analysis of Benjamin's allegory into the late twentieth century:

> The possibility of metaphor is disappearing in every sphere. . . . Economics becomes transeconomics, aesthetics becomes transaesthetics, sex becomes transsexuality—all converge in a transversal and universal process wherein no discourse may have a metaphorical relationship to another, because for there to be metaphor, differential fields and distinct objects must exist. But they cannot exist where contamination is possible between any discipline and any other. Total metonymy, then—viral by definition (or lack of definition). . . . Perhaps our melancholy stems from this, for metaphor still had its beauty; it was aesthetic, playing as it did upon difference, and upon illusion of difference. Today, metonymy—replacing the whole as well as the components, and occasioning a general commutability of terms—has built its house upon the dis-illusion of metaphor.[40]

Baudrillard is here writing hyperbolically, as is his custom. Even so, what he brings forward is the real or perceived threat that a lack of metaphor would bring about into the world. The loss of metaphor would be the loss of a vertical dimension to human understanding. Human orientation would become horizontal, of the earth, rather than connected to overarching themes such as Beauty, Truth, or God.

Intriguingly, several contemporary feminist theorists have picked up on the twin tropes of metaphor and metonymy as a way to work out a feminist mode of writing.[41] While a strict analysis of gender is lacking in Benjamin's work, there are further implications of the allegorical mode—particularly as it mixes metaphor with metonymy—that can be linked to feminist theories. As Benjamin and feminism are concerned with social change, such a linkage should not be surprising. In the work of Kristeva, and other feminist theorists and writers such as Luce Irigaray, Hélène Cixous, and Drucilla Cornell, metonymy works against the vertical, hierarchical aspect of the metaphoric, since "metaphor does imply metaphysics."[42]

Lesley Northrup nicely lays out the implications of a horizontally infused world, as opposed to the "masculine" verticality that dominates religious studies. Drawing on the work of ritual theorist Ronald Grimes, and feminist theologians such as Mary Daly, Northrup critiques the hierarchy of verticality found especially in Mircea Eliade's cosmology: "For Eliade, the sacred, in the form of a sort of invisible vertical shaft, breaks into the profane, horizontal world of 'religious man,' creating an *axis mundi* at the point of intersection—a holy place, a vital locus of access to the transcendent."[43] To the contrary, "women's rituals are supinely earthbound."[44] There are tendencies toward the essentialist impulse to equate women's experience with "nature," yet Northrup also makes clear that our cosmological structures of "up" and "down," even when "only metaphorical," have powerful political valence. Metaphor implies metaphysics, and metaphysical structurings of space are not innocent of ideology.

While the first wave of feminism may have worked within a metaphorical vein to replace the dominant masculine figures that rule society with feminine ones (a substitution that does not alter the fundamental structure of society), later feminism has worked in a more critical way to undo metaphor itself, and thus also to undo hierarchy. As Cornell puts it explicitly:

> And what tool or literary device do we use to bring women's "reality" into view if we cannot simply "unveil" it as inherent in maternity or women's reproductive capacity more generally? I want to suggest that the tool is primarily—and only primarily, because it is a mistake to think we can completely separate metonymy from metaphor—metonymy.[45]

Metonymy is not used simply to replace the metaphoric, for that would be a metaphoric process itself. Rather, it interrupts the metaphoric, flattening out the hierarchical dimension into horizontality. And so, we can find metonymy filtering through many of Cornell's works, since "metonymy is favored because it enacts the genealogical effort to uncover the structures of power that produce Woman."[46] ("Woman" here being an essentialized myth that must be deconstructed.)

Cornell picks up some of her ideas from Irigaray, who critiques metaphoric orientation, which in psychoanalytic terms is an orientation toward the phallic. So, while Jacques Lacan claims that the human subject acts his or her life out in a metonymic chain—what he labels the *objet petit a* (the little "a," as in *autre*, other)—he is in fact, as Irigaray reads him, actually always functioning within a metaphoric closed circuit. Lacan's desire is founded on a missing object—the phallus—and human desire proceeds with one representational substitution for that singular, primary object after another. Lacan is mistaken to think such a chain is metonymic, for as Irigaray correctly comprehends, this is a metaphorical process, a process of replacement always existing in a vertical structure. As she poetically rephrases it, "Erection is no business of ours: we are at home on the flatlands. We have so much space to share. Our horizon will never stop expanding; we are always open. . . . The sky isn't up there: it's between us."[47] Language is situated among interacting bodies, finding existence in the passage from one to the other.

Cornell is nonetheless pragmatic and realizes the importance of the metaphorization process, and argues that Irigaray does too. In spite of the dangers of essentialism that accompany metaphors (most prominently the metaphor of Woman as the "maternal"), they nonetheless enable the articulation of a utopian dimension to social life. All metonymy is contaminated by the metaphorical anyway, and human linguistic and aesthetic constructions are always already infused with the vertical—though what this vertical might point out may in itself prove to be nothing other than a further chain of metonyms. What Cornell argues for, which is of interest to those interested in the relations of religious practice and social change, is a *critical mythology*, offering a way out of the present system: "Utopian thinking demands the critical exploration and re-exploration of the possible and yet also the unrepresentable."[48] As long as that exploration continues, and does not stop with a metaphor that would pretend to fully capture "Woman," the vertical dimension of myth should be enacted. In a manner fitting Benjamin's project, Cornell states: "We re-collect the mythic figures of the past, but as we do so we reimagine them. It is the potential variability of myth that allows us to work within myth, and the significance it offers, so as to reimagine our world and by so doing, to begin to dream of a new one."[49]

To a very large degree, theology will always be metaphorical, always concerned with links between human language and a God beyond language. As such, its primary concern is not with the poetic potential of allegorical writing. Yet, by paying attention not simply to the metaphorical, but to the metonymical as well, it is possible to play with the capabilities of religious aesthetics. The implications of an allegorical thinking/writing for theology become particularly evident when one is looking at certain strands of "metaphorical theology." Despite the need to replace a theological metaphor such as "God the Father" with God as Mother or Friend,[50] a metaphorical approach to discourse reasserts the hierarchical structures, and does little to change the deep patterns of injustice in late capitalism.

Following Kristeva, Irigaray, and others, Rebecca Chopp shifts the feminist focus slightly when she argues not simply for a replacement of metaphors, but for a new social-symbolic structure. She states, "this is not to oppose changing images and metaphors but it is to argue that these terms and images are problematic because of the presuppositions built into the economy of the social-symbolic order that dispose feminism to correct rather than to transform bourgeois liberalism."[51] What Chopp implies here is that a replacement of metaphors is a metaphorical process itself, thus leaving the basic structure intact. As long as *substitution* (the action of metaphor) is the final aim of feminist or other theories of liberation, theology remains a patriarchal, capitalist, monotheistically ordered discipline. As long as metaphors are ordered and arranged within a monotheistic, hierarchical system, theology will continue to repeat itself. It may be *corrected* from time to time, but not *transformed*. What is needed instead is what Regina Schwartz calls for in her book *The Curse of Cain: The Violent Legacy of Monotheism*, and that is a revision of biblical religion in which she articulates an ethic of generosity, plenitude, and possibility that embraces "multiplicity instead of monotheism."[52]

For Cornell, Chopp, and Schwartz, as for Benjamin, somewhere between the metaphoric and metonymic is the place of *writing*. The dialectical force of allegory derives from the connection between the multivalent (possibly threateningly omnivalent) expressive qualities with the stability that comes through allegory's referential, conventional quality. Benjamin states: "[B]etween the cold, facile technique and the eruptive expression of allegorical interpretation . . . lies the essence of writing itself" (*OGTD*, 175). The heart of writing lies between the metaphoric and metonymic, between the hierarchies of metaphor and verticality of metonymy, and between a text and its interpretation.

Kristeva's notion of art and poetic language also relies on the interaction between the syntagmatic/metonymic and the paradigmatic/metaphoric. For Kristeva, the various "arbitrary," "concretized," and "metonymic" elements of the sign are combined to provide "a principle of *transformation*: within its field, new structures are forever generated and transformed." Furthermore, Kristeva's sign "does not refer to a single unique reality, but *evokes* a collection of associated images and ideas. While remaining expressive, it nonetheless tends to distance itself from its supporting transcendental basis (it may be called 'arbitrary')."[53] Expressive language, for Kristeva, is rooted in the semiotic body, and the subject who speaks is a subject *en procès* (in process/on trial), never settling with a singular set of symbols. Writing, particularly artistic and poetic writing, is endless.

All of these figures see in this interplay between the metonymical/horizontal and the metaphorical/vertical a chance for a transformational aesthetics. Even so, this occurs only when the materiality of the metonymical is stressed, where "new structures are forever generated and transformed." There is no creation out of nothing, nor is there a culminating telos. There is always some *thing*.

Word and Image

Up until this point it would be easy to imagine allegory specifically as a literary mode. After all, I have been referencing linguists and the literary tropes of metaphor and metonymy to explain allegory. True, Benjamin is deeply invested in literary studies, but allegory is not merely literal and literary, it is also material and visual. Benjamin shares such an understanding of language with Maurice Blanchot, who most embodied an aesthetic view of the materiality of language through the twentieth century, especially in works such as *The Writing of the Disaster* and *The Infinite Conversation*. Blanchot contrasts poetic language—sensual, material words—with ordinary language, which is "senseless," much in the same way Benjamin's allegory contrasts to the symbol. Of the poetic form of language, Blanchot states:

> My hope lies in the materiality of language, in the fact that words are things too, are a kind of nature. . . . A name ceases to be the ephemeral passing of nonexistence and becomes a concrete ball, a solid mass of existence; language, abandoning the sense, the meaning which was all it wanted to be, tries to become senseless. Everything physical takes precedence: rhythm, weight, mass, shape, and then the paper on which one writes, the trail of ink, the book.[54]

Blanchot and Benjamin are intrigued by the material nature of language and by the *visuality and materiality of texts*. This even brings Benjamin to some peculiar interests in graphology, which parallels allegory directly. Graphology, he suggests, "is concerned with the bodily aspect of the language of handwriting and with the expressive aspect of the body of handwriting" (*SW II*, 133). Through allegory and graphology, he reilluminates the premodern form of written texts, made up of handwritten language as a set of images to be looked at. Thus, what I wish to examine in this section is not the opposition of words *versus* images, but their conflation.

The origins of baroque allegory are found in the Middle Ages and in Renaissance commentaries on ancient hieroglyphs and various other "emblems" (German *Sinnbild*, literally "meaning picture"). These antecedent writers employed allegory as an exegetical tool, seeing hieroglyphs as "an image of divine ideas," as Marsilius Ficinus comments (*OGTD*, 169). Terry Eagleton suggests that the emphasis on hieroglyphs brings allegory around again to the materiality of aesthetics in Benjamin's thought and runs counter to the "phonocentrism" of Saussure and others: "the *Trauerspiel*'s preoccupation with script as against voice, its ceremonious arranging of matter-laden hieroglyphs like so many embalmed emblems, returns to us an awareness of the bodily nature of language."[55] By emphasizing the materiality of the baroque allegorical script, writing becomes visual: "Both externally and stylistically—in the extreme character of the typographical arrangement and in the use of highly charged metaphors—the written word tends towards the visual" (*OGTD*, 175–76). The dynamics of this aesthetic are provided by the overlay of the "highly charged" metaphoric dimension onto the metonymic dimension, here exemplified by the utterly material "typographic arrangement." In this overlay one finds the visuality of the written word, where language is not abstract, invisible, and interior, but thoroughly concrete and material, "a solid mass of existence." Language does not dissolve into the invisible, interior realm of the signified; rather, the signifiers exert their material force. Rainer Rochlitz comments on the extremes to which Benjamin would take this as he suggests how Benjamin "replaces the spirit with the word, the name, or, in a general way, the medium of communication, according them primacy over the subject."[56] Benjamin never eliminates the "spirit" altogether, that possibility remains perpetually open, but he does invert the Western metaphysical hierarchy of representation by giving great credence to the material/aesthetic.

What must therefore be dealt with in Benjamin's allegory is the relation between words and images, between the spirit and the word. Poet and literary theorist Gay Clifford's study of allegory suggests:

> One of the most important means by which interpretation is assisted and directed in allegory is its visual element. Narrative provides a basis of metaphor which expressed the ultimate purpose of the allegory and defines the limits of possible meaning. . . . But while both the energy and coherence of the work derive from narrative, it is often through visual detail and imagery that the clarity of particular parts of the system and their connection with the whole is established. Details of a character's appearance, of a landscape, of architecture, help us to interpret their essential nature and to fix them in our memory, while visual similarities and connections build up a pattern of thematic association.[57]

Easily detectable within Clifford's words here is the alignment of the metaphoric with the verbal, in contrast to the metonymic with the visual. But again, if the visual is connected to the metonymic, we could further say that the visual will threaten the verbal, narrative meaning, or rather will produce too much meaning.

In opposition to Gotthold Ephraim Lessing's distinction between poetry and painting (word and image) in his *Laocoön* as two "friendly neighbors," Benjamin's idea of allegory always reveals, as Benjamin quotes Carl Horst, "a crossing of borders of a different mode, an advance of the plastic arts into the territory of the 'rhetorical' arts" (*OGTD*, 177). In this act of transposition the visuality of the baroque allegory was seen as a mode of contamination on the literary. The romantics did not grasp this owing to their "excessively logical character," (162) which could not allow the disruptive, dialectical mode needed for allegorical interpretation. Far from being static, allegorical work, Benjamin is clear, is "a synthesis not so much in the sense of a peace as a *treuga dei* between the conflicting opinions" (177). The periods of gathering together are simply the eye of the storm, awaiting the next round of battle. Indeed, Michel Foucault has stated that "the relation of language to painting is an infinite relation,"[58] and this overproduction of meaning is characteristic of the relation of words and images within the arts, especially the avant-garde artistic practices of which Benjamin was so enamored. In an exhibition on Dada and surrealist word-images, John Welchman notes the disruptive power when these two media meet: Dada and surrealist artworks "sometimes exceed and sometimes deny analysis, but they always disturb it. Word-images demonstrate this disturbance with particular effectiveness, however, by virtue of their signifying not just from two codes but from two complex systems of signs: words and images."[59]

As a transposition of sign systems, the allegorical mode, as with Dada and Surrealism, has little interest in the unity of autonomous art such as that found in the formal-modernist aesthetics of Clement Greenberg. Following Kant's idea of the Beautiful as that which has "purposiveness without purpose," Greenberg, among others, saw purity and autonomy at the heart of "modern painting" (a stand-in for modernism as a whole), whose goal is "to eliminate from the specific effects of each art any and every effect that might conceivably be borrowed from or by the medium of any other art."[60] This purity of art leads to the autonomy of art, reliant on a perfect synthesis of form and content, creating a unified symbolic whole, and legitimized through its vertical relation to the divine: "As a symbolic construct it is supposed to merge with the divine in an unbroken whole. The idea of the unlimited immanence of the moral world in the world of beauty is derived from the theosophical aesthetics of the romantics" (*OGTD*, 160). Such logocentric "theoaesthetics" runs contrary to the hieroglyphic "other speech" of allegory.[61] (This is the further reason I began this chapter with the *Seinfeld* anecdote, since it was a visual-corporeal sign [George's wink] that disrupted a person's verbal speech.) The relation of word and image, and all the disruptive transpositions these two systems bring with it, display allegory's materiality, and the need for a sense-based, aesthetic reception of it.

Besides the aesthetic character there is also the religious character of this interrelation which surfaces particularly with an understanding of Kabbalah. When the Trauerspiel study was published, Benjamin gave a copy to his friend Gershom Scholem, himself almost solely responsible for rescuing the Kabbalistic tradition in the twentieth century. In the copy Benjamin inscribed: "To Gershom Scholem, donated to the *ultima Thule* of his Kabbalistic library," and in comments to others he specified that the book could be understood only by those familiar with Kabbalah.[62] In spite of the mystical orientation of the tradition, the materiality of the alphabet plays a vital role in Kabbalah. Divine energy is manifested in the ten elements (*sephirot*) discussed in the previous chapter, but also in the Hebrew letters. Thus the "Book of Creation" states, "In thirty-two wondrous paths of wisdom God . . . engraved and created his world."[63] The 22 consonants of the Hebrew alphabet, plus the 10 *sephirot*, become "building blocks" of the cosmos with which God engraves creation. Each character has its own set of symbolic meanings, yet each must also be seen in relation to the other characters, as well as astronomical cycles, human attributes, and other relational systems. "For the kabbalist, the paths to understanding are necessarily infinite, reflecting the boundless and infinite character of Divine energy."[64] Meditations upon the Hebrew letters thus have become part of the tradition, and spark the relation between language and image by showing how language *is* an image, a material object.

The Kabbalistic impulse to "read the world" because it is engraved by God is transformed under Benjamin's allegorical gaze into a sociopolitical aesthetic. As James McBride suggests, "Benjamin's fascination for allegory and his later experimentation with Marxist dialectics and Communist action represent his attempt to discover alternate methods of 'reading' the world in order to effect this Kabbalistically-inspired messianic vision."[65] The reason for Benjamin's relation of word and image and the concomitant emphasis on the "letter over the spirit" is precisely to remind us of the mediated nature of experience. An allegorical aesthetic finds itself working in the visible, material realm, challenging us to take note of our mediated reality, the very structures of creation. This reality is what prompts Benjamin to return to the baroque, and to the earthbound, in his search for a materialist basis for modernism. Under Benjamin's gaze, the world viewed becomes a text to read. To illustrate this, he discusses Albrecht Dürer's engraving *Melancholia*. Dürer's piece becomes a prime emblem for Benjamin, who suggests, "In it the knowledge of the introvert and the investigations of the scholar have merged as intimately as in the men of the baroque. The Renaissance explores the universe; the baroque explores libraries. Its meditations are devoted to books" (*OGTD*, 140). [cf. Kiefer's installation, Figure 1.3] Seeing the world as written text keeps us rooted in the material here and now, refraining from the escape into lofty transcendental flights of intellect.

To clarify, Benjamin does not pit the image against the word, nor does he simply merge them. Rather, he understands how the word tends toward the image, and the image offers itself as a "text" to be read. Through this imaging of the word, he is also able to displace the modern idea of literature, and by extension of the modern book, to offer comment on the visuality of texts. In Benjamin's day, as in the early twenty-first century, the modern book exists through its technological reproducibility, creating a quite peculiar visual object. Modern typesetting has created fonts for ease of reading (particularly seen in the refinement of the *serif* which moves the eye horizontally across the page), and perfectly justified margins make little rectangles of all the pages, leading inevitably to a practical invisibility of the word. The goal of modern typesetting is to print words that inevitably disappear as the reader becomes engrossed in the immaterial meaning behind the symbolic words. To imagine that words and images are split is to ignore the very visual nature of the printed word itself. Thus, in his emphasis on hieroglyphs and emblems, Benjamin is not merely romanticizing an age in which texts were handwritten, nor is it a matter of replacing the word with the image, or vice versa; instead, part of what he accomplishes is a highlighting of the very visual nature of written language itself, drawing attention, as well, to the medium of the printed book, which retains its dialectical nature between imaged words and the meanings beyond them.

A brief extrapolation of the allegorical aesthetic relation between words and images offers to shed light on a phrase that has become popular among those interested in interreligious dialogue in the early twenty-first century. The phrase, "people of the book," taken from the Quran,[66] has suggested itself to many as an exhortation to realize the commonality of the three Abrahamic, monotheistic, Western traditions: Islam, Judaism, and Christianity. However, the desire to link the traditions winds up reducing the traditions to their lowest common denominator, and actually even an inaccurate one. The problem is that the phrase, "people of the book," is understood from within a modern, highly literate society that has a massive system for the production and distribution of books. To be comprehended alone and silently, these books are very specific objects: handheld, produced by the thousands and hundreds of thousands, intended for individual readers. Walter Ong suggests of the medium of the printed book that "Print encourages a sense of closure, a sense that what is found in a text has been finalized, has reached a state of completion."[67] Importantly, this sense of closure is a *visual* sense, especially provoked by the technology of type: "typographic control typically impresses more by its tidiness and inevitability: the lines perfectly regular, all justified on the right side, everything coming out even visually."[68] The modern book is a finalized book, appearing complete unto itself, and thus mimics an art historical concept of "art for art's sake." Which is all a long way from the way most Muslims, Christians, and Jews use their "books," as these texts are chiefly contemplated visually, performed musically, and perceived by a community of people in a religio-aesthetic environment.

Ironically, there is a great deal of recent discussion that attempts to pit the image against the word.[69] It is with the modern, mass-produced book, however, that we find the distinction between the image and the word to be broken down as never before. The modern/postmodern "age of the image" does not begin with the invention of photography and the later rise of billboard advertisements, omnipresent video monitors, and company logos. Rather, it begins with the rise of print culture. The printed book, with or without illustrations, is a visual creation and, in its mass-produced form, has altered modern life (indeed, perhaps created it). It is one thing to note the word-image relation going on in Gustave Doré's illustrations for the Bible, or in medieval manuscripts with their images in one place and text in another; it is another thing altogether to approach the most literate component as itself being highly visual, something any typesetter knows. So, Benjamin's allegorical relation between the word and the image describes how the word is always visual, always material, even in its printed form. The modern "book" is not in opposition to the image, rather *it is an image*, a material creation, seen, felt, and sounded out.

Nature and History

As mentioned earlier, Benjamin does not work with binary *oppositions* so much as with what I suggest are "twin stars": two concepts that are actually distinct but sometimes so close that they are confused. Thus, symbols and allegories, metaphors and metonymies, words and images, are not, strictly speaking, opposed to each other, but are imbricated in each other's structures and ultimately inseparable from each other. The latter term in each pairing, within Benjamin's writings, exerts a distorting impact on the former.

In this section, I want to bring one more set of twin stars into the picture, and that is the way in which the baroque allegory also reveals a relation between space and time, and, relatedly, nature and history. What is revealed to be absolutely unique and vital to the allegory is "the decisive category of time" (*OGTD*, 166). Time is not an abstract conceptual category, but a "natural history" with all of its cycles of life and death. While the symbol exists in a fleeting instant of mystical unity, allegory is condemned to live out a physical, historical existence, susceptible to the exigencies of nature, including the limits imposed by death. This is emblematized by the image of a "death's head":

> Everything about history that, from the very beginning, has been untimely, sorrowful, unsuccessful, is expressed in a face—or rather in a death's head. And although such a thing lacks all "symbolic" freedom of expression, all classical proportion, all humanity—nevertheless, this is the form in which man's subjection to nature is most obvious and it significantly gives rise not only to the enigmatic question of the nature of human existence as such, but also of the biographical historicity of the individual. This is the heart of the allegorical way of seeing, of the Baroque, secular explanation of history as the Passion of the world; its importance resides solely in the stations of its decline. The greater the significance, the greater the subjection to death, because death digs most deeply the jagged line of demarcation between physical nature and significance. (*OGTD*, 166)

Benjamin mixes linguistics and myth together here, picking up on themes developed in his 1916 essay "On Language as Such and on the Language of Man." In that earlier and more theologically oriented period of his life, he articulated a theological linguistics in which the fall of Adam and Eve instituted the fall of language, the arbitrary split of signifier and signified. Since Adam was charged to name the animals, he originally spoke a pure language of naming, "in the name, the mental being of man communicates itself to God" (*SW I*, 65). There is no difference of word and thing, appearance and essence; it is pure, transcendental speech. "After the Fall, however, when God's word curses the ground, the appearance of nature is deeply changed. Now begins its other muteness, which is what we mean by the 'deep sadness of nature'" (72). With the Fall, not only does death enter the world, but language is forever split from its origin; death is bound up with the arbitrariness of the sign. Significantly, it is *lament* that best expresses humanity's fallen nature. "Lament, however, is the most undifferentiated, impotent expression of language. It contains scarcely more than the sensuous breath; and even where there is only a rustling of plants, there is always a lament" (73). Even though it is impotent, there is a sense in which it is a true form of speech, linking as it does an understanding of death with the inexpressibility of our language. Precisely because of the Fall, and the entry of death which is the demarcation "between physical nature and significance," there is the possibility of an ever greater significance, an unlimited rummaging through the metonymies of history.

So, while the ahistoricism of the symbol (its "mystical instant") pretends to cheat death by surpassing its own limits in a teleological unity, allegory instead plays out the lines and limits of physical history while it "inscribes death into signification."[70] This breaking point is the site of the origins of art. Art becomes a mode of repair of the world (*tikkun olam*), especially in its impotent expressions as lamentation, and is a way to break the Fall, to struggle to rebuild what was lost. Just as Kristeva notes, "Opposite religion or alongside it, 'art' takes on [the founding] murder and moves through it. It assumes murder insofar as artistic practice considers death the inner boundary of the signifying process. Crossing that boundary is precisely what constitutes art."[71] Allegorical art acts itself out in the space of between—between what is seen and what it means, between "physical nature and significance."

When Benjamin says of the lament-play that "what is vital is the *transposition (Umsetzung)* of the originally temporal data into a figurative spatial simultaneity" (*OGTD*, 81; emphasis added) he doubles the movement of Jakobson's metaphor and metonymy (the anachronism is noted) as well as furthers the synthetic definition of allegory given earlier. In the transposition, the chronology of history is flattened into an all-important synchronic dimension. The "strange combination of nature and history" is what Benjamin takes to be an alternative "natural history,"[72] a history grounded in space as well as time.

History thus renders itself to the senses, to be seen and perceived in the present. And as it is grounded in space, we reach a decisive trait of Baroque allegory: the "spatialization" of history is also the "secularization" of history. If linear time is bent into a spatial figure (which is, finally, an image), there can be no eschatologically redeemable time, no sense of teleological progress. What this amounts to is a "hopelessness of the earthly condition," "a flight into a nature deprived of grace," and a "rejection of eschatology" (*OGTD*, 81). Time does not steadily move upwards to some greater and clearer vantage point, rather natural history is one of decay and death. Benjamin's interest in the baroque rejection of progress is not merely due to its secularized vein: He sees such rejection as vital to any deconstruction of myth, whether from twentieth-century capitalism *or* from the mythical telos of Marxist utopias.

In the *Trauerspiel* book, Benjamin first discusses medieval mystery plays and then turns to Lope de Vega's "court plays." Such a shift marks the decisive historical turn that Benjamin is dealing with. Moving along in natural history, the divine elements of the mystery play become secularized in the court play (at least in the Spanish Counter-Reformation dramas), even if the overall vertical-transcendental structure remains: now the "king proves to be a secularized redemptive power" (*OGTD*, 81). So while the medieval mystery play found its *eschaton* in the final transcendence of Christ, the baroque drama, particularly exemplified by the Spaniard Calderón, attempts to "regain" an element of transcendence through reflection, through mirrors, crystals, and puppets (ibid.), in other words, through magic. "If history is secularized in the setting, this is an expression of the same metaphysical tendency which simultaneously led, in the exact sciences, to the infinitesimal method [of Leibniz]. In both cases, chronological movement is grasped and analyzed in a spatial image" (92). In the allegorical drama, the lament-play, we *see* history.

The lament-play, as opposed to tragedy, is set "in motion," by the simple fact that these dramas were performed in traveling theaters. "[I]n the European *Trauerspiel* as a whole the stage is also not strictly fixable, not an actual place, but it too is dialectically split. Bound to the court, it yet remains a traveling theatre; metaphorically its boards represent the earth as the setting created for the enactment of history; it follows its court from town to town. In Greek eyes, however, the stage is a cosmic *topos*" (*OGTD*, 119). Benjamin quotes from Nietzsche here on the mythical uniqueness of the Greek tragedy, including the permanence of the stage. In Greek tragedy, "the performance is never repeated identically," making each performance "a decisive cosmic achievement" (ibid.). Akin to the concept of the aura developed later, Greek tragedies were mythical and ahistorical, but the baroque lament-play lacked or at least had less of what might later be called the aura. Because it was a traveling show and because the same performance was repeated, the baroque drama becomes a precursor for Benjamin's interest in the mechanically reproduced art work, which "substitutes a plurality of copies for a unique existence" and "meets the beholder or listener in his own particular situation," to highlight a passage from "The Work of Art" essay we will explore further. This repetition is part of allegory's metonymical character, as opposed to the ultimately metaphorical character of tragedy grounded in myth.

The entwining of nature and history is duplicitous. On the one hand, the use of the term *nature* would pretend to posit a "natural origin" apart from the contingencies of history, but when we arrive at this origin we find its nature is not so pristine and/or prelapsarian. So on the other hand, the origin (or what we thought to be the origin) is found lacking and always already infected by natural decay and transience. There is, furthermore, no "creation out of nothing": "Origin [*Ursprung*], although an entirely historical category, has, nevertheless, nothing to do with genesis [*Entstehung*]. The term *origin* is not intended to describe the process by which the existent came into being, but rather to describe that which emerges from the process of becoming and disappearance. Origin is a whirlpool in the stream of becoming, and in its current it swallows the material involved in the process of genesis" (*OGTD*, 45). Nature is no origin, and is not permanent. But neither, of course, is history. The myth of origins is thus not a myth of creation, but of re-creation, of dealing in the cuttings and separations in the perpetually nascent beginning.

Within the depths of the dialectic of nature and history, materiality constantly threatens to swallow up meaning. Thus "the *eidos* disappears, the simile ceases to exist, and the cosmos it contained shrivels up" (*OGTD*, 176). With such a physical, secular quality of allegory we are reminded again that we are also in the realm of nature which, unlike the romantic symbol's universal unity, is within the scope of death and decay. Because of this, the allegory finds its greatest emblem (its own allegory) in the ruin. Physical script—being simultaneously sacred and profane, metaphorical and metonymical, language and image—brings history into physical nature.

> The allegorical physiognomy of the nature-history, which is put on stage in the *Trauerspiel*, is present in reality in the form of the *ruin*. In the ruin history has physically merged into the setting. And in this guise history does not assume the form of the process of an eternal life so much as that of irresistible decay. Allegory thereby declares itself to be beyond beauty. Allegories are, in the realm of thoughts, what ruins are in the realm of things. (177–178).

In the midst of these few sentences we come to several important points that constitute some crucial working themes through Benjamin's book. First, the aesthetics (religious and other) of the allegorical is a project undertaken in the physical world, a world that is susceptible to "irresistible decay." As such, allegorical aesthetics do not operate in the world of ideas, the world of transcendence, and are not a form of objective/subjective knowledge. Allegory is "beyond beauty," beyond the unity of form and content, or appearance and essence. With the ruin as the key emblem of allegory, allegorical aesthetics cannot create a total system, but must remain in the realm of fragments, of incompleteness. There is no lofty flight of thought, but rather the allegorical struggle is one of stumbling over ruins, of limping, and finally, of breaking the inevitable fall.

The problem with beauty is that it is reliant on socially inherited concepts of symmetry, perfection, unity, and harmony. What beauty forgets is its own mediated nature, and when it forgets its own artifice, ideology has its way with art. The modern world seeks beauty as a respite from the alienation of everyday industrial (and postindustrial) life, as a way to believe the world still exists as a cosmic whole. Yet, this is to forget the recreation of beauty, its own earthbound nature.

Working in the ruins shows the lack of control on the part of the artist/critic/individual subject. The allegorist may collect the ruins, but a unified structure cannot be (re)built. Instead, the *modus operandi* of the baroque was one of *invention*, of accumulating fragments "without any strict idea of a goal" (*OGTD*, 178) and hoping for a "miracle" to occur in their arrangement. Haphazardly collecting, the allegorist acts in faith as she or he arranges the pieces. *Accumulation* and *arrangement* are the two key processes of baroque allegory pointed out by Benjamin. Thus, the allegorist functions somewhat as an "editor" rather than an author,[73] and in this way "[l]iterature ought to be called *ars inveniendi*" (179). The way to invent is to accumulate and arrange, or, to put it in already rehearsed terms, to *select* and *arrange* (the actions of metaphor and metonymy, respectively, and, by extension, the Freudian condensation and displacement). In Benjamin's writings, allegory becomes a precursor to artistic practices with which he would later engage, practices such as surrealism, Brechtian theater, Proust's memory writings, and Eisenstein's filmic montage. Each of these practices is an *ars inveniendi*, dealing with already existing fragments and their arrangement.

Fragments and ruins are central to Benjamin's project, because they are situated at a liminal site, a site of transposition between some*thing* and nothing. They arrest, however fleetingly, the process of death and decay and offer an image to be melancholically contemplated. The melancholic gaze for Benjamin, however, does not wish for the whole structure again but productively rummages through the ruins, lighting upon lost objects that the unifying narratives of history have forgotten. Through this inventive allegorical mode Benjamin suggests the constructed nature of the work of art itself will make itself evident in the final product. A complete collection (a finished artwork) is not possible; instead, the baroque work of art is not polished and precise, but the "over-ripeness and decay" (*OGTD*, 179) of nature shows through. In the symbolic approach to the arts, the art(ificial) work that is created and finished with a smooth surface inevitably disappears and is swallowed up by its "inner necessity," its harmony of form and content, leading to its believed independence and autonomy. To the contrary, in the allegorical approach the artificial supplements the "natural," adding to and replacing the seemingly original term, and displaying the artificiality of nature. The finished work of art reveals its own process, shows the mortar in the walls, the infrastructure on which the superstructure rests. In the baroque allegory, the artifice of the edifice shows through, there is no recourse to an original nature.

Renaissance artists represented (i.e., imitated) nature; it was a nature "as shaped by God" (*OGTD*, 180). Baroque representation, to the contrary, is one of fallen nature, a nature bearing "the imprint of the progression of history" (ibid.). Tragedy, as opposed to *Trauerspiel*, is related to myth and thus to a vertical dimension that is not absent in the lament-play but is generally subverted by its "transposition into a figurative spatial simultaneity." Tragedy's mythic-sacred dimension lends it a strongly vertical character, or as Eliade claims, "the myth relates a sacred history. . . . But to relate a sacred history is equivalent to revealing a mystery."[74] Further, the myth is "the paradigmatic model of all human activities."[75] Eliade is here working in a metaphorical vein, prioritizing the vertical, paradigmatic element as the sacred and suggesting history itself is a reproduction of this sacred history. To the contrary, "the Baroque vulgarizes ancient mythology in order to see everything in terms of figures (not souls): this is the ultimate stage of externalization after the hieratic religious content had been aestheticized by Ovid and secularized by the neo-Latin writers. There is not the faintest glimmer of any spiritualization of the physical" (187). The allegory is an irruption, but not the simple downward movement of hierophanic myth. Allegory is the irruption of the profane into the sacred, the physical into the spiritual, death into the eternal, turning the mythic symbol *inside out*. If Eliade's idea of myth is paradigmatic, Benjamin's allegory pushes the paradigmatic into the syntagmatic.[76]

One of the prominent examples of syntagmatic myth found in the baroque are dramas based on the life of Christ, themselves reenactments of medieval Passion plays. Yet, as might be expected, a certain distortion occurs within their allegorized form:

> The mystical instant [*Nu*] becomes the "now" [*Jetzt*] of contemporary actuality; the symbolic becomes distorted into the allegorical. The eternal is separated from the events of the story of salvation, and what is left is a living image open to all kinds of revision by the interpretative artist . . . . It is an unsurpassably spectacular gesture to place even Christ in the realm of the provisional, the everyday, the unreliable. (*OGTD*, 183)

This is a radical theological insight on the part of Benjamin. As theology is freed from the symbolic—or rather, as the symbolic is distorted or mutated into the allegorical—the poetic writing of the "interpretative artist" opens on to a multivalent space of play in the field of ruins. A powerful poetic, even sublime, potential is invoked here, and Benjamin even quotes from Delbéne: "*La poésie n'était au premier âge qu'une théologie allégorique*" ["In the beginning poetry was simply allegorical theology"] (172). An allegorical approach to theology leads us back, which is to say forward, to this nonoriginary, original poetry, rooted in the decay of nature, of the everyday.

Another example provided by Benjamin brings more relations, more intertexts, into the picture. Lope de Vega's Spanish lament-play, *The Confused Court*, is referred to in a fleeting manner even as it "could be adopted as the model of allegory" (*OGTD*, 188). What Benjamin says about this royal "court" [*Hof*] is that it "is subject to the law of 'dispersal' [*Zerstreuung*] and 'collectedness' [*Sammlung*]. Things are assembled according to their significance; indifference to their existence [*Dasein*] allowed them to be dispersed again" (ibid.). What is interesting here is not necessarily de Vega's play per se, but the way Benjamin as allegorist interprets it. And in his interpretation, lasting about 10 lines, some key elements of allegorical interpretation are brought forward. First, there is the two fold process of the allegorical *ars inveniendi* that is made up of selection and arrangement, as noted earlier. However, we see a further process inscribed here and that is that after the collection and arrangement, the fragments are *again* dispersed. The creative, inventive practice of art cannot reach completion. Allegory ends in a dispersing indifference.

We should realize by now that Benjamin's criticism is bound up with an aesthetic practice itself so that the allegorist is also the artist, but hardly a master artist, for to write a song of lament entails the understanding that aesthetic production is founded on loss, and the sensuous breath of lament's expression is impotent. Instead, the inventive elements of allegory are recreative. By creating a new lamentation, the allegorist, who is also finally the poet, the inventor, or possibly the editor, attempts to open a space for redemption, even if it is unclear whether such a once and for all redemption will come. Beatrice Hanssen notes that allegory was not simply interpreted "as a historically specific trope but rather as a form of memory or historical commemoration."[77] Or as Benjamin states: "For an appreciation of the transience of things, and the concern to rescue them for eternity, is one of the strongest impulses in allegory" (*OGTD*, 223). And it was in the baroque observation of the impermanence of things, the decay of nature, and after the violence of the Thirty Years War that allegory surfaced as a mode of rescue, "where transitoriness and eternity confronted each other most closely" (224). Because allegory is concerned with the decay of nature and the "transience of things," it enacts a lament for a lost relation, a melancholic disposition that binds itself to nature, to the *nature morte*.

Redemption?

For the baroque allegorists, however, working within a Christian tradition (whether the Protestantism of the German lament-plays, or the Counter-Reformation Catholicism of the Spanish lament-plays) there always remained a theological/Christological redemption. How better show the work of God than to first show the extremes of profanity and decay of the world, and then God's redemptive force. So, after pages and pages of ruinous, death-bound nature, salvation is made possible. "Ultimately in the death signs of the Baroque the direction of allegorical reflection is reversed; on the second part of its wide arc it returns, to redeem. . . . For even this time of hell is secularized in space, and that world, which abandoned itself to the deep spirit of Satan and betrayed itself, is God's world. In God's world the allegorist awakens" (*OGTD*, 232). At the extremes of secularization, history would seem to finally realize its lack. Melancholically gazing at the world, the allegorist displays the hopelessness of the world and laments its loss. In this aesthetic action the "death's head" of the allegory turns into an "angel's countenance," as Benjamin quotes from Lohenstein. In this final and ultimate "collection," allegory itself is radically undone:

> Allegory, of course, thereby loses everything that was most peculiar to it: the secret, privileged knowledge, the arbitrary rule in the realm of dead objects, the supposed infinity of a world without hope. All this vanishes with this *one* about-turn, in which the immersion of allegory has to clear away the final phantasmagoria of the objective and, left entirely to its own devices, rediscovers itself, not playfully in the earthly world of things, but seriously under the eyes of heaven. And this is the essence of melancholy immersion: that its ultimate objects, in which it believes it can most fully secure for itself that which is vile, turn them into allegories, and that these allegories fill out and deny the void in which they are represented, just as, ultimately, the intention does not faithfully rest in the contemplation of bones, but faithlessly leaps forward to the idea of resurrection. (232–33)

What this ultimate reversal means in the context of the study of lament-plays is open to interpretation. Some studies see the redemptive ending as indicative of Benjamin's redemptive spirit.[78] They suggest that the combination of Benjamin's political interests and theological interests culminate in a final resolution, an ultimate redemptory moment. Thus making Benjamin into a negative theologian.

Certainly, the last few pages of the book bring us to a strange ending, an almost sappy, Hollywood ending tacked onto the fragments of broken relationships and ruinous structures. Can hundreds of pages of earthly hopelessness be redeemed in a final few? Is Benjamin agreeing with the Christian endings here? Hanssen's reading of the book is likewise one of puzzlement, and she comes to the conclusion, particularly by reading the *Trauerspiel* book alongside Adorno's views of history, that "through allegory, Benjamin essentially meditated on the possibility of reconciliation no less than on its illusionary nature."[79] Reconciliation could simply be something to ponder, a possibility to play with, while it is at heart an illusion. Or, as Rochlitz reads the ending, it is ironic in the sense that "irony and allegory are the aesthetic means for subjectivity's relativizing of itself from within the antinomies of the subject-object model."[80] There is no final collected self (*sich sammeln*), the subject is always susceptible to dispersal (*zerstreuung*).

While the language at the end of the *Trauerspiel* book is convoluted, Susan Buck-Morss offers an astute reading that demarcates Benjamin's position from that of the baroque playwrights. She notes how Benjamin himself was actually being critical of the final redemption, precisely because it "deserts both history and nature and (like the whole tradition of idealist philosophy that comes after it), takes refuge in the spirit."[81] As Benjamin put it, the baroque allegory "does not faithfully [*treu*] rest in the contemplation of bones, but faithlessly [*treulos*, "treacherously"] leaps forward to the idea of resurrection." Buck-Morss sees Benjamin to be critical of this faithless/treacherous move, and in the end, she argues, the allegory becomes indistinguishable from the unified ideology of myth.

We must add to these disagreements the difference between the dominance of Christianity in Europe (both in the baroque, and in Benjamin's day), and the marginalized status of Judaism. Benjamin himself was clear in his interests in Judaism, even if he did not commit to them. Thus, to see Benjamin as promoting the ultimate redemption at the end of the *Trauerspiel* book is to begin to suggest Benjamin promoted a Christian structure of redemption. Scholem makes clear that "Christian ideas never held any attraction for him. Indeed, he had an undisguised distaste for the type of neo-Catholicism which, at the time, was much in vogue among Jewish intellectuals in Germany and France."[82] And Wolin makes the point that such a redemption is, in fact, indicative of Benjamin's interest in the messianic elements of Kabbalah.[83]

The ending of the book, by whatever name, is twofold, ambiguous, holding open the dialectic process rather than dissolving it into one side or the other or synthesizing the two poles. Along these lines, Scholem recalls a conversation with Benjamin in the late 1930s that highlighted for him Benjamin's contradictory views of language and enlightens the ending of the book. Scholem says, "Benjamin was evidently torn between his predilection for a mystical theory of language and the equally strongly perceived need to struggle against it in the context of a Marxist view of the world."[84] At the time of writing the *Trauerspiel* book, Benjamin did not have a "Marxist view of the world," but he was interested in a material-aesthetic view of the arts. He was, moreover, aware of this contradiction and seemed to hold up this polarity, not in a dialectical way that might be resolved, but as a constellation and vanishing point for his thought, a point at which he could never arrive. The contradictory impulses left him, as Scholem called it, "Janus-faced,"[85] and the Janus face is one of the disguises of the allegorist. Indeed, Benjamin gives us his own interpretation, possibly his own self-critical interpretation, towards the end of the book:

> For a critical understanding of the *Trauerspiel*, in its extreme, allegorical form, is possible only from the higher domain of theology; so long as the approach is an aesthetic one, paradox must have the last word. Such a resolution, like the resolution of anything profane into the sacred, can only be accomplished historically, in terms of a theology of history, and only dynamically, not statically in the sense of a guaranteed economics of salvation. . . . (*OGTD*, 216)

What is clear here is Benjamin's criticism of the staticity of a "guaranteed economics of salvation" and eschatological myths of a redeemed world. Benjamin does not turn his back on theology, but argues for a theology of history and transposes the sacred into the profane, grounding theology in the realm of death and decay. In an opposite move, I would further suggest that Benjamin opens a space for aesthetics as a materialistic basis for doing theology. Might we then reread allegory from the perspective of religious aesthetics, an inventive space that retains irresolvable paradox, yet with a critical understanding? Might we find a religious aesthetic that is in process, that does not reach a final collection but instead is content with the continual writing of lamentations?

Precisely because there is the promise of completion, the collector is stimulated to keep collecting, gathering up the ruins. There is always something other. The vertical, unified myth, then, is not wholly denied, but transformed and transposed. Just as Drucilla Cornell has articulated the need for feminist thought and practice of a critical mythology, and its concomitant vertical relation, so too does the sociopolitical realm in general need such critical myths. Benjamin's allegorical mythology is not universal in the way of his contemporaries Klages and Jung. It is too infused with the metonymic, the poetic, and is caught up in the historical. The myth does not begin or end in a "beyond," it begins and ends in nature, and remains grounded there.

Allegorizing Allegory

Before fully advocating an allegorical aesthetics, however, it is essential to make clear the distinction between Benjamin's mode of allegorizing and that commonly understood within Christian biblical interpretation. In the book on lament-plays, Benjamin is clearly drawing on Christian modes of interpretation, and he links medieval Christian allegorical exegesis with the baroque; but he is not thereby attempting to continue Christian theology. He borrows the mode of operation but excises the content. How far this can actually be accomplished is a question I will need to leave open, for my interests here are in the aesthetic dimensions of creation and the arts.[86]

If allegorical interpretation gives a meaning to art that it was never intended to convey, then it runs several risks. George Costanza, in this chapter's opening anecdote, was betrayed by his own eye, which gave to his words meanings that he himself did not intend. This is indeed true and is what gives commentary and exegesis its poetic potential. Yet, because of its excessive nature allegory has received rather negative reviews in the last few hundred years. But it seems to me that the troubles have occurred not in what Benjamin would term allegory, but in an understanding of allegory that is more properly understood as a "figurative" or "typological" hermeneutic, and in other methods of interpretation that provide strict connections between the two layers of allegory.

So, in a sexually repressed Christian orthodoxy (the correlative to the repression of the body in general), the Song of Songs was reread and shifted from an outright erotic poem to a mystical desiring after God—in spite of the fact that "God" is nowhere mentioned in the text.[87] The placing of such limits on scripture (or any other text) circumscribes what should be a multivalency of poetic texts, sacred and otherwise. And while such a sexually repressive interpretation has negative implications, others lean into anti-Semitic interpretation. What has been called the allegorical approach toward the "Old" Testament is to treat it in light of the "New" Testament (even this naming cuts off a multiplicity of meanings among "testaments," or "covenants"). Supersessionist Christian interpreters might thus consider Noah's ark (Genesis 6) to typify the Christian church, outside of which there is no salvation; or Isaac's carrying of the wood for his own sacrifice (Genesis 22) to be a typology of Christ's carrying his own cross. In these examples, there is a strict one-to-one correspondence that effectively eliminates all other exegetical exercises. These interpretive strategies function within a (Christian) model of historical fulfillment—what was hidden in one time (to the Jews) is revealed at a later time (to the Christians). Such an approach, it should be clear by now, is precisely what Benjaminian allegory subtends.

Susan Handelman, in her early work *The Slayers of Moses*, discusses the rabbinical interpretive tradition of midrash in ways strongly akin to Benjamin's allegory. Unfortunately, she contrasts midrash with allegory, mainly because her understanding of allegory is based on this previous Christian model. In this model, allegory simply "uncovers" the supposedly true and invisible meaning lying underneath the form of the text. To the contrary,

In midrash, concepts exist only in particular forms, and this is one of the aspects in which midrash may be distinguished from allegory or figurative interpretation. The concept uncovered through interpretation never dispenses with the particular form in which it is clothed, nor does the midrashic meaning take any precedence over the plain, simple meaning. Furthermore, there is never any one single interpretation to which all understanding of the text aims, but a continuous production of multiple meanings. In midrash, one Rabbi can interpret a verse in several different ways, and conflicting interpretations are placed side by side with no concern for reconciling them. . . . There is no hierarchical scheme in midrash; no interpretation has more authority than any other.[88]

Of course, her retelling of midrash has strong resemblances to Benjamin's allegory, especially as midrash does not allow the text itself (writing/the material signifier) to disappear into the meaning, and it allows a multiplicity of interpretations with no hierarchical scheme, and no final reconciliation. Furthermore, like Benjamin's allegory, midrash has a strongly anachronistic element to it, since what is important is the scripture's relation to the present, how it "actualized." Thus, I would argue that Benjamin's allegory shares a strong kinship with rabbinic midrash.

Indeed, if the full potential of allegory is realized, one might approach, for example, the Song of Songs in an allegorical mode as Kyle Keefer and Tod Linafelt have done, claiming that allegorical

interpretation eroticizes theological discourse, with potentially very radical results. With the stroke of an allegory, God becomes both an object and a subject of desire. The world becomes the result of "an explosion of erotic energy, the ecstasy of a God who, in his act of creating, stands outside himself, perhaps literally 'beside himself' with Eros." By way of the allegorical interpretation, God is introduced into the vicissitudes of erotic existence. . . . [A]nd while the traditional allegorical interpretation will sometimes try to delimit the flow of Eros so that God remains unmoved by human desire, the effort seems ultimately vain. God desires the world; and God desires the world's desire.[89]

Allegory functions here to "profane" the sacred, to eroticize the divine, to pluralize monotheism, to turn any metaphor of God into a metonym. As allegorical desire enters the theological, God enters desire. Metaphor and metonymy move toward each other and cross.[90]

Such allegorical work (which is a work of art) is achieved only by keeping space open for otherness. Indeed, the etymological roots of the term itself speak of this otherness since allegory is literally, "other speech." And under the spell of psychoanalysis, this "other speech" of allegory is transformed in modernity, as Sigrid Wiegel argues, into the "speech of the other."[91] And as Hanssen concludes her work on Benjamin: If "Benjamin's gazes are turned earthward, they now no longer represent a melancholic self-absorption, which purely served to reaffirm the confines of the human subject. . . . Turned toward the creaturely, a radically different, dialectical side appears in Benjamin's melancholic gaze—one that fundamentally and resolutely resists incorporating the other."[92] The poetic nature of allegory involves an openness to the other. Gazing on the ruins of the past, allegory reconfigures what has been forgotten and re-collects for the present. Through the process of allegory, through the collection of ruins and the melancholic gaze of the critic, the lost other is given voice. Allegory never moves in the spirit of possession, it is not a knowledge, and therefore would seek to escape any interpretive work of "colonization."[93]

Joel Fineman, in an excellent essay entitled "The Structure of Allegorical Desire," nicely lays out what is at stake in our examination of the allegory. Though Benjamin is uncannily absent from his mostly psychoanalytic orientation, I quote Fineman's essay at length here because it inscribes so well the links I am arguing between Benjamin's work of art, his messianic history, and his "poetic" allegory:

> What we can say is that with its poeticality defined as structure superinduced upon metonymy, allegory initiates and continually revivifies its own desire, a desire born of its own structuring. Every metaphor is always a little metonymic because in order to have a metaphor there must be a structure, and where there is a structure there is already piety and nostalgia for the lost origin through which the structure is thought. Every metaphor is a metonymy of its own origin, its structure thrust into time by its very structurality. . . . The allegorical structure thus enunciated has already lost its center and thereby discovered a project: to recover the loss dis-covered by the structure of language and of literature. In thematic terms, this journey back to a foreclosed origin writes itself out as a pilgrimage to the sacred founding shrine, made such by murder, that is the motive of its movement. In terms of literary response, the structuring of the text holds out the promise of a meaning that it will also perpetually defer, an image of hermeneutic totality martyred and consecrated by and as the poetical. This is the formal destiny of every allegory insofar as allegory is definable as continued metaphor. Distanced at the beginning from its source, allegory will set out on an increasingly futile search for a signifier with which to recuperate the fracture of and at its source, and with each successive signifier the

fracture and the search begin again: a structure of continual yearning, the insatiable desire of allegory.[94]

Divided from its inception, from its *Ursprung*, or in Lurian Kabbalistic terms from its original *Ein sof*, allegory cannot maintain its own readings but ceaselessly deals in fragments waiting for a miracle of collection, some reversed thunder of a disaster that might bestow meaning. The work of the melancholy gaze, the song of lament, the work of interpretation, is the work of re-collection, allowing another re-binding to occur, and we are then able to see the ethical-religious function of the lament.

Allegorical Mythology, or Philosophy with a Screwdriver

The concern will be raised: If Benjamin works to "explode" (*sprengung*) mythic narratives, to deconstruct the unity of symbols, to destroy tradition itself, what can we say about him as a religious thinker? How can such destruction be religious? The beginnings of an answer, I believe, have to do with his difference from Nietzsche, whose proposal of a "philosophy with a hammer" is akin to Benjamin's intentions. In actuality though, I would suggest that Benjamin is much closer to doing philosophy with a screwdriver. You can destroy things quickly with a hammer, and it is quite a useful tool for such actions; but a screwdriver takes things apart, fragmenting the whole into its constituent pieces. The screwdriver simultaneously renders the whole unusable and maintains usable parts—similar activities are undertaken by Hannah Höch to create her photomontages. Taking the wholistic narratives of myths apart with a screwdriver does not simply destroy them, it scatters the whole, turning it into fragments, nonetheless leaving some of the pieces available for future use.

Religiously speaking, the difference in tools of destruction is the difference between *desecration* and *deconsecration*. Deconsecration is itself a sacred action, while desecration is antisacred. They may look alike, especially to the "thin phenomenologist"; but we must look closer to see the dual activity of deconsecration with both its destructive and creative purposes—it's scattering and collecting. Most importantly, however, the emphasis is placed on the action between these two poles, the *transposition* of the sacred. That is, if we place the emphasis not on the difference between the sacred and the profane, but on the *passage* (or the "threshold," *die Schwelle*, as Benjamin would say) from the one to the other—as religions inevitably do—then we might consider the passage from sacred to profane to be just as vital an action as that from profane to sacred. Allegorical aesthetics prompts religion to review its activities and performances, not its states of equilibrium, focusing on points of reform and movement.[95]

To point out the activities and movements of Benjamin's destructive creation, we might briefly look at his use of allegorical images. Benjamin stores up his metaphors and strings them along throughout his writings, making his entire corpus take on something of an allegorical structure, especially since these metaphors became shifted, altered, and distorted in their various locations. One of these is the image of the forest, which we have already seen through the romantic symbol's location in the "wooded interior" (*OGTD*, 165), an image probably taken from Baudelaire's "forest of symbols." Things can be kept hidden in a forest; secret societies meet in forests for esoteric rituals. Benjamin works against such interiority, against invisible meanings that disregard the materiality of their embodied signifiers. At the heart of allegory, we must be reminded, is the root *agora* (literally, marketplace), which refers to its very public presentation. Myths and symbols must retain their dialectical character, their form and their content, if they are to be of use in the historical present; they cannot hide in some transcendental, nonmaterial, invisible place beyond. Their historical and material situation must be taken out of hiding. Such revelatory activity can be seen in the *Arcades Project* where, at first, Benjamin seems to revive a rationalistic, Enlightenment critique of myth: "To cultivate fields where, until now, only madness has reigned. Forge ahead with the whetted axe of reason, looking neither left nor right so as not to succumb to the horror that beckons from deep in the primeval [*Ur*] forest. Every ground must at some point have been made arable by reason, must have been cleared of the undergrowth of delusion and myth," (*AP*, 456–57). From his critical toolbox he here chooses the axe of reason that would clear away such concealing forests, turning the esoteric inside out. The destructive allegorist reveals where myths and symbols have been hiding, bringing their physical existence to light. If the symbol moves inward, the allegory pushes meaning outward in a ruinous landscape.

But by no means is Benjamin an Enlightenment rationalist. The Enlightenment sought to distinguish between myth and truth and to place them in a hierarchical relation: Myth was a corrupted truth, subject to ignorance. To the contrary, Benjamin strikes to dissociate them even further, suggesting that they are in fact exclusory, and thus incomparable and incapable of being placed in a hierarchy. As Winfried Menninghaus puts it, "Benjamin refuses to reduce myth to either a form of truth or of falsehood, and thus rescues the autonomous dimension of myth."[96] Yet neither myth, nor the work of art nor the bourgeois individual is ultimately autonomous; rather, each is always bound up in material, historical circumstances. Clearing away the primeval forest, the interior space of symbols, makes meanings public. The allegorical process is one of clearing, of revealing, even of "stripping naked" (*OGTD*, 185), but this does not simply bring us to a singular core truth. Instead, in its publicity, its publication, that which was invisible is made physical—that is, is given body, and given to the senses of its public receivers, who continue to perceive and consequently disperse its meanings.

So Benjamin never throws anything away, never clears a forest and leaves it without remainder. He is a collector after all and he takes objects and ideas from the past, such as myth or allegory, and shines new light on them in the present. Thus, ultimately, by striking a difference, he can then turn around and create a montage between the ideas, lighting up previously unknown, concealed secrets about the ways rationality is mythical and myth rational. Joseph Mali has researched a little-known essay written by Benjamin in 1934, on a nineteenth-century Swiss scholar of mythology, Johann Jakob Bachofen. Bachofen's writings, like Nietzsche's, were eventually appropriated by National Socialist ideologies, and Benjamin's article was written in response, and further prompted by Erich Fromm's and Carl Jung's contemporary appropriations of Bachofen. Mali argues that Benjamin, in contradistinction to Bachofen, Fromm, and Jung, "wanted to show that history was not really determined by certain mythical beliefs, images, and tales but rather that certain historical conditions of material and anthropological necessities determined these mythic forms and compulsions."[97] By taking whole things apart and finding useful fragments among the ruins, Benjamin shows how myths operate from the ground up, how the whole, completed myth, symbol, or artwork is really a collection of material/historical components. Benjamin's remythologizing is an activity of *invention* in which "things are assembled according to their significance; indifference to their existence allowed them to be dispersed again" (*OGTD*, 188).

The allegorized and historicized myth also serves as a point of critique of the surrealist and psychoanalytic versions of myth (Freud and Jung), versions that are either oriented toward individualistic dream worlds, or are universalized. Benjamin would agree with Jung's "collective" notions of myth, and Benjamin suggests his own interest in wanting to "translate" psychoanalytic findings "from the individual to the collective" (*AP*, 844). Yet Benjamin is critical of Jung for lifting the collective out of historical time and space, and for theorizing on suprahistorical archetypes of human existence. Benjamin, to the contrary, seeks to dissolve "mythology into the space of history" (458). While borrowing surrealistic methods of juxtaposition, Benjamin nonetheless situates the realm of dreams in the land of time. Even so, it is importantly the passage *between* the two realms that retains his focus, the "threshold between waking and sleeping" (*SW II*, 208), as he puts it in his essay on surrealism published one year after the lament-play book.

The allegorical mode is a process of demythologizing and remythologizing without a final stable order. Benjamin may seek to transpose the verticality of myth that forsakes its historical existence, yet he shows the possibilities of what could be termed "allegorical mythologizing" (though he never called it such), a collective process working in the horizontal ruins of history. This is not a disregard for the past, but a high regard for what has been disregarded. The mythographer, for Benjamin, is an allegorist who reads culture, but instead of looking for symbols with their conventional meanings, as many anthropologists do, the allegorist looks for cultural allegories, those *mutated symbols* that unravel the presumed unity of religions and culture. The difference between the cultural observer who reads symbols and the one who reads allegories is brought forth in the classic Marxian analysis, according to which philosophers have only interpreted the world, whereas the point is to change it. By transposing word into image, time into space, metaphor into metonymy, the author into critic, the allegorical mode revalues what goes before it, repeats it only to change it, rewrites it to reactualize it. In this re-search for fragments, and the re-collection of them, the allegorist exposes what has been left out of the (illusory) narrative of myth and history. *Aesthetica artificialis* can never escape *aesthetica naturalis*.

In this chapter, I have attempted to rescue (or, possibly, reskew) allegory as a vital modality of religious aesthetics. Its vitality will be apparent only if seen as a contrast to traditional (most often, Christian) definitions of allegory. Allegorical desire might impel us to go back and reread allegory itself, to retrace its functions in a history of biblical/theological interpretation and reread that very history. Or, this desire may stimulate us to continue to search along a metonymic chain, tirelessly adding one term to the next, transforming old structures through destruction and re-creation. Or, it may induce us to continue our religion, understanding the past not as a smooth chain of operation, but as a series of fragments and distilled images that are perceived in the present.

What I am suggesting, as a writer attempting to actualize Benjamin, is that there is an allegorical mode of thinking/writing that takes fragments of the past (from its myths, rituals, paintings, or dramas) and rearranges them in regenerative ways. This function, which is a critical function, is both faithless and faithful: faithless because it does not respect coherence and unity, but destroys tradition by showing it to be a false construct from the beginning; faithful because among those fragments are the forgotten elements of history, which are brought to a perceptible level in the present. This is the point at which allegory becomes a way of thinking aesthetically about religion, and contributes to a furthering of religious aesthetics. These aesthetics are not oriented toward the logocentrism of Beauty, Truth, or God, but remain in the muddied, grounded matter of the earth. If most religious and theological aesthetics seek "the Beauty of the Lord" and permanent things beyond, Benjamin's aesthetics dwell among the earthly, the material, and thus, the transient. Benjamin's aesthetics are of transience, prompting himself and others to watch carefully, to pay attention, because we will miss something if we don't. Such aesthetics are not found in the interaction with great works of art in the static confines of the museum (though they may be), but found in the interstices where art meets life. It is not the masterpieces we should be looking for, but the mundane, the overlooked.

3
Working Art:
The Aesthetics of Technological
Reproduction

For the plate can only offer a negative. It is the product of an apparatus that substitutes light for shade, shade for light. Nothing would be
more inappropriate than for the image formed in this way to claim *fi-
nality* for itself.

Walter Benjamin[1]

The shorthand myth goes like this: Marcel Duchamp put a urinal in an exhibition and called it art. This is often cited in a disgruntled tone and set within a
general condemnation of modern art. But there is more to the story, much
more, and its retelling offers many inroads to Benjamin's key points in his classic essay "The Work of Art in the Age of Its Technological Reproducibility," as
well as showing a connection with an allegorical approach to the arts.

What really happened with Duchamp's art was this: In 1917 the American
Society of Independent Artists held an exhibition in New York. Duchamp's
contribution to the exhibition was to take a urinal, turn it on its back, label it
Fountain, and sign it "R. Mutt" (See Figure 3.1). Although the exhibition intended to highlight new artistic styles, the jury nonetheless took offense and
never allowed Duchamp's work to be shown, saying that it might "be a very
useful object in its place, but its place is not an art exhibition, and it is, by no
definition, a work of art."[2] Already the story is more complex, and in light of the
previous chapter we might say that Duchamp allegorizes the object by turning

Figure 3.1 Marcel Duchamp, *Fountain*. Photo by Alfred Stieglitz ©2004 Artists Rights Society (ARS), New York / ADAGP, Paris / Estate of Marcel Duchamp.

it into something other than what it was. While a urinal is a receptacle of liquid, a fountain is a dispenser of liquid; one is oriented toward input, the other toward output. In turning the object upside down, the artist ironically suggests that he is inverting the object's purpose. And as with the allegorical fragment taken from history, the object is taken out of a context and made to mean something new in another setting.

But that is also not all the story, for we are merely dealing here with an object and an artist. If seen from this perspective, we remain in the domain of traditional art and art history. What is perhaps the most significant element of this story is that there is no *Fountain*. The original object simply does not exist. In the fuller retelling we understand that Duchamp took the rejected artwork to the studio of his friend, the photographer Alfred Stieglitz, who made a photograph that was then published on the cover of an art journal, *The Blind Man*. An anonymous editorial titled "The Richard Mutt Case" (written by Duchamp himself, who was an editor of the journal) appeared in the same issue, as well as a critical analysis of *Fountain* entitled "Buddha of the Bathroom" by Louise Norton. Meanwhile, the original public toilet-*qua*-artwork was never again seen in public, and only years later did Duchamp go about replacing the piece of art when, through the 1950s and 1960s, Duchamp gave explicit instructions to various colleagues in various times and places to go and purchase urinals, which he then signed "R. Mutt." These multiple "artworks" are now owned by several museums, leading Dalia Judovitz to comment, "an original that is a documented copy leads to the proliferation of copies that are now documented originals."[3] At the heart of Duchamp's allegorical mythologizing are reversals of reversals, a repetition without origin—without singular origin, with many points "in the stream of becoming."

What is crucial to note is that Duchamp did not make history by putting a urinal in a museum and calling it art. This may have been a good story, but good stories do not survive simply because they are good stories; they survive because there is an entire apparatus in place to sustain and promote them. "Art," whatever that may be, is made by "artists," but it does not exist without critics of art, other artists, publishing outlets, institutions, collectors, galleries, museums, and a public to see and hear the story. There is no origin, no core thing at the heart of art, no singular artist creating *ex nihilo*, no single object.[4] Duchamp's antics were set in place to prove a point about *all* art. In a sense, the "Richard Mutt case" was meta-art—by producing something called "art," the project creates an allegory about how all art functions. (Even Michelangelo's *Pietà* (1498–1500), to take one example, as marvelously chiseled as it is, does not retain its status as a masterpiece without institutional support.) To study art in relation to religion and not take the social production of art into account is to risk setting art in a meaningless vacuum.

From Work to Work: Benjamin's Art

The dynamics of Duchamp's story usefully serve as an introduction to Benjamin's notion of the "work of art," a phrase that is strikingly different from what normally goes under the nomination. Early twentieth-century aesthetician Clive Bell provides a common understanding: "either all works of . . . art have some common quality, or when we speak of 'works of art' we gibber."[5] There is some essence to art, traditional aesthetics claims, some core entity, value, or force of energy shared from object to object—a quality typically named "beauty."

Benjamin's aesthetic theories of the artwork, on this account, are gibberish. That is because the emphatic word for Benjamin, and in the following, is *work* not *art*. That is, work is not to be understood as an object. Rather work is an activity; it is what art does. In the phrase "art work," we will understand art to be the subject and work to be the verb. Art works are then predicated by a host of other phrases, forming yet another of Benjamin's constellations: "Art works within culture," "Art works to change the perception of its viewers," "Art works with the help of technology to alter our social interactions." Art, if there is such a *thing*, exists only in reference to its work, to its functions in the world. One quickly notices too that there is a diminishment of subjective creation: there is no singular artist who accomplishes such work; it is a disseminated and dispersing activity.

Here I am mistranslating. In the preceding chapter I suggested the alternative translation of *Trauerspiel* as "lament-play," and that was still keeping within the semantic range of the German. Here, I am deliberating and unabashedly getting it wrong. The original title of Benjamin's essay that forms the backbone of this chapter is "Das Kunstwerk im Zeitalter seiner technischen Reproduzierbarkeit." The English language utilizes the term "work" in two ways, as an object and as a verb, while these can be separated in German: *das Werk* is a noun form, and the verb would be *arbeiten*. So, by stressing the *arbeiten* of art, I am distorting the translation in order to rethink what Benjamin might have meant here, and in so doing I am both getting it wrong and, I believe, getting it right.[6] Almost as if speaking directly to this dilemma, Benjamin himself, in a little sketch on translation, suggests, "The translation of important works will be less likely to succeed, the more it strives to elevate its subservient technical function into an autonomous art form" (*SW III*, 250). And in his well-known essay "Task of the Translator," he relates translation to the work of collecting fragments and putting the pieces together so that, "instead of imitating the sense of the original, [the translation] must lovingly and in detail incorporate the original's way of meaning, thus making both the original and the translation recognizable as fragments of a greater language, just as fragments are part of a vessel" (*SW I*, 260). Translation takes on allegorical functions. Or, as Betsy Flèche argues regarding Benjamin's shifts in meaning, "Translation functions metonymically in Benjamin's writings, in which terminology and style seem continually to transform. Words transform throughout each essay, being used later slightly differently, in 'translated' form."[7] Translation is always reproduction, representation, recreation, and is in other words a form of allegory. So to allegorize translation throughout this chapter, I will use the phrase "work of art" in speaking of the activities of art (its *arbeiten*) and "artwork" as the object of art (*das Kunstwerk*). Even when Benjamin discusses the *Kunstwerk*, I will be reorienting the emphasis as if he were talking of the *arbeiten* of *Kunst*.

In this chapter, I am interested in continuing some themes already highlighted in the *Trauerspiel* work, and I want to introduce a number of new stars in the constellation of aesthetics. Here, the stellar array is lit by the interrelation between art, technology, and society; the concept of the aura; the medium and the message; production and reproduction; the materiality of aesthetics and the related emphasis on the body and its senses; and aesthetic production and reception. One of the key theses of this chapter suggests that what allegory does for myth and symbol (i.e., distorts them), technological reproducibility does for the artwork and, in particular, for the artwork's aura. In other words, we move from artwork to the work of art, in a manner parallel to the *Trauerspiel*'s putting tragedy in motion. The "Work of Art" essay offers a political-aesthetic mode of analysis useful to a broad range of religious studies. For, to understand how the symbol gives rise to thought, we must also step back and understand how sense perception gives rise to the symbol, and how this occurs in historical settings.

Let it be said up front that Benjamin's essay is a strange essay, written in a dialectical format with shifting definitions of seemingly common terms like "reality," "art," and "perception." This, I take it, is part of what gives the essay its staying power and allows it to be frequently anthologized 70 years after its original inception.[8] The essay's strangeness comes in part from its very style: written as a series of theses, seemingly disconnectable, yet intimately linked. Such a style is found throughout Benjamin's *oeuvre*, and the format becomes inextricably bound up with the arguments themselves.

Not only are the essay's form and content strange, but its public history is somewhat convoluted (as if Benjamin were self-consciously trying to problematize the very origin and aura of the essay). It first appeared publicly in 1936 in French, translated by the surrealist writer Pierre Klossowski. Benjamin continued to work on the essay in various forms and today there are three known versions, but the only one published in his lifetime was that of 1936. A revised draft became the basis for the English translation by Harry Zohn and was included in Zohn's edited *Illuminations* in 1968; this is the version found in most anthologies. (*Illuminations*, with its introduction by Hannah Arendt, was the work that introduced Benjamin's writings to the English-speaking world, 28 years after his death.) Now, as part of Harvard University Press's publication of the multivolume *Selected Writings* in English, English readers have available the "form in which Benjamin originally wished to see the work published,"[9] an extended version of the one in *Illuminations*. The third version of the essay, recently translated into English for the Harvard series, represents Benjamin's continued unrest with the themes promoted in the essay. It is this version that Benjamin, as the editors note, "as late as 1939, could still regard as a work in progress."[10]

All of this confounds researchers, trained to find origins, leaving us with guesswork, having to piece together Benjamin's thoughts from 1935, 1936, 1938, and left to wonder whether the later work is more "accurate." Was there a singular Benjamin? Can we find what he really thought? Is there a beginning? Or is origin (*Ursprung*) always, as he himself suggested, "a whirlpool in the stream of becoming, and in its current it swallows the material involved in the process of genesis" (*OGTD*, 45)? Jumping into the stream now, I will primarily rely on the "second version," though referencing the others.

The Aura and Its Decline

Undoubtedly the most prominent and commented upon facet of the essay is the idea of the aura. And although it has been elaborated upon multiple times, I will briefly do so once more to contextualize it within my study and in relation to the study of religion. The concept of the aura was introduced in his 1931 essay "Little History of Photography," where Benjamin gives a definition similar to the one given in "The Work of Art": "What is aura actually? A strange weave [*Gespinst*] of space and time: the unique appearance or semblance of distance, no matter how close the object may be" (*SW II*, 518). And in the *Arcades Project*, Benjamin offers the contrast of the "trace" and the aura: "The trace is appearance of a nearness, however far removed the thing that left it behind may be. The aura is appearance of a distance, however close the thing that calls it forth. In the trace, we gain possession of the thing; in the aura, it takes possession of us" (*AP*, 447). Aura depends on a metaphysical distance from an object even though it may be physically close. Critically, the aura is not inherent in the object itself but is built up around the object through history and through social conditions: "The authenticity of a thing is the quintessence of all that is transmissible from its origin on, ranging from its physical duration to the historical testimony relating to it" (*SW III*, 103). Such reproducible testimony (its mediated communicability) is nothing new—"In principle, the work of art has always been reproducible" (102)—and in fact the imitating replicas of premodern reproduction actually served to preserve and promote the authenticity of the original, building up a thicker aura. As a result of historical and social conditions, the object is made to *seem* untouchable.

On one level, the case of Duchamp's *Fountain* would seem to be just what Benjamin is talking about, given the massive historical testimony relating to it. The critical difference is that the aura pertains to an actual object that exists in time and place. The *Mona Lisa* is perhaps one of the best examples, especially today, as directional signs are planted throughout the Louvre pointing the way to that most auratic of paintings, with its protective heavy frame. Duchamp understood the work of the aura, even painting a moustache on the *Mona Lisa* and including the verbal French pun of "L.H.O.O.Q." in his 1919 readymade. But with *Fountain* he goes further by inverting the whole structure and showing how powerful aura can be: The aura is so dominant in art that we no longer even need an original object.

Translating the aura into the language of religious studies is not much of a task, for the leap from aura to "sacred" or "holy" is quite short. Benjamin's application of aura to objects of art shares some similarities with Rudolf Otto's "idea of the holy" as that which is both mysterious and fascinating (*mysterium tremendum et fascinans*). Otto's idea of the holy is dialectical, consisting of two opposing energies. The holy is set apart from us; it is "wholly other," just as the aura institutes the "unique apparition of a distance" (*SW III*, 104–5). Yet, the holy on Otto's scheme is also fascinating: humans desire to get closer to it, for "it is no less something that allures with a potent charm."[11] Likewise, in regard to the art object invested with aura, "Every day the urge grows stronger to get hold of an object at close range in an image" (105). And just as the aura "takes possession of us," so does the mysterious and fascinating presence of the holy entrance those who perceive it: "he feels a something that captivates and transports him with a strange ravishment, rising often enough to the pitch of dizzy intoxication."[12] Regardless of whether Benjamin had Otto's work in mind, the relation between the aura and the holy is central to Benjamin's designs for his essay, and he continues to see the relation of the aura to its ritualized, sacred setting.

Clifford Geertz brings the relation even closer in his now classic definition of religion from his essay "Religion as a Cultural System," where he argues that religion is "(1) a system of symbols which acts to (2) establish powerful, pervasive, and long-lasting moods and motivations in men by (3) formulating conceptions of a general order of existence and (4) clothing these conceptions with such an *aura of factuality* that (5) the moods and motivations seem uniquely realistic."[13] The "aura of factuality" that Geertz goes on to discuss is evidently in place owing to a "prior acceptance of authority," and the symbols must be imbued "with a persuasive authority."[14] This authority has the ability to fascinate, to induce fear and/or laughter, and to mold people's behavior, particularly through the enactment of religious rituals. Fundamentally, Geertz is clear that the aura relies on a hierarchical authority structure.

Technological reproduction, however, changes the dynamic tensions between the mysterious authority of the aura and the desire to be possessed by it. While pretechnological reproduction (the handmade copy) actually serves to build up aura and retain the sense of distance, technological reproduction breaks it down and brings things closer. In this technological movement, reproduction usurps production, allegorizing the artwork by distorting the original meanings. In one of the most quoted phrases from the essay, Benjamin makes the implication clear: "what withers in the age of the technological reproducibility of the work of art is the latter's aura" (*SW III*, 104).

There are different types of reproduction, and Benjamin distinguishes what he means by technological reproduction from that of classical Western thought. The classical sense of reproduction and representation, as instituted by Plato in Book 10 of *The Republic*, is "imitation." In this model, there is an original of which replicas can be made, but the original retains prominence. In Plato's conception, life itself is at the origin, and art is merely a secondary, pale copy of an original. However, as Duchamp well knows, with technological reproduction the hierarchy is disrupted, the original becomes outmoded, and technological advances actually alter the very production of art in the first instance. If premixed tubes of paint allowed Manet, Monet, and other Impressionists to set up their easels in the great outdoors and "paint the moment," then photographic technologies allow reproduction to keep up with everyday life itself; film "could now keep pace with speech" (*SW III*, 102). The reproduction of the work of art now keeps pace with perception.

There are two immediate social implications to this movement, Benjamin notes, as the significance of the withering of the aura "extends far beyond the realm of art" (104). For one, technological reproducing technologies (especially photographic and filmic) enable a different way of seeing the original, thus altering human perception itself. For example, through the use of close-ups, shifting angles, and slow motion, the viewer can see the parts of the world in ways "which escape natural optics altogether" (103). Here Benjamin may have had in mind the legendary case of Leland Stanford's wager. In the 1870s, Stanford, then governor of California, gambled that at the gallop, horses actually have all four hooves off the ground at certain instants, an event that is not detectable to the rather slow human eye. The photographer Eadweard Muybridge, along with his high-speed shutter camera, joined Stanford in California and shot a series of images of one of Stanford's horses at full speed. There, sure enough, was a frame displaying all four legs of the horse off the ground, an event never before seen by the human eye.

This event is cleverly reconfigured in Dziga Vertov's 1929 film, *Man with a Movie Camera*. As the cinematographer follows a horse-drawn buggy down a Russian street, the horse suddenly appears to stop, frozen in time and space. The horse's gallop, seen in the "moving picture," is suddenly halted within the still frame. The unfolding of motion in the chronology of the "movie" is transposed into the spatiality of the still frame. In a second move, Vertov's film then cuts to the editing room, showing how the filmmaker is behind this presentation of reality. To make sure the viewer gets this point, Vertov intercuts a number of still images with live action sequences, (Figure 3.2) and in this way Vertov

Figure 3.2 Frame Capture from Dziga Vertov, *Man with a Movie Camera*, 1929

portrays precisely what Benjamin would articulate, that the "most powerful agent" in the "shattering of tradition" is film. Objects are taken from their natural, traditional context and given new coordinates through mechanical reproduction. The creativity of the camera is thus "inconceivable without its destructive, cathartic side" (*SW III*, 104). Photographic technologies allow viewers to see the world in new ways, in ways not originally thought possible, but only through a creative destruction of the originally perceived whole. As with allegory, there is no pure nature that can be reached; it is always mediated.

The second implication of reproducing technologies is that they can strip the authenticity of the original (its unique position in time and space) by putting reproductions in various contexts, enabling "the original to meet the recipient halfway, whether in the form of a photograph or in that of a gramophone record. The cathedral leaves its site to be received in the studio of an art lover; the choral work performed in an auditorium or in the open air is enjoyed in a private room" (*SW III*, 103). Reproducing technologies redistribute access to artworks by giving them over to the masses, effecting a democratization of images and other art forms. This second point has radical implications, for the technological reproducibility and mass distribution of artworks has effects greater than merely giving more people more access. Society itself is irrevocably altered.

The sociopolitical implications of the aura's destruction come to the fore in Benjamin's essay. He is ultimately interested in "the social basis of the aura's present decay" (*SW III*, 105) and believes—perhaps in a fit of utopian thinking that is less extreme in his other works—in the democratic desires of the masses, working hand in hand with the democratization of artworks made possible through their technological reproduction: "The stripping of the veil from the object, the destruction of the aura, is the signature of a perception whose 'sense for the sameness in the world' has so increased that, by means of reproduction, it extracts sameness even from what is unique" (ibid). Benjamin suggests that people want to bring things closer to themselves, and that a leveling effect occurs in that proximity with the result that no one thing is more valued than any other. Objects are put on a level field and evaluated by the masses who, through a retrained perception, see equality, sameness. No thing is "set apart" from any other, the sacred is made profane. The sociopolitical implications are clear, for as the auratic object is extracted from its traditional setting, so are judgment and taste taken away from the realm of the ruling classes. What might be intuited here is that Benjamin sees the desire for proximity instilled by the *fascinans* overtaking the distance created through the *mysterium*.

In this play of proximity and distance at the heart of the aura is the issue of *who* is in control of the relation. Quite simply, the class for which art is created supplies the traditional values of art and aesthetics, which up until the twentieth century was strictly the governing class. At one time this was the church and monarchy. Aesthetic control had traditionally been enforced through art's immersion in a ritual context, thus giving to the church and the monarchy policing powers in the realm of culture as well as in religion and economics. The authority eventually shifted away from the church to the bourgeoisie in the nineteenth century, even as the bourgeoisie created its own legitimating cultural authority. This class of people controls art's production and reproduction, utilizing the aura as a tool of legitimation—by legitimizing the art object, and thus a certain aesthetic style, the bourgeoisie can also legitimize the ruling class's authority on culture. Likewise, Geertz notes the reliance of the religion's "aura of factuality" on hierarchical power structures. Nonetheless, with the rise of technological reproduction in the twentieth century, the masses gained the ability to control their own interactions with artworks as they were given the potential to destroy the hierarchy of tradition and culture.

Here too, Benjamin merges the religious and political, and we find his mystical motivations underlying his political pursuits. The creation and destruction of the aura is not simply about art and politics; it is also about cosmogony. In the first chapter, I noted how Lurianic Kabbalism speaks of a God who, in the beginning, limits Itself and then attempts to create the world by pouring Its light into various "vessels" (*sephirot*), which break and shatter into pieces (*shevira*) [cf. Kiefer's work of art, Figure 1.3]. Some of the light from God falls to earth and becomes imprisoned in the realm of darkness, encaptured in *qlipot* (husks, shells). As Marc-Alain Ouaknin explains, "With the breakage, everything became disjointed. . . . The sparks of holiness fell into the world but were surrounded by the husks, which meant that they could not be reached; it was man's work to break the husks."[15] These sparks have a desire to be put back together, and the destiny of God's people is to liberate these sparks from their shell and lift them back to the divine realm. Just as humanity's activity is to work toward *tikkun*, so is the aura stripped of its "veil," creating a "sameness" of things, which on the Kabbalistic accounts is the underlying unity of the divine *Ein Sof*. By drawing on Kabbalistic thought, Benjamin is setting religion in the service of the social realm; mysticism is shot through with avant-garde notions about art, and a belief in the desires and work of the masses. Thus, it is not through reading Torah and performing *mitzvoth* that redemption occurs, but through avant-garde artistic practices connected to technological reproduction; and it is not Israel or the people of God who can pry the objects from their shells, but the masses who perceive the work of art. So, then again, Benjamin's cosmogony is really about art and politics.

What is absolutely vital to note at this point is that there is a two-pronged movement going on in Benjamin's analysis of the destruction of the aura, a movement that is a reworking of the allegorical movement he worked with at other stages in his writing. He explains the two processes thus:

> [T]he technology of reproduction detaches the reproduced object from the sphere of tradition. By replicating the work many times over, it substitutes a mass existence for a unique existence. And in permitting the reproduction to reach the recipient in his or her own situation, it actualizes that which is reproduced. These two processes lead to a massive upheaval in the domain of objects handed down from the past—a shattering of tradition which is the reverse side of the present crisis and renewal of humanity. (*SW III*, 104)

This is a significant quotation, and the two processes are often overlooked in studies of Benjamin's "Work of Art" essay. The critical suggestion made here is that it is not only the work of technological *reproduction* that shatters tradition, but also the *reception* of these reproductions on the part of the people. The masses play an active role.

Critically, Benjamin sees the masses not as an inert lump, but as a dynamic "mass *movement*." Samuel Weber notes how "Mass movements are the result, or rather, the corollary, of that movement of *detachment, ablösen*, that marks the decline of aura."[16] Whereas the aura situates an art object in time and place, technological reproduction detaches it from this tradition. Correlatively, the multiplying of artworks must be met by the multiplicity of the masses. The reception of the work of art by the mass movement destroys uniqueness just as the mass reproduction does. In this twofold movement of mass reproduction and mass reception, the work of art is shifted and shaken loose from its unique position. Traditionally, a human subject received the singularity of the art object; in Benjamin's mass movement, however, the object is multiple, as is the subject.

Looking more closely at Weber's remark, we find a further relation to Benjamin's concept of allegory. For within these two co-implicated processes attached to the withering of the aura, the reader is able to faintly detect the dual suggestive tropes of metonymy and metaphor. On the simplest level, as explained in greater detail in chapter 2, metonymy relies on contiguity and serves to complement what goes before it, while metaphor relies on similarity and serves as a substitute to what goes before it. So, we might see these tropes enacted by the way technological reproduction "substitutes" (metaphor) "a mass existence" (metonymy), and then by the way technological reproduction allows an art object to meet an observer "in his or her own situation" (the synchronic aspect of metonymy) and thus "actualizing" the reproduced object (the paradigmatic aspect of metaphor). And through these activities, the thing itself is made to seem other than itself. Just as allegory is reception based, relying prominently on the critic to extract its various meanings, so do the sociopolitical implications of the work of art rely on the masses. The two-part play of reproduced art also mimics the lament-play since the baroque dramas were performed by traveling theatrical companies, meeting the audience in their own particular situation, as opposed to the singular stage of the Greek tragedy. "The spectator of tragedy is summoned, and is justified, by the tragedy itself; the *Trauerspiel*, in contrast, has to be understood from the point of view of the onlooker" (*OGTD*, 119). The audience of the lament-play parallels the allegorical critic, who parallels the perceiving mass of people, all detaching the core meaning of the "work of art" from the "artwork" and relocating it in an external public setting: in the transference from art object to perceiving subjects.

The Work of Art

Benjamin's emphasis on the work of art, rather than the artwork, brings out the dynamic movement between art and reality. In Munich, Benjamin studied, however briefly, with Heinrich Wölfflin, sometimes called the father of modern art history and a pupil of the historian Jacob Burckhardt, not long after Wölfflin had published his *Principles of Art History* (1915). Among other things, Wölfflin is credited with rescuing the baroque as a demarcated style and period of art, legitimate for study—before him the term had been used pejoratively—and Benjamin clearly picked up on this rescue operation. He was nonetheless critical of his teacher, since Wölfflin disregarded the relation of art to life. The problem was that Wölfflin saw the art object *qua* object and neglected its reception, its productive interactions with life. Thus, the "Work of Art" essay begins with a radical notion that we have already seen implicit in Duchamp's work of art: "creativity and genius, eternal value and mystery" are outmoded concepts (*SW III*, 101). In other words, the entire conception of what constitutes art and traditional theories of aesthetics are immediately put into question.[17] What is emphasized instead is the *work* of art.

Providing a brief history of art's relation to ritual, Benjamin suggests how early artworks "originated in the service of rituals" and "the unique value of the 'authentic' work of art always has its basis in ritual" (*SW III*, 105). At this point, art had "cult value." Through time, the ritual that gave art its context, function, and meaning, shifted from being a religious ritual into a secularized, albeit still ritualized, cult of beauty in the Renaissance. Severed from the transcendence of magic and religion, art turned *beauty* into a transcendent quality and ended with the inevitable isolation of *l'art pour l'art* (art for art's sake). Just as art began to lose its auratic, ritually grounded nature in the nineteenth century, the doctrine of *l'art pour l'art* arose, setting it in the context of its "exhibition value." No longer connected to external religiosocial conditions, this doctrine turns in on itself, finding an inner unity to art that guarantees its own worth— much like the romantic symbol, and it is no secret that the two movements arose at roughly the same time. This leads to a "negative theology" of pure art, dissociated from all other realms, which "rejects not only any social function but any definition in terms of a representational content" (106).

Even at this point, it must be observed, there is still an aura enacted, since it is the aesthetic judgments of the upper classes that maintain the cultural institution of art, and most importantly, create the *veil* around the artwork by framing it and placing it in the museum. In the modern age, the value of art shifts from its basis in religious authorities to socioeconomic authorities— from the church to the museum. In the midst of this shift, there is actually no substantive shift, for socioeconomic authorities are structurally no different from religious authorities. The shift is a metaphorical one, a replacement of vertically-directed "heads," rather than a metonymical one, which is what the technologically reproduced work of art does by expanding the meanings of art and replacing its singular location in time and space. Art on exhibition, for its own sake, instead of making images more democratic, "is coming to be defined in the only way that it ever achieves definition—by expressing the perceptions, interests, and values of the class for which it is produced,"[18] suggests Joel Snyder. The politics of the upper class now manages the affairs of art, and shapes a society's perception.

In spite of his protests, the doctrine of *l'art pour l'art* continued on and reached its zenith well after Benjamin's essay. It could be said to have reached its limits, and thus its death, in the formalist aesthetics of Clement Greenberg in the 1950s and 1960s, and later in Michael Fried's art theories in the 1960s through the 1970s. Greenberg's prominent 1960 essay "Modernist Painting" lays out the aims of modern painting and, by implication, of modernism altogether. While similar to Benjamin in certain of his Marxist convictions, and a belief in the transformative potential of the avant-garde, Greenberg was strikingly different from Benjamin in many ways. Greenberg's championing of an independent and pure art was miles away from the aesthetics put forward in "The Work of Art." Greenberg contended that through self-criticism, as instigated by Kant, "each art would be rendered 'pure,' and in its 'purity' find the guarantee of its standards of quality as well as of its independence."[19] Furthermore, at the end of "Modernist Painting," he gives a view of history at the opposite end of the spectrum from Benjamin. Greenberg states, "Nothing could be further from the authentic art of our time than the idea of a rupture of continuity. Art is, among many other things, continuity."[20] Such an anaesthetizing of history is anathema to Benjamin, who seeks to explode tradition and continuity as well as the isolated artwork.

To the contrary, Benjamin's essay steps over the autonomous limits imposed by art as he reads *l'art pour l'art* within its historical context, emerging with an optimistic statement about art in the age of technological reproduction: "[F]or the first time in world history, technological reproducibility emancipates the work of art from its parasitical subservience to ritual" (*SW III*, 106). He might concur with Greenberg on the importance of art's independence from ritual, but he sees that the "cult of authenticity" serves similar ends: "But as soon as the criterion of authenticity ceases to be applied to artistic production, the whole social function of art is revolutionized. Instead of being founded on ritual, it is based on a different practice: politics" (106). Having applauded *l'art pour l'art*'s ability to help sever art's ties to ritual, he notes how art can now be disseminated across the perceiving abilities of the masses. Benjamin's utopian suggestion is that in the age of technological reproduction, the aura is held under the control of the masses: since art is democratized in the age of technological reproduction, it is made present to all. Although this admits to an authority for art, it is an authority that is at bottom unstable, dispersed among the many. Technology is able to put reproducing power into the hands of the masses and let them manage themselves.

In an age in which exhibition value has all but replaced art's cult value, he suggests that "the work of art becomes a construct [*Gebilde*] with quite new functions" (*SW III*, 107). Benjamin's philosophy of the arts argues how the essence of the work of art is not unchanging and does not hold universal truths. Instead, the meaning of the work of art shifts throughout history depending on social conditions surrounding the work of art. This is especially the case when the dominant media are those of technological reproducing technologies. As Rochlitz comments, "In a certain way, for Benjamin—at least in this essay—the medium is already the message; the significance of art is reduced to the medium through which it addresses the public."[21] Art *qua* object disappears, is liquidated. There is nothing significant about art itself, and it cannot rely on some self-authenticating theory. It is valuable only as it is put into motion and made public in and through the work of the masses and technology. And now that technology mediates cultural experiences, the perception of the world itself shifts: "The way in which human perception is organized—the medium in which it occurs—is conditioned not only by nature but by history" (104). Perception is subject to space and time. Anticipating McLuhan, Ong, and others, Benjamin turns to emphasize the *medium* over the *message*. In so doing, Rochlitz also notes, he

> Replaces the spirit with the word, the name, or, in a general way, the medium of communication, according them primacy over the subject. . . . The move from the spirit to the letter brings together philosophy and literature: The literary work is the quintessential medium where the spirit has no existence independent of the letter. In remaining at this symbolic "materialization" of the spirit, Benjamin has contributed to the effacement of the boundaries that make the philosopher-writer a "creator of concepts."[22]

The Benjaminian poet/artist/allegorist keeps the artwork from disappearing, from flying beyond itself, from dissolving into an idealist unity. Benjamin has no use for art as a separate category. Instead, he is interested in the *work* of art, how it labors to explode that which was thought to be universal. For art to work in this way, its materiality must be emphasized, its existence as objects in space and time.

Allegorizing the Museum

Though Benjamin does not mark it in this essay, the move to the independence of the artwork's exhibition value coincides with the birth of the museum in the eighteenth and nineteenth centuries. A brief look at this development offers new dimensions in understanding Benjamin's essay on the work of art, for there are material, institutional reasons behind the rise of the doctrine *l'art pour l'art*, and they are very much bound to the emergence of the museum.

Commentators on Benjamin have often made note of his use of the ruin and the fragment, yet it is important to make the further note that fragments are always connected to the action of the collector; they are not fragments for the sake of fragments. Collection played a crucial role throughout Benjamin's thought, and his final, grand, incomplete *Arcades Project* was nothing less than a decade or more of collections of literary fragments, many written by him and many by others. Therein lies section "H," otherwise known as "The Collector," where we see the ways in which the collector both destroys the aura of an object by "detaching" it from "its original functions" (*AP*, 204), and ends up reinstituting another shell: "It is the deepest enchantment of the collector to enclose the particular item within a magic circle, where, as a last shudder runs through it (the shudder of being acquired), it turns to stone. Everything remembered, everything thought, everything conscious becomes socle, frame, pedestal, seal of his possession" (205). While objects invested with aura (holiness) "take possession of us," the collector possesses the object. Nonetheless, the collector works toward establishing a "new, expressly devised historical system: the collection. And for the true collector, every single thing in this system becomes an encyclopedia of all knowledge of the epoch, the landscape, the industry, and the owner from which it comes" (ibid.). The collector ultimately labors toward completeness, to recreate a past in the present. Having been pried from its original shell, the object may now take on a new value in its exhibition. But a brief history of the museum shows the limitations of such collecting.

Many claim that the first real museum was the Louvre in Paris, after the private collection of Louis XVI was taken over by the public in the midst of the Revolution. But the first museum, built *as* a museum—an architectural site in the midst of a city—was the neoclassical Berlin museum built in the

1820s designed by Karl Friedrich Schinkel, architect of much of modern Berlin. In *On the Museum's Ruins*, Douglas Crimp points out that Schinkel was a friend of Hegel's, and the construction of the museum took place while Hegel was delivering his seminars on aesthetics in which he sketched the "cult of beauty" of romantic (i.e., Christian) art that was to be roundly rejected by Benjamin. Hegel values romantic/Christian art, for "in its efforts to free itself from the immediately sensuous as such, in order to express a content that is *not* inseparable from sensuous representation, romantic art becomes indeed the self-transcendence of art itself."[23] Here, as elsewhere in idealist aesthetics, we see the effacement of the material in the sought-after unity of form and content, inner and outer. In Hegel's schema, "immediate" sensuous perception must be taken up into a final "absolute knowledge," a unity of consciousness and self-consciousness. The materiality of art and aesthetics is ultimately left behind.[24]

By detaching artworks from ritual, the museum recreates a new auratic status of art by placing it in a building that is set apart from the world, preserving art in specific places and times, set on pedestals, framed, and specially lit. Schinkel himself thought of the museum as a "sanctuary," cordoned off from the other parts of life, and there was a great deal of debate over whether the new Berlin structure should be called a "museum." Friedrich Schleiermacher, father of modern theology and hermeneutics, called it a "*treasury* for sculpture and painting distinguished by their age and their art."[25] Meanwhile Adorno sees the implications of such ways of thinking as he brings out some of the hesitations around the word museum:

> The German word *museal* [museumlike] has unpleasant overtones. It describes objects to which the observer no longer has a vital relationship and which are in the process of dying. They owe their preservation more to historical respect than to the needs of the present. Museum and mausoleum are connected by more than phonetic association. Museums are the family sepulchers of works of art.[26]

As with the coincidental and co-implicated independence of art from ritual, Benjamin might have on one hand praised the rise of the museum, but he would see its shortcomings because it remains a structurally separate element in society. Picking up on Benjamin's thoughts, Crimp points out the correlation of modernist theories of art and practice and the birth of the museum. In doing so he too connects, against autonomous art's own interests, the social setting to the practice of art, thereby deconstructing the autonomous impulses of *l'art pour l'art*: "When art is thought to be naturally lodged in the museum, an institution of the state, it is an idealist rather than a materialist aesthetic that is served."[27] Crimp also declares that a move out of modernist aesthetics necessitates the "museum's ruins" and asserts that "we must still struggle for a materialist aesthetics and a materialist art."[28]

The museum is a collection (*Sammlung*), creating a coherent experience of the past by making history visible in the present. Pieces are selected from the past and brought forward and arranged in the present space, and for this Benjamin would be sympathetic to the activities of the museum. Yet, they go too far with their collections and wind up positing a unified narrative of the past that can be experienced as whole and seemingly complete. The modern museum is constructed to reenact the experience of *Erfahrung* (a unified, narrativized experience that reasserts a continuity of history through second-order reflection), while Benjamin's allegorical history opens up a place for *Erlebnis* (the more immediate and intuitive singular experiences that disrupt the present), to leave the fragments as ruins that, while re-creating something new, nonetheless remain incomplete. Betsy Flèche comments on Benjamin's critical urge to destroy the continuity of tradition, a tradition that would include the modern museum: "the impulse to look for resemblances homogenizes history, makes it a story, a narrative, with easy connections. History that is all of a piece is also a viable a tool of the totalitarian state."[29] Simply put, the collection must always be subject to dispersal, or it becomes a tool of the totalitarian state.

Benjamin's distrust of unified collections is not merely abstract leftist criticism, but is instead terribly prescient. Indeed, as Richard Cohen charts in *Jewish Icons*, the totalitarian use of a museum collection is precisely what happened with the development of Jewish museums in modern Europe. After emancipation in the nineteenth century, Jews in Europe were faced with problems of assimilation into the broader society. One of the strategies among Jews was to visibly display their material culture, and thus their identity, showing to the broader public that they had and have a past and a present. Thus, they began to shift their collections of Jewish ritual objects out of synagogues and private homes into museums, and the first Jewish Museum was created in Vienna in 1895, followed by museums established in Prague, Danzig, and Budapest. Paralleling Benjamin's language on the collection, Cohen notes how the Prague museum in particular provides an important case history, suggesting how "[t]ransformation of meanings is an ever-present phenomenon in the history of museums and built into their very nature."[30] For not long after the Prague museum was finished, with its fine collection of Judaica, National Socialism arose, and in 1942 the Nazis ordered the takeover of the museum, using it for their own purposes and creating of it a giant storehouse called the "Central Jewish Museum." Cohen tells the story:

> As Jews were deported from their hometowns, their objects were assembled and sent to Prague, where they were carefully examined and

classified. Prague's museum was transformed into a unique collection. Its holdings covered objects from all over the Czech lands, ranging from the finest Torah ark curtains to everyday objects created by unskilled craftspeople. Moreover, it paradoxically, and cynically, pursued the goals of its creators—both in its national character and in its desire to prevent the destruction of objects that had been preserved for generations in families and synagogues, about to be demolished. Members of the museum and additional staff from other Jewish museums in the former Czechoslovakia, who continued to fulfill their museological functions, could not know of the eventual goal of the Nazis—to create a permanent museum of Jewish art, from cradle to grave, that would be a constant reminder to the world of the decadent nature of Jewish civilization. This museum, so some National Socialist theorists claimed, would become even more essential following the destruction of European Jewry, for with their demise one needed to guarantee their ideological centrality to National Socialism. Objects were to vindicate and legitimate National Socialist policy on the "Jewish question." Thus emerged one of the most important repositories of Jewish art in the world today.[31]

In many ways, Cohen's synopsis of the Prague museum echoes Benjamin's critical concerns: that in the end it depends on *who* is in control of cultural meaning that makes the difference. Just as the aura of the artwork is disseminated for and by the masses, so should the museum be dispersed. What becomes vital, then, is to note the way Benjamin's discussion of the collector shifts through section "H" in the *Arcades Project*. What we find is a relation between the collector and the allegorist—becoming another set of those twin stars found throughout his writings. While the collector "takes up the struggle against dispersion [*Zerstreuung*]" and "brings things together that belong together," the allegorist "dislodges things from their context and, from the outset, relies on his profundity to illuminate their meaning."

> Nevertheless—and this is more important than all the differences that may exist between them—in every collector hides an allegorist, and in every allegorist a collector. As far as the collector is concerned, his collection is never complete; for let him discover just a single piece missing, and everything he's collected remains a patchwork, which is what things are for allegory from the beginning. On the other hand, the allegorist—for whom objects represent only keywords in a secret dictionary, which will make known their meaning to the initiated—precisely the allegorist can never have enough of things. With him, one thing is so little capable of taking the place of another that no possible

reflection suffices to foresee what meaning his profundity might lay claim to for each one of them. (*AP*, 211)

What is revealed is that collectors, against their better hopes, are always only allegorists, always dealing with incomplete collections. Chronologically, the collector seeks to bring on the eschaton, a time when all will be collected and arranged in an order, "an encyclopedia of all knowledge of the epoch." But that end time is always deferred, and allegorist and collector alike live in unfulfilled, incomplete time in which they never get enough of objects. The final line here suggests again the metonymic character of the allegorist, who must illuminate the meaning of each one of the objects collected. The collection never comes together as a whole, but remains a patchwork—against the metaphoric, substitutional structure, no thing can take the place of another.

As Benjamin well understood, objects take on meaning according to their context, their position in space and time. He writes of the work of art as a process of continuously shuffling the pieces so that they cannot become static and confined to a particular point in space and time, and thus become usable under totalitarian ideologies. He even quotes from Marx on the subject of collecting in relation to aesthetics: "Private property has made us so stupid and inert that an object is ours only when we *have* it. All the physical and intellectual senses . . . have been replaced by the simple alienation of all these senses, the sense of having" (*AP*, 210). Collecting is attractive, we want to possess. But possession alienates us from our body, and the myth of a total collection can serve the wrong ends. This too is why Benjamin emphasizes the technological reproducibility of art, for it becomes more public, more subject to the dispersing power of the masses. As the masses made public the collection in the Louvre as part of a democratic revolution, so does technological reproduction allow the masses to disperse the work of art even further.

Subjectivity Collected and Dispersed

To destroy aura, to detach the artwork from its privileged location in order to meet the masses halfway, is not as simple as it seems. What must be accounted for and destroyed is the myth of the individual subject, who would pretend to be in control of cultural meanings. In the context of film and photography, we find the aura of the individual particularly in the continued presence of the human figure, and especially the face. Benjamin points out how early photography was focused on portraiture, and further how photographs of humans, "dead or absent," bring with them the continued presence of an aura: "In the fleeting expression of a human face, the aura beckons from early photography for the last time. This is what gives them their melancholy and incomparable beauty. But as the human being withdraws from the photographic image, exhibition value for the first time shows its superiority to cult value" (*SW III*, 108). Benjamin reasserts here what religious iconographers have recently come to argue: that it is the *face*, and especially the eyes, in an image that constitutes its mimetic pull, its aura. This is true for South Asian traditions as it is for Christian.[32]

Because Benjamin is so insistent on championing the new age of the work of art, he also tarries to rid the new age of the aura of its humanity. It was because of this incessant housecleaning of aura that Scholem suggested to him, "You have swept art out of the corners of its taboos."[33] Not that Benjamin is antihuman, but humanism too is an ideology maintained by the cultural elite. Significant for Benjamin was the work of photographer Eugène Atget and others at the turn of the century in which the human form is taken out of the photograph, leaving images that look like "scenes of crimes" and thus they "unsettle the viewer" (*SW III*, 108). This new, humanless form and style of depiction detaches the image from its existence in a particular space and time, leaving the viewer struggling to find a new mode of response. Nonetheless, the powers of media soon sedated viewers by providing captions, thus imparting a particular orientation for the viewers. Words surrounding the image make them safe for viewing by reinstilling a sense of stability. Benjamin continually sees arresting images as having a social function that might shock the viewers, bringing them to a heightened consciousness, but political forces that insist on cohesion create captioned images.

If photography eventually freed itself from the human countenance, films did not do so quickly. Because film relied, and continues to rely, on actors who exert a certain presence, Benjamin means to erase any allusion to an aura for the actor. To do so he must splinter the presence of the actor, keeping any recourse to an aura of the human at bay. While the lament-play put actors in motion, film pushes the motility even further, and Benjamin compares the human presence on film and on stage. As opposed to the screen actor, the film actor feels alienated, or as Benjamin quotes Italian writer Luigi Pirandello, the actor "feels as if exiled" (*SW III*, 112). First of all, in film, "many shots are filmed in a number of takes" (111). The director and the editor then select and arrange these shots, removing authority from the actor, consigning him or her, in the words of Rudolf Arnheim, to the role of a "prop" (112). Such exile, such metonymic replication, connotes a loss of aura: "For the first time—and this is the effect of film—the human being is placed in a position where he must operate with his whole living person, while forgoing its aura. For the aura is bound to its presence in the here and now. There is no facsimile of the aura" (ibid.). Through the many layers of technological reproduction, the aura of the "character" of the actor disappears: "His performance is by no means a unified whole, but it is assembled from many individual performances" (ibid.). Consequently, a general fragmentation of the actor occurs through the numerous layers of production.

The exile of the film actor from the audience, along with the resulting decay of aura, becomes, in turn, an exile within the actor's own self. The results, Benjamin argues, are "highly productive" (*SW III*, 113). He goes on to say that the estrangement of the actor from her or his self "is basically of the same kind as the estrangement felt before one's appearance [*Erscheinung*] in a mirror—a favorite theme of the Romantics. But now the mirror image [*Bild*] has become detachable from the person mirrored, and is transportable. And where is it transported? To a site in front of the masses" (ibid.). Technological reproduction detaches the art object from its auratic place, allowing the masses to meet it in their own place, and here we note how the subjectivity of the actor is also disseminated and given over to a perceiving public.

Though Benjamin was most likely unaware, the "Work of Art" essay was published in the same year that Jacques Lacan presented the first version of his "Mirror Stage" essay in Marienbad. Chances are Lacan did not know about Benjamin's work either, though by the time he did publish "The Mirror Stage" he may well have come to know Benjamin's work, for they certainly traveled in similar circles in late-1930s Paris. That both of these texts were originally presented in the same year, and that both have been pivotal for late-twentieth-century aesthetics—particularly for film studies—is somewhat uncanny and a brief comparison not only casts significant light on each but raises the implications on the relation between subjectivity and aesthetics.

In the later published version of "The Mirror Stage," Lacan points to the initial separation of an infant from the world surrounding the infant, leaving a permanent rift residing within the subjectivity of the human. At the age of 6 to 18 months, the infant, "in a flutter of jubilant activity," overcomes "the obstructions of his support and, fixing his attitude in a slightly leaning-forward position, in order to hold it in his gaze, brings back an instantaneous aspect of the image."[34] Lacan's myth of origins suggests that an infant sees the self as whole, or, more accurately, imagines her or his image to be whole and complete. This results in the initial (pre)formation of the identity of the infant, the "transformation that takes place in the subject when he assumes an image."[35] This original "image" of the infant's own body precedes a consciousness of "otherness," and there is in reality no separation yet of the infant from the world around the self—the infant cannot actually stand alone and is still dependent for sustenance on parent or caretaker. Because this initial image yet gives the *appearance* of independence, the infant creates an image of a personal Ideal-I and thus "situates the agency of the ego, before its social determination, in a fictional direction."[36] The infant misrecognizes its own independence—the unified self is an illusion—and will do so for the rest of her or his life. Furthermore, Lacan pins his theory on the idea of a "stage" (French: *stade*) which is read in two ways: first diachronically as a "period of time," but second synchronically, as in or on a theater stage. The human subject is an actor, depicting her or his own fragmented identity on stage through history and is simultaneously gazed upon by an audience whose members provide their own determined recognition of the subject. Identity, for Lacan, is forged from the image the actor-subject displays in the world, met by the gaze of the others.[37]

The connection to Lacan's theory of the mirror stage furthers my argument for a religious aesthetics apart from an individual and singular authentic consciousness and toward to the multiplicity of the masses in the public realm. Later, as filmmaker Maya Deren labored on her unfinished film *Divine Horsemen*, an attempt to translate Haitian vodoun rituals into film, she would come to note a similar element of dispersed subjectivity within ritual:

> [A] ritual is characterized by the de-personalization of the individual. In some cases it is even marked by the use of masks and voluminous garments, so the *person* of the performer is virtually anonymous; and it is marked, also, by the participation of the community, not as a series and an accumulation of personalities, in the romantic sense, but as a homogenous entity in which the inner patterns of relationship between the elements create, together, a larger movement of the body as a whole. The intent of such a depersonalization is not the destruction of the individual; on the contrary, it enlarges him beyond the personal dimension, and frees him from the specializations and confines of "personality."[38]

Subjectivity in and out of ritual, in and out of film, is not dependent on the individual alone, but is only created "on stage" in front of, and together with, a public. The theater and film actor, the ritual participant, and the person on the streets, all enact their identity in public, and in turn others mutually create their identities through the reception of their bodily image. The subject is put in a continual fluctuation between collection and dispersal, mimicking something like Kristeva's psychoanalytic renderings of the *sujet en procès* (in process/ on trial).[39]

Even so, as the film actor's now fragmented self is taken to new levels of estrangement, the film production studios reassemble the pieces, creating a cult of personality and turning the actor into a commodity. With the capitalistic control of the actor's alienation, there can be no social change, no revolutionary movement in film: "[T]here can be no political advantage derived from this control until film has liberated itself from the fetters of capitalist exploitation" (*SW III*, 113). Benjamin even goes further to footnote that the external appearance of the actor is not unlike that of the politician. Thus, "the crisis of democracies can be understood as a crisis in the conditions governing the public presentation of politicians" (128, n. 23). Just when Benjamin seems to be going too far with his idealism, particularly in relation to the function of the masses, one realizes how shrewdly he perceived the ways in which changes in media affect not just art, but politics. He would no doubt have been alarmed by the political situation in the contemporary United States, where cultic media icons are increasingly elected to prominent political positions, just as he was concerned with the propaganda machine of National Socialism in his day in Germany. One can imagine Arnold Schwarzenegger, Joseph Goebbels, and Ronald Reagan between the lines when he states: "Radio and film are changing not only the function of the professional actor but, equally, the function of those who, like the politician, present themselves before these media. . . . This results in a new form of selection—selection before an apparatus—from which the champion, the star, and the dictator emerge as victors" (ibid.). The image of the Hollywood film star promotes a universalized concept of humanity, and ultimately a monomythic one, which sets up simplistic dichotomies between insiders and outsiders, good and evil, the civilized and the barbarians.[40]

Benjamin nonetheless continues to insist on the work of the masses, and on their abilities as "quasi-experts" (SW III,114) to champion the democratic potential latent in the medium of film. Film, like the print media in the late nineteenth century, becomes a radically democratic tool. Just as the rise of "letters to the editor" sections in newspapers made it possible that "[a]t any moment the reader is ready to become a writer," so the film makes it possible that "[a]ny person today can lay claim to being filmed." "Thus, the distinction between author and public is about to lose its axiomatic character" (ibid.). In response to studio creations of an actor's cult of personality, Benjamin sees the power of films in which the actors playing roles are not "actors in our sense but people who portray *themselves*" (ibid.). If anyone can be an actor, the medium of film alters the circumstances of everyday life and wrests the power of subjective portrayal from the studio heads, offering the masses the chance to represent themselves. Clearly in mind here is the work of Russian filmmakers Sergei Eisenstein, V. I. Pudovkin, and Vertov. Particularly pertinent would be Vertov's project of *kino pravda*, translated into *cinema verité*, and taken for the name that stands at the heart of the documentary tradition. It is as if Benjamin saw Eisenstein's *Battleship Potemkin* (1925) and *October* (1927), and believed that the masses, if only they saw these films, would rise up like the masses depicted in those films and take film away from the capitalistic interests of the film industry.

Disseminating Contemplation

So far, I have attempted to show how the singular artwork is transformed into the *work* of art through its technological reproducibility and ability to meet the masses in a variety of spaces and times. Similarly, the individual subjectivity of the actor is dispersed through the apparatus of cinema and through the potential for the masses to lay claims to being filmed. Now we must account for the dissolution of subjectivity on the part of the viewers as well. In the end, no singularities remain, nor does any recourse to basing aesthetics in transhistorical subjective judgment, engaged with an autonomous object.

Benjamin provides a straightforward, though radical thesis: "The technological reproducibility of the artwork changes the relation of the masses to art" (*SW III*, 116). Unlike painting, which is not intended to be viewed simultaneously by a collective—even the museum consistently frames, hangs, and lights paintings for single point perspectives—film is viewed by the masses, and for this reason it is the medium favored by Benjamin. When coupled with another of his ideas, namely, "The painter's is a total image, whereas that of the cinematographer is piecemeal, its manifold parts being assembled according to a new law" (ibid.), we see how in both production and reception, film pluralizes the possibilities of meaning, value, and political power within society. As long as the ideological power of the work of art remains scattered across producers and receivers, the masses may resist the encroachments of totalitarian control.

Before continuing in this discussion, I want to take a step back and bring to the foreground the distinctiveness of Benjamin's approach to the arts for a religious aesthetics. Many publications and exhibitions attempting to connect (or, perhaps, reconnect) religion and the arts in the modern age focus on the "spiritual," contemplative works of Mark Rothko, Wassily Kandinsky, Barnett Newman, Piet Mondrian, and a few other abstract painters.[41] Benjamin's examination of the modern age brings out a strikingly different way of relating religion and the arts. By denying that which is thought to be most vital to a religious aesthetics—that is, contemplation that becomes submerged in a "wooded interior" as with the romantic symbol—Benjamin resituates the interdisciplinary focus from the interior to the exterior, from a religious experience based on one's personal, subjective feelings, to a social interaction in the material world.

Stemming from the radicality of the Dadaists, the destruction of contemplation is important for social change. Contemplation is associated with the inner life of the individual, and Benjamin sought "to put an end to the myth of interiority."[42] The contemplation invited by painting, as a medium in general, lends itself to subjective, individual abandonment in which individual viewers are isolated from others, from society, and from their own aesthetic bodies—just as the art object is surrounded by an aura, so is each individual viewer cordoned off from the rest of the world in rapt contemplation. The uniqueness of the artwork is matched by the unique experience of the individual viewing the artwork: the artwork becomes a symbol, met by a transhistorical subject, both submerged in what Benjamin would metaphorize as a "wooded interior." This contemplative approach has long been valued by the bourgeoisie and finds its heritage in religious contemplation where one is left alone with one's god. The emphasis on the individual subject in a moment of repose, of collection, is rejected by Benjamin in favor of the material, social conditions and connections of art.

Benjamin believes that what the Dadaists attempted—destruction of contemplation—film achieves. For while Dadists "turned artwork into a missile," it is yet film that metonymically puts the art in motion by constantly changing the scenery: "The painting invites the viewer to contemplation; before it, he can give himself up to his train of associations. Before a film image, he cannot do so. No sooner has he seen it than it has already changed. It cannot be fixed on. The train of associations in the person contemplating it is immediately interrupted by new images. This constitutes the shock effect of film, which, like all shocks, seeks to induce heightened attention" (*SW III*, 132 n.33). In metonymical fashion, film shocks and interrupts the previously contemplative single viewer and puts her or him in a receptive space with other viewers.

Film also offers the ability for many people to see the same image simultaneously. This situation affects each individual's response, and in fact, what could be called an individual response no longer exists. Rather, in the cinema, the reaction of the individual and the collective "regulate one another" (*SW III*, 116). While the individual nature of observing a stable art such as painting may lead to a "reactionary" stance (single viewer observes total image), the simultaneity involved in observing film can lead to what Benjamin labels a "progressive" response: "The progressive attitude is characterized by an immediate, intimate fusion of pleasure—pleasure in seeing and experiencing—with an attitude of expert appraisal" (ibid.). Pure entertainment through conventional means is emotionally enjoyable for people, while any jarring and unexpected artistic work causes a decrease in enjoyment by heightening the criticality of the viewer.

Duchamp's *Fountain* was all about a critical distance, and the jury found no pleasure in it. But with film Benjamin believes there is a dialectic of the conventional and the new, allowing the masses to come to an enjoyment of film, even as they also become film's actors *and* critics. Mass reception is dynamic, and can be both enjoyable and critical at the same time. Rather than allowing the artificiality of the artwork to pass for reality—for *aesthetica artificialis* to pass as *aesthetica naturalis*—Benjamin contends: "The most important social function of film is to establish equilibrium between human beings and the apparatus" (*SW III*, 117). Art, its enjoyment, and its temptation toward disembodied contemplation, is a vital component in human life, but its allure can lead to an anaesthetized existence in which ideological apparatuses do the work for the collective social body. However, the hope is (and it really is more a hope on Benjamin's part, than a descriptive fact) that a critical dimension might be maintained through the medium of film so that ideology and the ideologies of myth, while inescapable, might at least be recognized.

To bring to light the social potential of the mass reception of film, he turns to an analogy with Freudian theory, and notes how the publication of *The Psychopathology of Everyday Life* changed the public's perception of everyday life. Suddenly, slips of the tongue demonstrated the existence of another reality, distinct from the reality people thought they were perceiving, and making them conscious of their own unconscious perception. Likewise, "a similar deepening of apperception throughout the entire spectrum of optical—and now also auditory—impressions has been accomplished by film" (*SW IV*, 265).[43] With film, people perceive behavior and existence in a way they never have before; they become conscious of their own perception and are able to see a different world lying below the surface of the world of appearances. Which is not to say the underlying world is truer than the surface. For by allowing a vision of everyday life in an innovative, challenging way, film changes the perceptions of the familiar. What were once overlooked structures—"our bars and city streets, our offices and furnished rooms, our railroad stations and our factories" (*SW III*, 117)—are brought into a new focus, from a new angle. "With the close-up, space expands; with slow motion, movement is extended. And just as enlargement not merely clarifies what we see indistinctly 'in any case,' but brings to light entirely new structures of matter" (ibid.). The world is understood anew.

And so, the consequences of film as a technologically reproduced medium of art are not trivial. Technological reproduction alters the structures of society (the masses have more control over cultural representation), and renders reality relative to perception. The world we believed to exist does not look like we thought it did:

> Clearly it is another nature which speaks to the camera as compared to the eye. "Other" above all in the sense that a space informed by human consciousness gives way to a space informed by the unconscious. . . . This is where the camera comes into play, with all its resources for swooping and rising, disrupting and isolating, stretching and compressing a sequence, enlarging or reducing an object. It is through the camera that we first discover the optical unconscious, just as we discover the instinctual unconscious through psychoanalysis. (*SW III*, 117)

As an allegorical critic, Benjamin seeks out the "other nature" that may be brought into the here and now to disrupt the perceived coherent view of the world, a coherence that is an instrument of political powers. Altering reality itself, the camera intervenes into the seemingly smooth structure of space and time—analogized to a surgeon cutting into the human body. Painting merely represents the surface of things, and thus cannot provoke viewers to rethink reality, but the camera "penetrates deeply into its tissue" (*SW III*, 116). Within the ability of technological reproduction to "keep pace with speech," and thus, with the ability for reproduction to usurp production, new images of reality are created. As Joel Snyder comments, "[t]he resulting work does not reproduce the world so much as it makes a world."[44] Here, we move most forcefully to the disruptive potential for the new arts, the radical revolutionary potential: the recreation of the world.

None of this is far from religious ritual. As film theorists David Bordwell and Kristin Thompson note regarding the work of cinema: "Whatever its shape, the [camera] frame makes the image finite. The film image is bounded, limited. From an implicitly continuous world, the frame selects a slice to show us. . . . Characters enter the image *from* somewhere and go off *to* another area —offscreen space."[45] With this language we are only a step away from that of ritual, as Mary Douglas succinctly suggests, "A ritual provides a frame. The marked off time or place alerts a special kind of expectancy, just as the oftrepeated 'Once upon a time' creates a mood receptive to fantastic tales."[46] The world, through film and ritual, is selected and therefore created, but only as it is recreated. Seen in this way, we might understand Benjamin's emphasis on the *work* of art to pick up on dimensions of ritual activity, even after he has affirmingly noted the severing of art from ritual. However, this is no retro-activity on Benjamin's part, for in his modern cinematic ritual any singular object loses its magic power, its aura. And in the "desire of the present-day masses to get closer to things," the uniqueness of the object is disseminated until all is profane. Again, the parallels Benjamin strikes between traditional religious structures and the work of art are enlightening, but diverge at certain key points.

So in the cinematic ritual, rather than contemplation of a singular, auratic object, the film brings with it, in an often misunderstood phrase, a *reception in distraction*: "Distraction [*Zerstreuung*] and concentration [*Sammlung*] form an antithesis" (*SW III,* 119). The commonplace view, and especially that seen in religious traditions, takes this opposition and prioritizes concentration (the word used here is *Sammlung,* the same word used earlier and translated as "contemplation" and "collection") over distraction. But Benjamin is not dissuaded by conventional thought, and he turns to upset the opposition between contemplation and distraction. The difference between contemplation and distraction is that primarily within a mode of contemplation the viewer/reader/observer is "absorbed" by the work of art—just as for Otto, the Holy is alluring and intoxicating—whereas in a distracted mode the observers absorb the work of art into themselves. This is the desire of the masses, to take hold of the thing itself and see its "sameness." In this absorptive reception the work *qua* object is multiplied and dispersed. Relatedly, Benjamin uses the singular "person who concentrates" as opposed to the "distracted masses" (ibid.). The masses, to repeat, are not inert and passive, but active "movements," and their distraction is an active state of affairs.[47]

Almost at the end of "The Work of Art," a significant difference emerges among the various versions of the essay. In the widely distributed English version of the essay, as translated by Harry Zohn, the final line before the epilogue reads: "The public is an examiner, but an absent-minded one."[48] The same line is repeated in the "third version" of the essay on which Benjamin worked until 1939 and considered unfinished. The second version, from which I have been quoting, provides a different ending. I will deal with the other ending soon, but let me briefly unpack this better known statement.

This strange last phrase about absent-mindedness is certainly not an attractive notion to many English-using readers of this essay in an era with soaring ADD rates, and it is difficult to understand the sense of revolutionary potential involved here. Much of the problem is the straightforward translation given by Zohn. The German *ein Zerstreuter*, is the term translated as "an absent-minded one" (or, in the recently published third version as "a distracted one"). As already mentioned in this and the previous chapters, the term *zerstreuung* (or variants) shows up consistently in Benjamin's work and is translated variously as "distraction," "dispersion," and here, "absent-minded." Yet, Benjamin's use of the German word is more active than the passive translation of "absent-minded" might suggest, particularly in light of the other ways Zerstreuter is used throughout the essay. The root of the word, *Streuen,* is a cognate to the English "strewn" and carries connotations such as: "disperse," "dissipate," "spread," "scatter," "disseminate," "banish," "distract," and "amuse." Thus, this final sentence could be translated, "The public is an examiner, however a disseminating one." Howard Eiland describes the active nature involved here in his discussion of the seemingly paradoxical phrase "reception in distraction" by relating it to jazz improvisation:

> The improvising jazz musician himself listens to the improvisations of others in the group—both *as* a group and as other individuals—and responds to the surprises. The musician must have at his disposal a set of (variable) moves, to paraphrase Benjamin, in order to perform his task, which involves equal measures of spontaneity and knowledge, or receptivity and productivity. The deflection of attention here is manifold and concentrated, for the player is both carried away and in control.[49]

The masses and their movements are able to receive the work of art, becoming, in turn, producers who continually disperse any singular symbolic meanings, any static way of playing a note. In other words, the masses are improvisers, allegorists.[50]

This "reception in distraction," or this "disseminating reception," is so important to Benjamin once again because of its relation to fascism, and it is on this note that he ends the essay. Fascism "sees its salvation in granting expression to the masses—but on no account granting them rights" (*SW III*, 121). Benjamin realizes that to resist these fascistic impulses means to never allow the masses to be represented, never be made the object of a picture, never be stabilized into the specific time and place that is endemic to the aura. In the contemporary age of "reality television," we find a parallel example whereby "[a]ny person today can lay claim to being filmed" (114); yet, it is the studio editors and producers who control the final image on screen. And by labeling it "reality," they have hidden the apparatus. Audio visual technologies today control much of our mythological constructions about our society and ourselves. Fascism, as well as capitalist-controlled media, offers up an image of identity for people, but only as an appearance. There are no rights granted, no alterations of society. Metaphorically the world looks different, but the change is not systemic. Capitalist controlled media gains power by building up an aura around people, making them *appear* to have power, choice, social sway, but this does not connect to the material conditions underlying the surfaces. Thus again, the need to strip the veil of aura is not merely motivated by art theory, but has direct consequences in political life.

In Benjamin's conception of the work of art in the age of its technological reproducibility, the mass movement scatters/is scattered, leaving no space or time in which subject and object might be collected, for as soon as subject and object are seen as whole and complete, ideological powers have the potential to recreate social life and identity in whatever way the wish. The Judaica collection of the Prague museum may be used in the service of National Socialism, just as the perceived body image of the individual is created and packaged by media conglomerates selling fast cars and skinny people. Any hint of stabilization that might lend itself to a sense of identity (for either subject or object) must be rejected. Thus, mass reproduction is the corollary to mass reception. Just as the stability of the singular art object is broken down in its mass reproduction—it is no longer "authentic," or "original," and is not connected to any sense of a cult value—so the stability of the singular receiver is broken down: No stable subject exists to contemplate the art object.

Technological reproduction reanimates our relation to the world. It stretches time and condenses spaces, chops up the afilmic world, and offers reformed fragments. Benjamin's utopian hope—ultimately, and unfortunately somewhat of a failed hope since commercial cinema has succeeded to the point of remythologizing the world in its own image—was in the ability of reproducible technologies to fragment the perceived whole of the world, and to show the world is actually an imposed whole. But we can always see otherwise, we can always allegorize the world, finding meaning in another arrangement of space and time. Thus we are brought back to the aesthetic, that site where perception is a process of collecting and bringing together, but also of dispersal.

Aesthetics

Another ending to the essay takes us in other directions. In the second version, instead of the language of an "absent-minded/disseminating" public, the penultimate section ends thus:

> Reception in distraction [*Zerstreuung*]—the sort of reception which is increasingly noticeable in all areas of art and is a symptom of profound changes in apperception—finds in the film its true training ground. Film, by virtue of its shock effects, is predisposed to this form of reception. *In this respect, too, it proves to be the most important subject matter, at present, for the theory of perception which the Greeks called aesthetics.* (*SW III*, 120; emphasis added)

Benjamin shifts a philosophical analysis of the arts into an aesthetics of materiality, of sense perception; and film is the training ground for modern aesthetics. Significantly, Benjamin evokes the Greek use of aesthetics (i.e., related to sense perception) rather than writing about it in the Germanic Idealist vein. And in so doing, he is not far from the early Marx, who sets the senses within social life, noting their historical constructions and deconstructions. Social power is regulated in and through manipulating the material structures of life, and at the level of the senses we find an important basis for understanding ideology, cultural life, and religious constructions. Further, if sense perception is relativized by historical developments, aesthetics too is relativized and cannot found itself on seeming universal structures such as mystery, creativity, or genius, not to mention truth and beauty. Benjamin's aesthetics are constantly pushing at their own borders, querying their connections to other social, philosophical, and technical structures.

The revolution inaugurated by technological reproduction was not merely to take place in the outer world, for there is also a revolution to occur within the conscious and unconscious workings of everyday life. Benjamin, intrigued by surrealist art, even as he saw its limitations, was also interested in psychoanalysis and the possibilities it provided for its rethinking of human behavior. Briefly noting the relation between the conscious and the unconscious in the Freudian schema, we find in *The Ego and the Id* (published in 1923) the aesthetically pertinent idea that "consciousness is the *surface* of the mental apparatus" and that "[a]ll perceptions which are received from without (sense-perceptions) and from within—what we call sensations and feelings—are conscious from the start."[51] According to Freud, perception is located at the conscious level, and with consciousness we are brought to similar limits as those that aesthetics itself interrogates: the passage between inside and outside. From this liminal point, bodily sense organs also become some of the most vital structures in the constitution of personal identity, the "*I*," the ego: "The ego is first and foremost a bodily ego; it is not merely a surface entity, but is itself the projection of a surface."[52] A footnote to this statement—provided by the English translator, James Strachey and approved by Freud—brings the ego even closer to our interest in aesthetics: "the ego is ultimately derived from bodily sensation, chiefly from those springing from the surface of the body. It may thus be regarded as a mental projection of the surface of the body."[53] As with Lacan's "mirror stage," Freudian accounts of the ego suggest how sense perceptions serve as foundational to identity itself. Indeed, identity is formed at the nexus of inside and outside, of the ego's projection of the body's surface, met by the aesthetic perceptions of others. But individual identities, like mythologies, are illusions and the whole *imago* of the self is a narcissistic fantasy that, for Lacan, is always threatened by nightmares of a fragmented body (*corps morcelé*). The true subject is a composite, with many layers of projected images. And so there is an implicit concern on Benjamin's part not only to deconstruct the world of external political apparatuses, but also to explode the myth of the complete individual. Narcissism and fascism have intricate relations, both relying on the power of the aura.

Yet what happens when, in the modern world, we are constantly exposed to shock? Why would anyone want to be shocked in the cinema when there is plenty of shock in the "real world"? Susan Buck-Morss highlights some of the relations between Freud and Benjamin's essay, particularly emphasizing the work of the conscious to buffer shock. Psychological buffering is a healthy thing for persons exposed to the catastrophes of war or sexual abuse, but shock, according to Benjamin, has become the norm in modern life. And in the everydayness of shock, people cannot experience the world, or their own memories —memory is replaced by conditioned response. The system of industrial factory work and modernity in general is designed to "numb the organism, to deaden the senses, to repress memory."[54] Modern life has *an*aesthetized people. In response, Benjamin's aesthetic work, as paraphrased by Buck-Morss, is "to *undo* the alienation of the corporeal sensorium, to *restore the instinctual power of the human bodily senses for the sake of humanity's self-preservation*, and to do this, not by avoiding the new technologies, but by *passing through* them."[55] In this "passing through," we come around again to the aesthetic experience in relation to the work of the camera. Conscious perception has been overworked, thus technological reproduction is revolutionary in its ability to stand in for the conscious; it does the work of the conscious to bring about a deeper "penetration" into the unconscious. As Freud's "dream work" sought to make the latent content of the dream manifest, Benjamin's work of art seeks to make the unconscious conscious, destroying the anaesthetizing aura built up around individuals in modern life.[56]

At this point, the aesthetic importance of sense perception, must be amended. To a very real degree, if we merely relied on what was given to us through our bodies as they are, we could not understand many of the functions of the universe, or of our own bodies at their cellular level, much less the workings of atoms, quarks, and neutrons. We humans can neither sensually perceive the image of atomic particles, nor hear frequencies above 23,000 hz, nor detect the planet Pluto with our own eyes. What Benjamin's essay brings to light is the way in which our aesthetic construction of the world is transformed through new technological tools. Optical inventions such as the camera, the telescope, and the microscope, or audio inventions like the radio and radio telescope, operate as "prostheses" to our senses, enabling us to see farther, and see closer. Thus, the site of the body as that which is enveloped by our skin must be expanded—theories of aesthetics as "embodiment" bring us only so far—so that we do not forsake the critical locus of the skin itself, and especially the sense perception of the skin, and the other sense organs at the surface of the body. How we construct our worlds may indeed have much to do with how we sensually perceive the world, but those "natural" senses are themselves reliant on the "artificial" creations of art and technology. There is no *aesthetica naturalis*, in the sense that there is no natural basis for sense perception. Just as history becomes spatialized in nature, so is nature bound to the contingencies of technologized history. Technology remakes the world.

The Religious Desires of Aura

Benjamin fairly consistently puts religious ideas—particularly Kabbalistic ones—in the service of politics. By way of concluding this chapter, I want to temporarily reverse this flow to shed light on Benjamin through movements in religious history. When he considers "the desire of the present-day masses to 'get closer' to things," we might usefully and briefly review a few points in the history of religions to rethink both the aura through religion and religious movements through the destruction of aura, noting the role of new technological media in these movements. In other words, while the "Work of Art" essay often tends toward the suggestion that the destruction of the aura is a secularizing movement—as do many of Benjamin's interpreters—I reexamine this assumption and hypothesize that this desire of the masses is in itself a religious movement that has already been enacted throughout religious histories, specifically at points of religious *reformation*. What we are here dealing with is again the emphasis on deconsecration, which in other terms might be a way of rewriting the "secularization thesis": The masses aren't becoming secularized; they are instead reformers who must deconsecrate that which has been built up with too much aura and made inaccessible. Sacredness is the result of a process of consecration, yet paradoxically, to access the sacred, a certain level of deconsecration must take place. And in the history of religions, one of the places deconsecration seems to occur is alongside new technological developments of media.

The desire for closeness or proximity might be seen in two totally unrelated religious movements. The *bhakti* "movement" in South Asia and the Protestant Reformation in Europe are both, more or less, democratic movements made possible through the development and use of new media, and thus resulting in a reorientation of the masses to the sacred. The orientalizing mode of relating these movements—that *bhakti* came about only because of its contact with Christianity—has been well discredited, but I wish to parallel them here briefly without the equally orientalizing search for origins.[57] I am also ignoring the theological dimensions (i.e., *bhakti*'s monotheistic dimensions) and focusing on religious practices and media uses. By seeing the two movements as disconnected fragments of past histories, I wish to expand on Benjamin's ideas about sacred distance and proximity. Each of these religious movements marked a time of upheaval and renewal, and the repercussions of both are still being felt into the twenty-first century.

The *bhakti* (devotional) movement has hazy origins, but most historians date its beginnings to the sixth century of the Common Era in what is today southern India. And although the current denomination of *bhakti* as a "movement"—as in a formalized system with leaders and clearly defined manifestos and dogmas—is not quite accurate, the broader picture from the privileged place of the present does allow a few interesting observations. First of all, like most religious reform movements and paralleling Benjamin's aesthetic interests, the *bhakti* movement was, and is, democratic, seeking to flatten hierarchical structures. Simply put, it allowed more people to have access to the sacred. This is achieved most especially by the elimination, or at least the diminution, of the intermediaries of religion: priests, texts in ancient dead languages, and set-aside sacred times and spaces. Noting the absolute sense of the sacred of the earlier Vedic system in India, Philip Lutgendorf notes:

> Although belief in the power of the oral sacred word dates back to the earliest period of Indo-Aryan culture, the notion of the social role of sacred text has changed considerably during the past two millennia. The preservation of the Vedic corpus was insured by an elaborate system of education within Brahman lineages, by the notion of the text as an efficacious mantra that could never be altered, and by the evolution of the spoken language, which fossilized and fixed the Vedic forms. The result was the extraordinary oral preservation of much of Vedic literature. But preservation and transmission need not imply propagation

and dissemination. Oral performances of Vedic texts were not, apparently, fully public occasions; large segments of the population—notably, all women and Shudras—were forbidden ever to hear the sacred words. Indeed, the insistence on oral transmission in the Vedic educational system (which continued even into the period when writing had become commonplace and other religious texts were being written down) presupposed the view that texts such as the *Rig veda* were not merely too sacred to be written down but also too powerful to be made generally available. Access to the texts had to be restricted not only to specific persons but also to persons in specific conditions—to twice-born males who had entered a ritually pure state. Thus, even though Vedic literature was an "oral tradition," it was not, within historical times, a "popular" one.[58]

Noticeable here is the way a certain aura is built up around Vedic literature through a class (caste) system, marking distance from the sacred text for some, and proximity for others. In this way, society remains hierarchically structured, and the dominant class retains power by controlling means of access to the sacred.

In response, the idea of *bhakti* as a means to liberation (*moksha*), arises initially in the *Bhagavad Gita*, a thousand years after the *Rig-Veda*. As Karen Pechilis Prentiss considers in ways that correlate with Benjamin's destruction of tradition and aura, "Unlike classical law books, which sought to legislate correct human action, and unlike formalized prayers and ritual manuals, which located worship in a specific time and place, *bhakti* is represented in the *Gita* as a religious perspective that can inform all actions, at any time and in any place."[59] The desire of those adherents to *bhakti* was to engage the sacred on their own terms, to "bring things closer." This was achieved through an emphasis on personal devotional actions—"at any time and in any place"—rather than the performance of ritual, guarded over by priests, in the space of the temple, and with a singular sacred text. *Bhakti*, we might consider in Benjaminian language, allows the sacred to "meet the recipient in his or her own situation."

In a manner akin to the traveling baroque lament-plays, the medieval *bhakti* movement produced a number of poet-saints who traveled from village to village, reciting poems/hymns in vernacular languages, which were in themselves renditions of sacred texts such as the *Mahabharata*, the *Ramayana*, or the *Vedas*. By embodying and translating the texts, these poets enacted a transference of religious media, from book to body, and from eye to ear. Here the aura of original sacred texts is disseminated in order to meet people in their own place and time—which is not to say the originals were disregarded. Further, the devotional poetry was full of images of human love, and as Nancy M. Martin considers, "This love is mediated through the body, experienced through the senses, with devotees employing metaphors of sight, sound, taste, smell, and touch."[60] *Bhakti* practitioners, across social locations, were thus able to translate between the universal and the local, between the spiritual and the corporeal.

The emphasis on devotional democratization in the Hindu context has continued through to the twentieth and twenty-first centuries, where it has met up with the technologies of mass reproduction. Whereas the medieval period produced wandering poet-saints who brought the sacred closer to the masses, the modern age has extended this, making it possible for people to set up shrines in their own homes, to perform *puja* to the devas and devis manifested in mass-reproduced icons, posters, calendars, comic books, and television. The phenomena surrounding many of these contemporary permutations are taken up in a critical collection of essays entitled *Media and the Transformation of Religion in South Asia*. Introducing the volume, Lawrence Babb mimics Benjamin's ideas and suggests, "When symbols pass through such 'sticky' media as writing, they tend to eddy backward into relatively stable social memory. Thus the content of tradition can accumulate and grow. But nothing is truly fixed; time inevitably deposits new layers over previously stored materials, and each generation finds its own ways of construing the deposits of the past." In contradistinction, new media affect the "mobility" of symbols through tradition, and "the increased social mobility of religious symbols has had a socially 'disembedding' effect on religious traditions."[61] What Babb speaks of as "mobile symbols" triggers Benjamin's notions of allegory as "distorting symbols," and as I suggested in the previous chapter, allegory puts the symbol in motion. In the allegory, as in technological reproduction, tradition is fragmented, objects are disembedded from their shells, from the presumed continuity of history's accumulations, thus freeing them to be made effective in the here and now.

Relatedly, the Protestant Christian Reformation is founded on the printing press, as developed by Johannes Gutenberg in the fifteenth century in Germany (though much earlier in East Asia),[62] and furthered through Martin Luther's translation of the scriptures into the vernacular (i.e., German), thus clearly enabling the "reproduction [of the Bible] to meet the recipient in his or her own situation." The mythical foundation of Protestantism finds its origins, its original act, with Luther's tacking of the Ninety-five Theses onto a door at his monastery in Wittenberg in October 1517. His theses were a protest, and thus as verbal, auratic history tells us, they enacted a reformation across European Christendom. Yet, as historian Elizabeth Eisenstein points out, church doors were common places for disputes to be made public; Luther did nothing original and even expressed surprise himself at the controversy that followed. Indeed, controversy followed his theses not so much because of the content of the message (though that was necessary) but because of the medium —for the "theses" were very quickly taken up by print shops, translated, and disseminated to the masses. In December 1517, Eisenstein notes, "three separate editions [of the Ninety-five Theses] were printed almost simultaneously by printers located in three separate towns." Further, "As Maurice Gravier pointed out, it was largely because traditional forms of theological disputation had been transformed by entirely new publicity techniques that the act of the German monk had such a far-reaching effect."[63]

Although the Roman Catholic Church, to which Luther had taken vows as a monk, conducted services in Latin (a dead language) and understood the means of access to the Word of God (i.e., Jesus Christ) to be through the church, Luther ultimately preached the "priesthood of all believers" and became known for the democratic visions he instilled in Christianity. Among other theological ideas, he emphasized the importance of scripture as a more direct access to the Word of God. However, before one can accept his theology, one must understand the material grounding on which his intellectual theories are built. Crucial to note is how foolhardy it would be to promote a sacred text as democratic if it remains bound to a language that the masses neither speak, understand, nor read. It would be equally imprudent to stress a text's centrality if the people do not have access to these texts—before their mass reproduction through the printing press, Bibles were scarcely to be found. Luther understood the power of the medium and began to use it to his advantage. The result was a mass movement that craved proximity to the sacred.

By disseminating the once-auratic Christian and Vedic traditions, the masses were able to bring things closer, thus displaying their desire to detach sacred objects from their traditions and make them accessible in the here and now. These two examples, plucked from religious history, are undoubtedly too brief to provide full evidence, but it should not be too controversial to suggest how the impulse to reform is part and parcel of religious traditions themselves: Reform is indigenous in religion, and reform is reliant on changes in material culture. Religions do not survive through their conservation (their conservatism), but through their adaptability, and it is translations in media that bring this about, allowing more people access to the sacred. Yet, there may be limits to this.

The Limits of Benjamin's Art

Benjamin seemed to believe that if the auratic play of presence and absence was in the hands of the disseminating masses, then a certain heterogeneity might be maintained. Fascistic (and most other) power structures in societies operate through controlling a hierarchy of auratic value of objects. The masses respond with their "sense for sameness in the world." As I have tried to indicate, this tension is as political as it is religious.

At the same time, we must halt the dialectic, questioning Benjamin's insistence on the "fascinating" side of the sacred (the desire for proximity and sameness) over and against the "mysterious" side (the wholly Other, distant). We can find many examples of the impulse to reform, to bring things closer, to make the world of things more democratic, but does the other side simply disappear with no more mystery, no more objects "set apart"? Do the revelatory activities of technological reproduction simply let all the secrets loose? Is it possible then to retain some sense of limits, however shifting they are? Does not the aesthetic, as well as religion, need limits?

Benjamin's theory of art in the "Work of Art" essay is highly idealistic, its political potential greatly overrated. I am not the first to argue how utopian the essay is, how extreme some of Benjamin's positions become at this point in history, this era during which he lives as an exile in Paris while the Nazis triumph over Europe. Although his contemporaries criticized Benjamin for his utopian visions on the eve of the Holocaust, we can hardly do so today. Adorno said of the essay in a letter to Benjamin, "You under-estimate the technicality of autonomous art and over-estimate that of dependent art."[64] And Miriam Hansen's critical commentary on Benjamin's essay shows how Benjamin's stance toward the decline of the aura was somewhat more ambivalent during the 1930s than the "Work of Art" essay would have us believe, and indeed the aura "plays a precarious yet indispensable part."[65] (Immediately following his completion of the first version of the essay, Benjamin himself turned to write another essay, "The Storyteller," which strikes an almost opposite pose, showing a somewhat conservative and nostalgic view of the loss of the medium of storytelling.) Nonetheless, the essay remains crucial to an understanding of twentieth-century art and art theory. Perhaps it is the extremities of the thought itself that makes it so impossible to ignore.

In the desire to bring Benjamin's writings closer to the present age, I must also argue that what Benjamin misses in his account of the masses in this particular essay is the way we humans simultaneously and continually crave the auratic and the sacred, as embodied in objects set apart from us and made mysterious. Humans desire the mystery and the distance as much as the reform and proximity. The history of religions shows us how democratic reform movements work to bring things closer. What we can find at the same time, however, are instances in which religions have continually returned to acts of consecration, setting things apart from our ordinary existence if only to raise us, from time to time, beyond ordinary existence. Certainly we want it both ways: to touch it all, and to be restricted from touching. The polished marble sculpture in the museum is made all the more beguiling, seeming to crave a caress, because of the museum guard standing nearby.

Indeed, while technological reproduction has brought things closer on religious and aesthetic bases, the sacred and the auratic continue to reassert themselves. Even in Benjamin's most promising medium, film, we can see the ways in which a sense of the holy has been reenacted in South Asian film theaters, continuing the impulses of *bhakti* in an age of technological reproducibility. Lutgendorf discusses this with regard to the 1975 hit film, *Jai Santoshi Maa*, about the goddess Santoshi Ma. At the screenings, "Audiences were showering coins, flower petals, and rice at the screen in appreciation of the film. They entered the cinema barefoot and set up a small temple outside."[66] Likewise, through the mass reproduction of the Bible, Protestantism provided a "revelation" accessible to the masses. Although Luther was clear that the "Word of God" was Jesus Christ and that the Bible merely served to point toward the incarnation, mass reproduction winds up inverting the hierarchical structure, and in the nineteenth and twentieth centuries we find the emergence of fundamentalist Christianity that essentially deifies the scriptures themselves.[67] So as *bhakti* and Protestantism both show the desire of the masses to brings things closer, they concomitantly show the equal force of the masses working to erect the sacred—oftentimes functioning uncannily like Duchamp by taking the reproduction to hold even more sacred status than the "original." And it is not necessarily the ruling classes who are here instituting the aura/sacred.

By idealizing the work of the masses and championing the decline of the aura, Benjamin temporarily (the "Work of Art" essay is somewhat anomalous) forsakes one pole of the sacred dialectic between mystery and fascination, repulsion and attraction. Anthropologist Michael Taussig has noted what is the more common two part dialectical movement in Benjamin's writings, and in the structures of religion itself, suggesting that it is *transgression*, and its related dimensions of negativity and taboo, that remain so crucial to the aesthetic practices of religion. Among other activities, religions set limits in place, demarcating space and time, and separating the pure from the impure. In doing so, they maintain power by regulating things, spaces, and times. Yet built into this very structure are the possibilities of crossing the limits, of negation: "The salient property of danger present in this fascinating complex of negation, with its mutually nourishing oppositions, is its considerable if undefinable power to attract and repulse."[68] Religious people are tempted toward transgression, and often ritually enact the negation of the taboo, because of the power registered there. Clearly, limits must be in place for such activity. Taussig, in another study, further suggests how "defacement," rather than destroying something sacred, actually brings its power to light: "It brings insides outside, unearthing knowledge, and revealing mystery. As it does this, however, as it spoliates and tears at tegument, *it may also animate the thing defaced and the mystery revealed may become more mysterious*, indicating the curious magic upon which Enlightenment, in its elimination of magic, depends."[69] Taussig ably translates between Benjamin and the study of the sacred, showing how the stripping of the aura/sacred reveals the sacred in a new form and, crucially, makes it public. Rather than creating a sameness of things, the transgressive act shows a further, more mysterious power.

As the next chapter will further indicate, Benjamin usually emphasizes the threshold between things, between spaces, and between times. His focus is on the active nature of bringing things closer. When things actually are closer, the whole activity ceases to be interesting and enjoyable. It is in the process of destruction that the energies are found. In between, at the threshold of attraction and repulsion, fascination and mysteriousness, perhaps is the real focus of the sacred, or at least the source of its power, and this is where Benjamin typically understands it as well. Without the taboo there can be no transgression, and if all things are seen for their sameness, then nothing stands out, and religion dies. Not that Benjamin is necessarily concerned to salvage religion per se; but he does understand the radical potential of artistic creation as a catalyst for social and political change. The possibilities for change are located in the movement between the sacred and profane, that is, in the activities of consecration and deconsecration. Power and meaning are not found in the thing itself, but at its margins, in the passages between art and reality, object and subject, and among the physical accretions that build up on the object's skin (from kumkum powder on icons of Shiva to leather bindings on Bibles) and the metaphysical accretions built up through history, if only to be stripped away once again. In like manner, the freeing of the object from this meta/physical shell is both deconsecrating of the object and a sacred activity in itself. The threshold is the nonstable location from which energy is derived. Potential power is not found in some stasis on one side or the other.

4
Aesthetics (II):
Building the Communal Sense

As the events unfurled on September 11, 2001, I found myself unfolding an old article I had tucked away in my files. Gently prying open the pages of the now-brittle newspaper so as not to disturb the printed words, I read again the prophetic phrases of *New York Times* architecture critic Herbert Muschamp. Just after the bombing of the Twin Towers of the World Trade Center in 1993, he had stated:

> Exploding buildings are [the contemporary global] community's landmarks—its inverted arches of triumph, its sinister Taj Mahals. They provide images of a collective experience that is otherwise elusive. Traditionally, we look to buildings to provide symbols of social cohesion. Exploding buildings now perform an equivalent symbolic role.[1]

Muschamp's words construct an intriguing and powerful statement, one that has much in common with the equally powerful theory of scapegoating, particularly as articulated by René Girard.[2] That is, in speaking of "inverted arches of triumph" Muschamp turns the exploding building into a scapegoat. In a scapegoat economy, the negativity of the sacrifice occurs and reaches completion, and the community is then established or reestablished in its place. On Girard's view, such sacrifice is a foundational event for human society, and for religion. True to their Hegelian roots, theories of the scapegoat revolve around the negative being "taken up" into a new positivity. The (positive) community must believe itself to exist apart from the (negative) sacrifice and can be founded only upon the dissolution of the sacrificial conflict. The community comes together only to view the rubble; the victims and the victimizers are always elsewhere. To put it in other words, the community constitutes itself by displacing something to the "outside" (negative) whereby it can legitimize itself as "inside" (positive). Destruction and creation form polar opposites that constitute each other, yet they remain opposed.

Although there is much here that is suggestive and many more directions to go with Muschamp's and Girard's ideas and those of scapegoating, I rather wish to skew the perspective slightly and highlight a different relation between architecture and community, one that leads into Benjamin's writings on the subject. This final concluding chapter will take several of Benjamin's ideas from the previous chapters, bringing them to bear on the *aesthetic community*, and to tenuously rethink the *sensus communis*. The stars of this communal constellation will include memory, architecture and urban space, and the prominent place of the passage, that between space which is ultimately neither here nor there but remains a site for transformation and the ground of community. This is, however, a community, as Maurice Blanchot would have it, that is "unavowable," or as Jean-Luc Nancy would have that is "inoperative."[3] Such a community, I will state up front, retains the status of a collection (*Sammlung*), but always only in juxtaposition with its dispersal (*Zerstreuung*).

In contradistinction to the origin-positing activity of the scapegoat sacrifice, I want to suggest, particularly following Benjamin's ideas on both architectural ruins and passages, that a more fecund space of community may be that created through the ruins that are already and continually among us. The catastrophe is ongoing: "The concept of progress must be grounded in the idea of catastrophe. That things are 'status quo' *is* the catastrophe. It is not an ever-present possibility but what in each case is given. Strindberg's idea: hell is not something that awaits us, but *this life here and now*" (*SW IV*, 184–85). Benjamin's melancholic reflections on the catastrophic ruins were not articulated to reconstruct some coherent mythic past now gone, but to bring parts of the past into the present as an interruption, as a shock that jolts the mythic continuum of history, making us aware of our material surroundings and thereby uncovering our collective unconscious (sans the Jungian universal archetypes). History, on Benjamin's account, is not a continuum, but rather a collection, an endless contiguous collection, of ruins of the past. His allegorical gaze looks backward while being taken into the future in order to recollect, to put pieces together always and only in the present. To enter into history, into life itself, is to enter into the fragmentary, to stumble on ruins, and to participate in a re-creation of the world, *tikkun* without end. Within these catastrophic ruins, the community remains in a liminal state.

Indeed, it is at the point of liminality where, as Victor Turner has suggested, we find the formation of *communitas*, due mainly to the danger and ambiguity of this particular state of being. Turner is clear that this "non-place" is relatively unstructured, even as it is overseen by ritual elders and within the overarching context of a rite of passage.[4] Benjamin desires a mass-mediated movement that takes apart hierarchies and in which art is working toward the revolution. Like the surrealists who sought to blur the line between art and life, Benjamin works to blur the line between the sacred and the profane. The focus continues to be on the limin, or the threshold (*die Schwelle*) between the two realms, yet the hierarchical structures and the mythic origins of religious structures are replaced by the material realities in the here and now. What is needed is something of a "*profane illumination,* a materialistic, anthropological inspiration" (*SW II*, 209). Richard Wolin explains this as follows: "Like religious illumination, profane illumination captures the powers of spiritual intoxication in order to produce a 'revelation,' a vision or insight which transcends the prosaic state of empirical reality; yet it produces this vision in an *immanent* manner, while remaining within the bounds of possible experience, and without recourse to otherworldly dogmas."[5] This aesthetic vision gathers pieces of the past, bringing them into the present in order to review the world as it is.

Before continuing with Benjamin's community of sense, however, I want to return to the site of sacrifice, thinking back through it via other writers who have broken down the quest for the Ur-sacrifice (apparent in Girard's views) and who stress the liminality of the ritualizing process, albeit in a profane way. It is in the very everydayness of the ruins that we find a different way of responding to the past and the future, a response not seeking the otherworldly but grounded in the now. So in contrast to the origin-seeking scapegoat point of view, Julia Kristeva argues "that the habitual and increasingly explicit attempt to fabricate a scapegoat victim as foundress of a society or a counter-society may be replaced by the analysis of the potentialities of *victim/executioner* which characterize each identity, each subject, each sex."[6] From this psychoanalytic perspective, the sacrifice has not passed us by, and the society has not been permanently founded on its remains. Rather, the sacrifice exists in a nascent state. We are, each one of us, bound up within an economy of victims and victimizers. They have not simply fled the scene, or suicided in a plane; we are they.

The physical site of the sacrifice is also not very clear cut, in spite of society's attempts to erect walls and barriers of delineation. Jacques Derrida begins to point us toward a reconsideration of the threatening liminality of sacred space and sacrifice in his treatment of the scapegoat:

> The ceremony of the *pharmakos* [the scapegoat] is thus played out on the boundary line between inside and outside [of the city.] . . . The origin of difference and division, the *pharmakos* represents evil both introjected and projected. Beneficial insofar as he cures—and for that, venerated and cared for—harmful insofar as he incarnates the powers

of evil—and for that, feared and treated with caution. Alarming and calming. Sacred and accursed.[7]

Derrida points to the passages inherent in the ceremony of the scapegoat and shows that the lines between inside and outside, good and evil, poison and cure, sacred and accursed, are under continual negotiation. With Derrida we begin to move toward a sense of sacred space that is in a perpetual state of *in-between*, whereby the evil never fully leaves the city, and the abject is never thrown far enough over the wall. The community cannot found itself on a past event now completed, for the remains always remain; even if the rubble were to be cleared from the devastated architecture, they would not go away.

Derrida and Kristeva, on this view and others, are indebted to Georges Bataille who wrote extensively on the sacred space of architecture. During the 1930s, Bataille worked in the Bibliothèque Nationale in Paris at the same time Benjamin was spending his exilic years there, perusing nineteenth-century historical documents in the search for quotations with which he would build his mammoth *Arcades Project*. In the late 1930s, Bataille was one of the founders of the short-lived "College of Sociology," and even shorter lived, quasi-surrealist, esoteric group *Acephale*. (*Acephale*, apparently, attempted to revive a sacrificial economy themselves, though it seems they struggled to find a volunteer to play the scapegoat.) Bataille was interested in the relations of urban space and sacrifice and, I suspect, found some camaraderie with Benjamin, who occasionally showed up and even lectured at the College of Sociology gatherings.[8]

Bataille, for his part, works out his readings of urban space partially in response to Émile Zola's writings on urban planning, but his divergences from Zola's thought are instructive. Zola was a proponent of the modernization—and hence *sterilization* on Bataille's view—of Paris in the nineteenth century. A modern Paris would be one that accommodated good, hard, and clean labor. In the modern city everything is useful, and everyone is busy; there is no laziness, no waste, nothing unused. Because waste is associated with inutility, part of the modernization process was to move the slaughterhouses out of the city, to keep the excess blood and guts outside a smoothly functioning economy. Yet this does not mean that just any structure can take their place. In an 1867 article entitled "The Squares"—written after the Parmentier square was built on the former site of the Popincourt slaughterhouse in Paris—Zola reacted to the unnaturalness of the public urban square.[9] Nature—and the associated inutility of persons idling around in nature—Zola argued, should also be left outside the gates of the city, for the city is the place of labor, of efficiency. Leisure and slaughter are necessary excesses, but the urbanite should excise their vision of them for productive labor to continue.

Only on Sundays, on the day of rest, should the worker delight in idleness. Zola strongly favored the rest and pleasure of the Sabbath, as long as it was a "real" pleasure, a pleasure that could not be purchased. "The joy of the people is a good and beautiful thing," Zola states. "When poor people are having fun poverty vanishes from the earth."[10] Also vanished are any connections between pleasure and shame. Such idle pleasure was to be enjoyed at the site of "real" nature, that is, outside the city, and only on Sundays. Work was done during the weekdays in the city, and leisure was had on Sunday outside the city. Sharp distinctions were made, and again the walls were erected so that the clean and proper citizen was not confronted with excess waste. Denis Hollier comments:

> Zola's "city of concord and peace" celebrates the Sunday of life. No emptiness remains. But there is no loss. Nothing is lacking after lack and nothing have been eliminated. There is nothing that would make you notice that nothing is missing. Lack is abolished and leaves no mementos. There is no madman to disturb the secular harmony with Nietzsche's message that God is dead.[11]

Zola's city is a mythical place, a collectivity without disruptions. No madmen, no disruption of the boundaries exists. When the walls are in their place, when the excess waste is relegated to outside of the city and all that is useful is established inside, then harmony ensues. There are no mementos, nothing to remind us of waste.

As Zola reacted to the unnatural public squares in the midst of the city, Bataille followed suit by pointing out the strangeness of the space of the museum within the city. Bataille's early writings display a fascination with the ordering—indeed, "cosmicizing"—forces of architecture and the historical shifts that can be read through the remains. One of these shifts is the move from religion to art, in the modern age, seen through the replacement of the church with the museum. He offers several ideas on how to think about the ruins of architecture. In separate essays written in the late 1920s, Bataille writes about the twin architectures of the *abattoir* (slaughterhouse) and the museum, and these are both implicitly contrasted with the function of the church/temple. To Bataille,

> The slaughterhouse relates to religion in the sense that temples of time past . . . had two purposes, serving simultaneously for prayers and for slaughter. . . . Nowadays the slaughterhouse is cursed and quarantined like a boat with cholera aboard. . . . [T]he victims of this curse are neither the butchers nor the animals, but those fine folk who have reached the point of not being able to stand their own unseemliness, an unseemliness corresponding in fact to a pathological need for cleanliness.[12]

These are the same people who wind up in the museum during their idle time. Bataille observes them "[o]n Sundays at five o'clock, at the exit to the

Louvre," where he "admires the stream of visitors visibly animated by the desire to be similar in every way to the heavenly visions still delighting their eyes."[13] One architecture supplies something the civil person wants to mimic; the other is what civility casts out. The slaughterhouse, because it is reminiscent of the otherness of death and excess, is cast beyond the walls, to the outside. The museum, because it provides a site for internal reflection, is left inside. Ultimately, however, the architectures of the museum and the slaughterhouse depend on each other, are constituted by each other, and contain within them the heart of the other. And at the tensed space between the two, in Bataille's economy, lies the passage that is the sacred.

Bataille grew up in a quite dysfunctional Catholic home and even studied to be a priest before renouncing his faith. Nonetheless, he devoted a good deal of his life's writings to concerns about the limits and bounds of religion. He disdained religion for the most part, but never fully separated from it. Modern religion took on many of the bad habits of the modern city, and it was precisely the clean and proper ideas of the city, and the corresponding clean and proper modern ideas of the church, for which Bataille had little tolerance. Stating an obvious but usually overlooked relationship between slaughterhouses and churches, Bataille writes, "The sacrifice of the mass is a reminder but it only rarely makes a deep impression on our sensibility. However obsessive we find the symbol of the Cross, the mass is not readily identified with the bloody sacrifice."[14] He then goes on to say, "Cattle being slaughtered or cut up often makes people sick today, but there is nothing in the dishes served at tables to remind them of this. So one might say of contemporary experience that it inverts pious conduct and sacrifice."[15] According to Bataille, modern life (in the city and in the church) is based on a strict economy of exchange in which separations and borders are maintained. The slaughterhouse, because it reminded people of the formerly living nature of that which was embodied (in other words, "food"), was moved out of the city. The museum, because heavenly visions were presented to the public, was established on its ruins. In a secularized economy, Sunday was the day for the museum, the day for renewal and rebirth. And, as Hollier's comment earlier points out, this secularized economy leaves no traces to even remind us that God is dead.[16]

Building Memory

If Lacan has famously suggested that "the unconscious is structured like a language," we may amend this by putting the following words in Benjamin's mouth: "The collective unconscious is built like a city." Benjamin understood that our spatial environment constructs and consequently reveals who we are. Painting and cinema, in the end, are both media that can come and go in their influence on social life, but architecture has been from the beginning, and no doubt always will be. As long as humans are corporeal entities, architecture will be the predominant public art. Of course Benjamin would not suggest that topography totally confines and defines us, but he is concerned with the overlooked, that which turns invisible in spite of its all too prominent visibility. To make the unconscious conscious and understand the forgotten fragments of the past and how they invisibly affect the present, one must become an urban physiognomer who reads by touch, who feels the spatiality of the city.

In the third chapter, I neglected one critical paragraph toward the end of Benjamin's "Work of Art" essay. To help rethink the polar opposition between contemplation and distraction, he brings an analogy to architecture into the argument: "Buildings are received in a twofold manner: by use and by perception. Or, better: tactically and optically. . . . For the tasks which face the human apparatus of perception at historical turning points cannot be performed solely by optical means—that is, by way of contemplation. They are mastered gradually —taking their cue from tactile reception—through habit" (*SW III*, 120). Although it is possible to concentrate/contemplate a building visually, there is no tactile counterpart to visual contemplation. Benjamin here breaks apart two senses and briefly highlights the importance of tactility. The visual sense, so dominant in the modern age, is associated with the bourgeois reaffirmation of contemplation, a contemplation that reinstills the distance of the auratic object. Tactile use of a building is one of habit, everydayness, thus bringing the object closer. People *use* buildings and thereby break down any "husk" that might encapsulate a building as an artwork.

During the writing of the "Work of Art" essay, Benjamin was also hard at work on his final, incomplete project on a peculiar excavation of the nineteenth century, seen through the urban spaces and architectures of Paris. Translated into English as the *Arcades Project*—Benjamin tended to call it the *Passagenarbeit*—it is Benjamin's literary stab at allegorizing the city, at translating Vertov's *Man with a Movie Camera* or Walther Ruttmann's *Berlin: Symphony of a Great City* (1922) into words, metonymically strung out along a seemingly never-ending axis. Talmudic in its construction, the *Arcades Project* operates between textual space and spatial textuality, extending well beyond its initial parameters.[17] What we are left with are around a thousand pages of fragments made up of quotations from architects, poets, critics, philosophers, politicians, and others, grouped together into thematic sections that, when read through, form something of an argument. Here Benjamin has fully come to terms with the allegorical method, actually embodying the form, rather than offering a critique on it. In this manner, Benjamin is something of a critical mythmaker who reconstructs the present out of the ruins of the past.

We also find the demythologizer, the destructive character, embedded here. Having an allegorical structure, the *Arcades Project* could easily be claimed to be incomplete because such a "book" could never be completed. Maurice

Blanchot shares with Benjamin the emphasis on the function of the fragment —especially in the *Writing of the Disaster* and *The Infinite Conversation*—and discusses this as the difference between the work (*l'oeuvre*) and the book (*livre*), showing the always incomplete nature of the work. As Blanchot states, "The Book always indicates an order that submits to *unity*, a system of notions in which are affirmed the primacy of speech over writing, of thought over language, and the promise of a communication that would one day be immediate and transparent."[18] Blanchot's book is therefore kin to Benjamin's collection (*Sammlung*), but both are always subject to disaster and dispersal that render the whole into fragments, however usable. A similar thing occurs with the baroque allegory, "Things are assembled according to their significance; indifference to their existence allowed them to be dispersed again" (*OGTD*, 188). The creative activity of putting together is constantly followed by the collection's never-ending dispersal.

Through his work in the 1930s, Benjamin demonstrates how the city becomes the "discovery site of the personal."[19] For Benjamin, however, this is not an individual, subjective discovery, but an uncovering of one's life situated within a vast social-spatial fabric. Indeed, his "autobiographical" writings ("Berlin Chronicle" and "Berlin Childhood Around 1900") are not about remembering his past life so much as they are a revealing of himself in the present, within the urban spaces of Berlin. Here, as in the baroque allegory, chronological time is transposed into spatial dimensions, "a past become space" (*AP*, 871). As Graeme Gilloch puts it, "the urban setting shapes, and is in turn shaped by, the work of remembrance."[20] And like the allegory, the city and its ruins do not mean anything by themselves; they must be read or, to be more sensually inclusive, *perceived*.

One of the modern city's best-kept secrets (especially seen in Paris, though visible as well in the major metropolitan centers of Europe) was the development of elaborate interior space. The conceptual rise of the isolated, bourgeois individual coincides with the rise in domestic space that cordons one off from the world: "The nineteenth century, like no other century, was addicted to dwelling. It conceived the residence as a receptacle for the person, and it encased him with all his appurtenances so deeply in the dwelling's interior . . . " (*AP*, 220). Benjamin's language of the interior is analogous to that of the aura, in which "the dwelling becomes a shell" (ibid.). Further transposing the language of aura from art to architecture, and inflecting it with a Kafkaesque mood, he states, "To live in these interiors was to have woven a dense fabric about oneself, to have secluded oneself within a spider's web, in whose toils world events hang loosely suspended like so many insect bodies sucked dry. From this cavern, one does not like to stir" (*AP*, 216). This shell, or web, isolates the individual from the world, anaesthetizing them.

We must recall here that such interiority is also structurally similar to the "wooded forest" into which the symbol disappears and in which the ahistorical, primeval myth can be found. Thus, as might be suspected, Benjamin works throughout the *Arcades Project* to explode the buildings, to reveal the interiors. The destructive allegorical response is to take it outside, to read the presumed individuality as a collective unconscious that is unmasked in the public realm. As mentioned before, at the heart of allegory is *agora*, the "public," and this public has an etymological history that denotes the marketplace. (Indeed, the "agora"was the political-social-economic center of ancient Athens.) The marketplace that was the Parisian arcades provided Benjamin with a text to read, since they were simultaneously interior and exterior, even as in Benjamin's day they were already in a state of decay. These were city streets covered by glass, offering people places to shop while remaining in the comfort of the inside. The "passage," therefore, is not so much between individual buildings as it is between the inside and outside: "Streets are the dwelling place of the collective. . . . More than anywhere else, the street reveals itself in the arcade as the furnished and familiar interior of the masses" (*AP*, 423). Within such liminal spaces myths are revealed.

How to turn things inside out on such a large scale? In the city, the allegorist most prominently takes on the guise of the *flâneur* who wanders the streets, ambling through its passages, and revealing undisclosed secrets. Becoming distracted among a crowd, the flâneur nonetheless makes unconscious and unwitting connections within the streets, thus putting into practice a "reception in distraction." Relating the metonymic meanderings of the flâneur in relation to film, Benjamin suggests, "Couldn't an exciting film be made from the map of Paris? From the unfolding of its various aspects in temporal succession? From the compression of a centuries long movement of streets, boulevards, arcades, and squares into the space of half an hour? And does the flâneur do anything different?" (*AP*, 83). The flâneur is himself (it is explicitly gendered in Benjamin's writings)[21] "on the threshold" (*AP*, 10) and thus offers a unique and privileged position from which to understand modern capitalist society, and to bring to light the mythological structures on which the present stands. Myths, Benjamin argues, have merged into the physical setting, becoming topographical. Intimately paralleling Freudian dreamwork, the flâneur reveals the mythical secrets of society, especially when society has forgotten about them and they function unconsciously. The *Passagenarbeit* is also *Traumarbeit*. As such the flâneur undergoes a process of re-collection, not for the sake of the individual (as with psychoanalysis) but for the collective.

History and Memory, Monuments and Memorials

The urban setting does not exist in some pure spatial form divorced from the accretions of time. And so one of the most prominent themes throughout the *Arcades Project* is the function of memory and its relation to history. The activity of making history is fundamentally an aesthetic activity for Benjamin: "To write history means giving calendar dates their physiognomy" (*SW IV*, 165). Allegorical readers-cum-flâneurs must take up a Braille-like reading in which past time is made spatial in the present and offered to the senses to perceive. This is the proper activity of memory, as opposed to keeping track of the facts of history. Memory is oriented toward the interactive dimensions of keeping the past alive aesthetically, not for its own sake but for the sake of the present.

Contemporary Jewish historian Yosef Hayim Yerushalmi discusses such an idea of Jewish memory in a manner similar to Benjamin's interests and sees "the essence of collective memory as a dual movement of reception and transmission, successively propelling itself toward the future. It is this process which forges the *mneme* of the group, the continuum of its memory, which is that of the links in a chain and not that of a silken thread. The Jews were not mnemonic virtuosos. They were, however, willing receivers and superb transmitters."[22] Yerushalmi points toward a historical "continuum" in a way that may be anathema to Benjamin. Yet key here is the metaphor of links in a chain, rather than an unbroken thread; history is created from the metonymic fragments culled together over time, a continuous activity of collecting that may never end. And this chain of links is continued because it is aesthetic— the past is transmitted "more actively through ritual than through chronicle."[23] Jewish life has continued through time not by keeping good records, but reactualizing the past in the present through the interactive aesthetic drama that is ritual.

Benjamin, we have seen, is not interested in religious rituals with their reaffirmations of aura, their hierarchies of power, and their otherworldly concerns. But he does not forsake the active, material basis of ritual either. Commenting on Benjamin's writings on Baudelaire, Rainer Rochlitz suggests, "Contrary to the theses in 'The Work of Art,' it is in ritual form that art is placed in the service of social life. . . . Benjamin can no longer abandon the idea of a reactualization of ritual."[24] In his quest for a profane illumination—that may take on a ritual form—his gaze lights on the built environment, and the spatialization of the past. Indeed this is not far from the Jewish tradition, and going way back to the scriptures of the ancient prophets we find the necessity for solid structures in the activity of memory:

> "Take twelve stones from here out of the middle of the Jordan, from the place where the priests' feet stood, carry them over with you, and lay them down in the place where you camp tonight." . . . When your

children ask in time to come, "What do those stones mean to you?" then you shall tell them that the waters of the Jordan were cut off in front of the ark of the covenant of the Lord. When it crossed over the Jordan, the waters of the Jordan were cut off. So these stones shall be to the Israelites a memorial forever. (Joshua 4:3, 6–7)

In such places, memory is built; past historical events and personages are kept alive by preserving them in a spatial structure, usually of a solid substance like stone, marble, or metal. History is created from hard materials; it is seen, felt, or heard, and provokes an interaction with the questioning generations to come.

Extrapolating on the idea of Jewish memory, I want to suggest that there are two varieties of such built histories, and the difference between them triggers several of Benjamin's "twin stars." That is, they appear similar, but when read by the allegorist their differences are highlighted. These two constructions are the *monument* and the *memorial*. Scholarly and popular parlance alike tends to conflate the two, and even when differences are noted, there is little consensus about the distinction. An increasingly vast and disjunctive literature treats the differences between the monument and the memorial, and it is not my intention to establish any firm definitions here, but simply to suggest a point at which Benjamin's thought might enter into the discussion.

Let me then start with part of Arthur Danto's distinction, stated in response to Maya Lin's Vietnam Veterans Memorial: "Monuments commemorate the memorable and embody the myths of beginnings. Memorials ritualize remembrance and mark the reality of ends."[25] Similarly, Marita Sturken offers this difference: "Monuments tend to use less explanation, while memorials tend to emphasize texts or lists of the dead."[26] This difference can be readily seen in Washington, D.C., as both Danto and Sturken note, with the difference between the Washington Monument and the Vietnam Veteran's Memorial.

The Washington Monument is a closed structure, leaving little chance to interact. It is a striking erection in the middle of the city, capable of being seen from great distances, and it is the distance that is of note. Interaction is limited to an entrance, a smallish portal at its base, through which one can enter in order to be transported upward. At the top, the viewer takes on the role of the seeing eye of the obelisk, a homunculus who loses the ability to interact with its body, and capable only of looking at the city beyond (exclaiming something like, "Look I can see the airport from here!"). The monument is thus not far from Benjamin's visual notion of concentration/contemplation on the auratic object that retains an "appearance of semblance or distance, no matter how close the object may be" (*SW II*, 518). The monument is invested with aura, distant from the viewer, even while inside its space. "A person who concentrates [*sich sammelnde*; also connotes "to gather oneself"] before a work of art is absorbed by it; he enters into the work" (*SW III*, 119). It is not so much that the object is spatially distant, but that the temporality of the mythic event is meant to evoke is kept at a distance. The primeval myth is perfectly formed, existing as a foundational past. We can enter, we can look, but we cannot touch.

The Vietnam Veterans Memorial, to the contrary, is cut into the ground, creating a negative space that actually becomes invisible from behind. No heroes or victors are here, nor mythical events, only the expression of lament. Two walls come together at a corner, invoking an open book to be read. Here reading becomes blind reading, done by the hands, as family and friends of the deceased participate in and with the memorial by touching the names of the deceased etched into the black granite (the traditional substance of monuments). The memorial works allegorically, appearing at first like a symbol (monument) with a fixed meaning, but it finally remains open and finds meaning only within its subsequent aesthetic interaction with the public in the present. The catastrophe is not in the past, separated; it is now, here with us.

Yerushalmi, in discussing the importance of the ritualized dramatic structure of the Passover Seder, with its interactive storytelling and eating, notes precisely this kind of time travel in memory work. "Both the language and the gesture are geared to spur, not so much a leap of memory as a fusion of past and present. Memory here is no longer recollection, which still preserves a sense of distance, but reactualization."[27] Religious history, it would seem, shows a constant attempt to memorialize, yet keeps getting stuck in monumentalizing, hence the need for open structures, for rereadings and reritualizings.

Even with the foregoing distinction, the memorial and the monument would not be opposed to each other in Benjamin's view, for as with many of his binary terms, through the allegorical activity the one is distorted by the other. There is ultimately no completely stable monument, incapable of interaction. All is susceptible to the gaze of the allegorist, and in this reception-orientation even the monument is made into a memorial. Just as the singularity of the artwork is exploded by the *work* of art in its cultural/social setting, so too is the monument exploded by the active work of memory. The monument erects a myth, a myth set in stone and thus petrified, meanwhile giving off the illusion of stability and permanence through the contemplative calm of vision. Benjamin's work is to show forth its transitory nature, to ruin the myth. He looks, for example, at the Egyptian obelisk in the Place de la Concorde in Paris, noting "what was carved in it four thousand years ago today stands at the center in the greatest of city squares. Had it been foretold to him—what a triumph for the Pharaoh! The foremost Western cultural empire will one day bear at its center the memorial of his rule."[28] Thus, as Gilloch notes, "Once the symbol of Egyptian rule, Pharaoh's monument now proclaims the colonial power of France. The meaning of the monument changes in the course of its own history." In this way, "The monument has an 'afterlife' which negates the original intention."[29] The monument is allegorized in its new setting; its old meaning is distorted.

Sensing Memory

> All we have to open the past are the five senses . . . and memory.
>
> **Louise Bourgeois**

> All these things, each one of which came into memory in its own par-
> ticular way, are stored up separately and under the general categories of
> understanding. For example, light and all colors and forms of bodies
> came in through the eyes; sounds of all kinds by the ears; all smells by
> the passages of the nostrils; all flavors by the gate of the mouth; by the
> sensation of the whole body, there is brought in what is hard or soft, hot
> or cold, smooth or rough, heavy or light, whether external or internal
> to the body. The vast cave of memory, with its numerous and mysteri-
> ous recesses, receives all these things and stores them up, to be recalled
> and brought forth when required. Each experience enters by its own
> door, and is stored up in the memory.
>
> **Augustine, *Confessions X.8***

Ultimately, however, even the memorializing of the monument is not what
Benjamin is after with regard to memory. He alternatively points toward another way of experiencing the past that escapes what has been said here about
both memorials and monuments. In the end, he articulates buildings and
urban spaces that remain open to interaction, but most importantly he
searches for interactions that lead to chance encounters, especially seen
through the movements of the flâneur. It is the memory work revealed in the
profane, sensual world that intrigues Benjamin, and here his work on Marcel
Proust becomes central.

What rises out of the ruins of the past is a particular form of memory, a
memory most closely related to Proust's *mémoire involontaire*. Indeed, in the
Arcades Project, just after his discussion of the collector as allegorist, Benjamin
places a fragment from Proust's *Le temps retrouvé*. Commenting on this,
Benjamin suggests, "A sort of productive disorder is the canon of the *mémoire
involontaire*, as it is the canon of the collector" (*AP*, 211). The memory work
Benjamin lights on here is that which comes without warning. The collector
collects and arranges, as best he or she knows how, even with the knowledge
that all will always remain incomplete, perpetually an unfinished project, open
to the future. Within these openings, one comes across the whiff of the
madeleine that brings everything rushing back. Allegorical collecting allows a
"productive disorder," not unlike Kafka's leopards that break into the temple to
drink the sanctified drink, only to be incorporated later into the ritual itself. In
other words, memory work becomes something of an invention, an orientation

toward the future that can nevertheless not predict that future. We have experiences, but they are only made meaningful in their afterlife. The invention (*l'invention*) of collection occurs in the here and now, even as it is oriented toward the future (*l'avenir*), toward an event through which the future might come to us.

In 1929 Benjamin published "On the Image of Proust" and worked on translations of Proust's writings (including part of the massive *À la recherche du temps perdu*) into German. The memory experience that Proust famously had through his sensual encounter with the madeleine was precisely what Benjamin sought as the aesthetic disruption of time and space, literally bringing him to his senses and through them to the buried, hidden world of the past, a sensed shock that wakes one from the dreamworld of modern life. But although the mundane, sensual shock that triggered Proust's memory—and, eventually, his enormous "memoir"—intrigues Benjamin, Proust's conclusions marked a warning to Benjamin, and his commentary continually circles around metaphors of Proust's interiority, finally bringing it to bear on Proust's asthmatic medical condition. The asphyxiating illness, Benjamin suggests, can be read in his very style of inward writing, and ultimately his memory writing brings him to a mythical, timeless past, secluded as in a "wooded interior." John McCole comments, "Proust did not so much capture time as annihilate it, attempting to flee from the consequences of transience."[30] The catastrophic ruins of progress are rebuilt by Proust into a distant, nonhistorical monumental memoir. In architectural terms, the building (noun) has forgotten the building (verb); it merely appears to exist as if it always was and will be. To the contrary, McCole aptly synthesizes Benjamin's interest in the inventive memory of the present: "New perspectives will continue to emerge from the vantage point of a constantly changing present moment. For a life (or a society) whose future has not been foreclosed, the past can never become a closed book. It will always be subject to revision, in principle, from the standpoint of the present."[31] While rescuing the involuntary experience of memory from Proust, along with its productive disorder, Benjamin must leave behind his interiority, his ordered monument of memory, and turn outward.

To do so, Benjamin picks up on the sensual basis of Proust's memory.[32] In a Benjaminian way, Fredric Jameson refers to Baudelaire's and Proust's modes of connecting the body and memories, rephrasing their ideas thus: "That memories are first and foremost memories of the senses, and that it is the senses that remember and not the 'person' of personal identity."[33] Augustine, as quoted in this section's epigraph, like many others, also understands the sensual dimension of memory. Yet his theological orientation has little of the disorder about it and, in fact, is deeply representative of a Greek ratiocinated worldview. For Benjamin, as for Jameson, any coming together of personal identity is always subject to dispersal. Indeed, as Benjamin reads Proust, "Only the *actus purus* of remembrance itself, not the author of the plot, constitutes the unity of the text. One may even say that the intermittences of author and plot are only the reverse of the continuum of memory, the figure on the back side of the carpet" (*SW II*, 238). The aesthetic basis of memory turns the interior life inside out, and the focus is on the "act" of memory (memory *work*) not anything in itself.

The senses, like the streets of Paris, are passages between inside and outside, existing in social-spatial dimensions. Anthropologist C. Nadia Seremetakis highlights the liminal nature of the senses:

> The senses represent inner states not shown on the surface. They are also located in a social-material field outside of the body. . . . The sense organs function in the same manner that the material artifact can also function, that is as *semíon*, track, which one senses and a medium by which one senses. Thus the sensory is not only encapsulated within the body as an internal capacity or power, but is also dispersed out there on the surface of things as the latter's autonomous characteristics, which then can invade the body as perceptual experience. Here sensory interiors and exteriors constantly pass into each other in the creation of extra personal significance.[34]

The senses operate in liminal space, in the passage between interior and exterior, and are continually being crisscrossed back and forth. They read the world and can be read by the world. We offer images of ourselves—through our dress and body appearance, certainly, but our inner state can also be read through our eyes—and we also offer scents and sounds, tastes and touches, to others. At the same time we perceive the world and others around us through our senses and gain knowledge about another's identity and the construction of the world through our senses. This may smack of a warmed-over empiricism, yet it is also vital to continually reassert the cultural variations of the senses, the manifold ways in which we perceive the world. People across various cultures may share the physiological capacity for vision, but to turn this biochemical activity into "seeing" as a meaningful experience is a culturally situated activity. The meanings of what we sense are created from out of cultural locations. In other words, aesthetics are not simply empiricism, for they are always a combination of the *aesthetica naturalis* and the *aesthetica artificialis*, the senses and their cultural construction, including (perhaps especially so) the role that art and architecture play.

Besides the spatial dimension of the senses and their liminal status between interiors and exteriors, the senses are also imbricated with a temporal dimension, in the passage between past and present. Again, Seremetakis is excellent on the topic and has effectively articulated such an aesthetic function:

There is no such thing as one moment of perception and then another of memory, representation, or objectification. Mnemonic processes are intertwined with the sensory order in such a manner as to render each perception a re-perception. Re-perception is the creation of meaning through the interplay, witnessing, and cross-metaphorization of co-implicated sensory spheres. Memory cannot be confined to a purely mentalist or subjective sphere. It is a culturally mediated material practice that is activated by embodied acts and semantically dense objects. This material approach to memory places the senses in time and speaks to memory as both meta-sensory capacity and as a sense organ in itself.

Memory as a distinct meta-sense transports, bridges, and crosses all the other senses. Yet memory is internal to each sense, and the senses are as divisible and indivisible from each other as each memory is separable and intertwined with others. Memory is the horizon of sensory experiences, storing and restoring the experience of each sensory dimension in another, as well as dispersing and finding sensory records outside the body in a surround of entangling objects and places. Memory and the senses are co-mingled in so far as they are equally involuntary experiences. Their involuntary dimension points to their encompassment by a trans-individual social and somatic landscape.[35]

Memory would seem to be a "sixth sense," tying the other senses together as well as organizing sensual stimuli from the outside world. Yet we must be careful to recall that this memory is not anything specifically internal to the human; it is triggered by material culture. It is also somewhat out of the control of the individual reasoning self, giving way to involuntary experiences.

Forgetting, on this understanding, is not far from anaesthesia. The inability to feel becomes the inability to remember. In the modern world, the human being has become anaesthetized and alienated as a result of the division of labor, and the triumph of rationalization and its coconqueror, visuality (here vision prevails at the expense of the other senses). As I have previously suggested, the reason-vision nexus begins not in some postmodern "age of the image," but rather with the printed, mass-produced, mass-disseminated, completed *book*. The *logos* of reason has met the *logos* of the word in the modern world. Logocentrism is not merely about disembodied metaphysical thought; it is also about technologies and their reframing of the human sensorium (which further helps explain the significance of Benjamin's *Arcades Project*, not as a "book," but as an unfinished "work" of fragments.)

And so, particularly in the aftermath of the Holocaust, we attempt to "never forget," and the response is to create museums and memorials that aid in our remembrance. These constructions aid in memory, giving us something to touch, and offering a passageway for the past to come to us in the present. This too is not without its price. "The less memory is experienced from the inside," Pierre Nora warns, "the more it exists through its exterior scaffolding and outward signs."[36] Nora's comments are of course not far from Socrates' well-known comments in Plato's *Phaedrus* about how the technology of writing will destroy memory. Architecture (or any material technology) cannot become a substitute for memory. The building cannot be a metaphor for the past. What is no doubt needed is architecture that allows for interiors and exteriors to be connected, with passageways that retain metonymic, and therefore open, dimensions.

Religion is a "chain of memory," as Danièle Hervieu-Léger has put it. And the "scholar of religion is, therefore, concerned with dimensions of memory and remembrance," as Jonathan Z. Smith suggests.[37] What the scholar of religion must then become attentive to are the sensual bases for memory, the ways in which memory functions between the internal and external worlds, between the past and present, as well as the material technologies that enable memory to take place. No doubt much work along these lines has been achieved in ritual studies, yet the field often remains within a phenomenological framework and becomes blind to the specificities of media, technology, and the physical impact of material culture on the body. Benjamin's allegorical aesthetics provoke reflection on this aspect of religion, as these aesthetics particularly showcase the passages through which a culture's symbols become distorted, memories are brought to light via material objects, and cultures believe their political and religious myths to exist in an ahistorical wooded interior.

The Community of Sense: Inventing the Messiah

Benjamin's memory work is not really about the past. It is very much about the present, even as it points toward the future, albeit in a blind and backward way: His "angel of history" is famously "turned toward the past" and is caught up in a storm that "drives him irresistibly into the future" (*SW IV*, 392). From among the catastrophic ruins, the strewn wreckage that is progress, may come the hoped-for Messiah, a ubiquitous figure in Benjamin's writings. This is, nonetheless, a strange character that may come to us at any moment and not via some eschatological horizon of progress. Still, what Benjamin meant by the figure of the Messiah is open to many readings, the most convincing being that the Messiah is the Revolution that would come through historical materialism. His writings on the topic were oriented toward an otherworldly being coming in not from beyond, but from within. Thus, transposing his religious, political, and aesthetic ideas, and based on the preceding chapters, what I want to suggest in the end is that the awaited Messiah is none other than the aesthetic community. The Messiah may be equated with the Revolution, but what Benjamin meant by this had to do with collecting, re-collecting, and interacting with others in and through the passages of material life.

Reminiscing on the College of Sociology meetings in the late 1930s, Pierre Klossowski has commented on the uneasy exchange Benjamin had with this group of philosophical surrealists, noting especially that Benjamin thought their brand of atheological aesthetics left too much ambiguity, opening the door to varieties of fascism similar to what was then evident in Germany. Tyrus Miller mentions Benjamin's brief engagement with the College of Sociology and notes Benjamin's contrary insistence on an "antipatriarchal libidinal politics" that would enable a "communist gynocracy."[38] Seeing him "between Marx and Fourier," Klossowski recalls Benjamin's pushing for a "phalansterian renaissance," an "esoterism that would be both 'erotic and artisan.'"[39] And in the *Arcades Project*, Benjamin devotes one of the sections to Charles Fourier, bringing to light the utopian's dreams of founding a phalanstery, a socialist space where individual talents and passions (especially valuing the artistic type) are put to use for the good of the collective. Friedrich Engels, writing to Marx and quoted in the *Arcades Project*, likened the phalanstery to the Messiah: "it will be the 'new Heaven' and the 'new Earth'" (*AP*, 638).

On the revolutionary tone, Terry Eagleton suggests how "the aesthetic is a dangerous, ambiguous affair . . . [because] . . . there is something in the body which can revolt against the power which inscribes it."[40] This is certainly Benjamin's Marxian hope for the aesthetic body. Refocusing aesthetics away from judgments about art and toward material, corporeal interactions allow us to see the passages between the subjective ego and the art object, between interiors and exteriors, and between humans, as it opens the world to liberative possibilities. Benjamin, like other materialist writers, understood the power of the body stripped of the aura of the imago. The body image produced by consumer capitalism creates an anesthetizing veil, a narcissistic narcotic, an opiate for the masses that disallows interconnection in the world. Meanwhile, it is precisely *through* the thresholds of the body (amended by certain new technologies) that revolutionary processes occur. By stripping the aura of the art object in its unique time and place, and without the myth of the singular individual subject to contemplate the object, the aesthetic experience becomes diffused across space and time. I suggest that this conception of aesthetics, with its "origin" in the materiality of the media of art and the sense perceptions of the masses, is opened to a form of community. The *sensus communis*, in opposition to most Western philosophical accounts, is not situated in the interior of the individual, but in the external world. It is socially located.

Even if we continue to insist on some subject-object relation, what must be accounted for are a series of *passages* that intercept any and all communications between subject and object. The tradition of aesthetics, and certainly that of theological aesthetics, is largely concerned with a connection between a disembodied mind in communion with symbols, disappearing in an otherworldly wooded interior. This quasi-mystical experience forgets all that takes place between these two entities. When these passages are denied or repressed, the illusion of immediacy (literally "without medium") takes precedence, an illusion preferred by theological aesthetics working in the romantic vein as well as by the functions of fascism and modern capitalism. The allegorical aesthetics we have discussed throughout instead emphasize two main passages: the *medium* of the artwork and *sense perceptions* at the border of the body. There is never any simple transmission of information from one point to another; no message arrives undistorted. Further, these passages are themselves constructions in historical space and time, and are subject to alteration. There is no such thing as immediacy; rather the medium becomes the message (the "work" becomes the art), and the bodily sense perceptors become the ego. The artwork and the perceiving subject are turned inside out.

It is precisely because of this emphasis on the liminality of the aesthetic, the openness to the other, that we must return to the passage that perhaps takes precedence over all other passages: death. Death stands at a critical juncture in the community of sense. One of the key consequences of the alienation of the modern individual is that she or he dies separate from the community, and increasingly often in the midst of the professional death industry, keeping us alienated from our own mortality, and in that way, from each other. Benjamin's 1936 essay, "The Storyteller," tells of such a perceptual distance in relation to modern death. Benjamin's essay emphasizes the communal (and communicable) aspect of oral storytelling, and the artistic craftsmanship that is necessary for this sharing. This is somewhat in opposition to the rise of the novel as a production of and for privatized interests—the novel is read alone, in the interior of one's domestic space. Benjamin is not nostalgic for some lost oral culture in this essay, but he is interested in a recouping and recollecting of the *communication* of tradition. In its very communication, the past remains unfinished, open to the present:

> It has been evident for a number of centuries how, in the general consciousness, the thought of death has become less omnipresent and less vivid. In its last stages this process is accelerated. And in the course of the nineteenth century, bourgeois society—by means of medical and social, private and public institutions—realized a secondary effect, which may have been its subconscious main purpose: to enable people to avoid the sight of the dying. Dying was once a public process in the life of the individual, and a most exemplary one. . . . In the course of modern times, dying has been pushed further and further out of the perceptual world of the living. It used to be that there was not a single house, hardly a single room, in which someone had not once died. . . . Today people live in rooms that have never been touched by death—dry dwellers of eternity; and when their end approaches, they are stowed away in sanatoria or hospitals by their heirs. (*SW III*, 151)

Modern capitalist modes of production have isolated people from each other —through the building of interior space, the rise of the novel, and the division of labor—and one of the effects is the way modern humans become closed off from death itself. Death was once *public* and *perceptual*; now it is interior, invisible.

Oral stories and baroque lament-plays alike work around allegories of death, and the readily perceptible image of death becomes a form of "public speaking," turning the individual experience into a collective one. In commenting on Bataille, Blanchot suggests as much, "'the basis of communication' [for Bataille] is not necessarily speech, or even the silence that is its foundation and punctuation, but the exposure to death, no longer my own exposure, but someone else's, whose living and closest presence is already the eternal and unbearable absence, an absence that the travail of deepest mourning does not diminish."[41] The perception of death is a public activity and serves as a source of communication, bringing the community together. Recollecting death— through storytelling and memorializing—gathers others together in response. Ultimately, a tinge of the aura returns through death's untouchable yet present absence. And yet, in the invented community, because of the negativity of death, "Things are assembled according to their significance; indifference to their existence allowed them to be dispersed again" (*OGTD*, 188).

Notes

Prescript

1. Good introductions to Benjamin's life and writings include Richard Wolin, *Walter Benjamin: An Aesthetic of Redemption* (Berkeley: University of California Press, 1994); Graeme Gilloch, *Walter Benjamin: Critical Constellations* (Blackwell, 2002); Howard Caygill's illustrated *Introducing Walter Benjamin* (New York: Totem Books, 1998); and Bernd Witte, *Walter Benjamin: An Intellectual Biography* (Detroit: Wayne State University Press, 1991).
2. Susan Buck-Morss, *The Dialectics of Seeing* (Cambridge, MA: MIT Press, 1989), 339–40.
3. See Hans Ur von Balthasar's multivolume *Glory of the Lord* (New York: Crossroad Press, 1983–1991); Alejandro Garcia-Rivera's *The Community of the Beautiful* (Collegeville, MN: Liturgical Press, 1999); Frank Burch Brown's *Religious Aesthetics* (Princeton, NJ: Princeton University Press, 1989), and *Good Taste, Bad Taste, and Christian Taste* (New York: Oxford University Press, 2000); Jeremy Begbie's *Voicing Creation's Praise* (Edinburgh: T & T Clark, 1991); and Edward Farley's *Faith and Beauty* (Burlington, VT: Ashgate, 2001).
4. For a nice overview of these variant positions, see James McBride's article "Marooned in the Realm of the Profane: Walter Benjamin's Synthesis of Kabbalah and Communism," *Journal of the American Academy of Religion* 57.2 (Summer 1987): 241–66.
5. Gershom Scholem, "Walter Benjamin and His Angel," *On Jews and Judaism in Crisis* (New York: Schocken Books, 1976), 201.
6. See Mark C. Taylor, *Disfiguring: Art, Architecture, Religion* (Chicago: University of Chicago Press, 1992).
7. Significant works on Benjamin from a religious studies standpoint include Brian M. Britt's *Walter Benjamin and the Bible* (New York: Crossroad, 1996); Margarete Kohlenbach's *Walter Benjamin: Self-Reference and Religiosity* (New York: Palgrave Macmillan, 2002); Tomoko Masuzawa's *In Search of Dreamtime: The Quest for the Origin of Religion* (Chicago: University of Chicago Press, 1993); and Roland Boer's "The Bowels of History, or The Perpetuation of Biblical Myth in Walter Benjamin," *Journal of Narrative Theory* 32.3 (2002): 370–89.
8. See "A Berlin Chronicle," *SW II*, 629.
9. Momme Brodersen and Martina Dervis, *Walter Benjamin: A Biography*, trans. Malcolm R. Green and Ingrida Ligers (London: Verso, 1996), 42–43.
10. Quoted in Bernd Witte, *Walter Benjamin: An Intellectual Biography*, trans. James Rolleston (Detroit: Wayne State University Press, 1985), 27.
11. Ibid., 28.
12. Daniel Gold, *Aesthetics and Analysis in Writing on Religion: Modern Fascinations* (Berkeley: University of California Press, 2003).

Introduction

1. The notion that there are "five senses" is not universal. In the West, the number was chiefly derived from Aristotle's philosophy. Many other thinkers in the West have had different ways of counting the senses, however, and other cultures continue to divide the world into two, three, or more senses. For interesting overviews on this, see David Howes, *Varieties of Sensory Experience: A Sourcebook in the Anthropology of the Senses* (Toronto: University of Toronto Press, 1991); Constance Classen, *The Color of Angels: Cosmology, Gender, and the Aesthetic Imagination* (New York: Routledge, 1998), and *Worlds of Sense: Exploring the Senses in History and Across Cultures* (New York: Routledge, 1993); and Louise Vinge, *The Five Senses: Studies in a Literary Tradition* (Lund: LiberLäromedel, 1975).

   As I researched for this book, I kept an eye out for studies on the senses. Intriguingly, as I did several searches for the "five senses," a vast majority of the listings (at least 80 percent) came out under the headings, "juvenile audience" or "poetry." One can hardly imagine two more specialized fields for showing the acculturated dimensions of the senses: Our children are educated to learn this pattern of sense perception and to experience the world through this bodily structuring, and our poets draw on what they believe to be universal and fundamental ways of sensing the world. And yet, to draw on a prominent Western metaphor, there are other ways to *see* the world, and the five senses are not the only way.

2. David Chidester, *Word and Light: Seeing, Hearing, and Religious Discourse* (Urbana: University of Illinois Press, 1992), 1. The well-known aphorism by Paul Ricoeur is from the conclusion to his *Symbolism of Evil*, trans. Emerson Buchanan (Boston: Beacon Press, 1967).

3. William Paden, *Religious Worlds: The Comparative Study of Religion*, 2d ed. (Boston: Beacon, 1994), 51.

4. Ibid., 52.

5. Edwin Diller Starbuck, "The Intimate Senses as Sources of Wisdom," *Journal of Religion* 1.2 (1921): 145. Following the psychological theory of his day, Starbuck discusses ten senses that he believes can stand as a basis for understanding religious experience in a quasi-empiricist way.

6. My aim here is not to deny or affirm a transcendental experience beyond the bodily senses, but I do wish to broaden the reigning religious studies definition of experience as being only that which is transcendental. Note, for instance, Ninian Smart's descriptions of experience in his widely used textbook *Worldviews: Crosscultural Explorations of Human Beliefs*, 3d ed. (Upper Saddle River, NJ: Prentice Hall, 2000), 55–70. "Experience" is almost equivocal to "feelings" (i.e., emotional states, not sensual feelings), and there is barely a hint that this might have anything to do with a real sensuous body. Similarly, Robert Sharf's overview of "experience" also suggests its common understanding as residing in the subjective minds of the practitioners ("Experience," in *Critical Terms for Religious Studies*, ed. Mark C. Taylor [Chicago: University of Chicago Press, 1998], 94–116). Timothy Fitzgerald problematizes the vagueness of the term, though he too sidesteps the issue of sensual experience (*Guide to the Study of Religion*, eds. Willi Braun and Russell T. McCutcheon [London: Cassell, 2000], 125–39). Wayne Proudfoot challenges William James's analogy between religious experience and sense perception, confounding the way beliefs and experiences act together (*Religious Experience* [Berkeley: University of California Press, 1985], 155–89).

7. Bhatt discusses Kumarila's understanding that there are six sense organs: the five commonly conceived in the modern world, plus *manas* (typically translated as "mind," but the Sanskrit is somewhat more nuanced). See Govardhan P. Bhatt, *The Basic Ways of Knowing: An In-Depth Study of Kumarila's Contribution to Indian Epistemology*, 2d ed. (Delhi: Motilal Banarsidass, 1989), esp. 162ff.

   Geaney discusses the ways in which ancient Chinese philosophers often kept to "five senses," though they differed on what exactly those five were, and shows how in some cases the "heart-mind" is understood as a sense organ. See Jane Geaney, *On the Epistemology of the Senses in Early Chinese Thought* (Honolulu : University of Hawaii Press, 2002).

8. Kathryn Linn Geurts, *Culture and the Senses: Bodily Ways of Knowing in an African Community* (Berkeley: University of California Press, 2002), and Robert R. Desjarlais, *Sensory Biographies: Lives and Deaths Among Nepal's Yolmo Buddhists* (Berkeley: University of California Press, 2003). See also the new series from Berg Publishers, *Sensory Formations*.

9. See Classen, *The Color of Angels*.

10. See, among other places, cognitive scientist Donald D. Hoffman's *Visual Intelligence: How We Create What We See* (New York: W.W. Norton, 1998). Hoffman notes, "To understand visual intelligence is to understand, in large part, who we are," and "Vision is not merely a matter of passive perception, it is an intelligent process of active construction" (xii).
11. See "The Background: Ancient Theories of Vision," in David C. Lindberg, *Theories of Vision from al-Kindi to Kepler* (Chicago: University of Chicago Press, 1976), 1–17.
12. Colin Renfrew, *Figuring It Out: What Are We? Where Do We Come From? The Parallel Visions of Artists and Archaeologists* (London: Thames & Hudson, 2003), 7.
13. Derek Attridge, "Innovation, Literature, Ethics: Relating to the Other," *PMLA* 114.1 (1999): 23.
14. Franz Kafka, *Parables and Paradoxes* (New York: Schocken Books, 1961), 93.
15. Ronald L. Grimes, *Deeply into the Bone: Re-Inventing Rites of Passage, Life Passages* (Berkeley: University of California Press, 2000), 3.
16. Jacques Derrida, "Psyche: Inventions of the Other," trans. Catherine Porter, in *Reading De Man Reading*, eds. Lindsay Waters and Wlad Godzich (Minneapolis: University of Minnesota Press, 1988), 46.
17. *American Heritage Dictionary*, 3d ed. (Boston: Houghton Mifflin, 1992); emphasis added.
18. This is one of the key ideas Theodor Adorno took from Benjamin, and it stands at the heart of Adorno's "negative dialectics" (*Negative Dialectics*, trans. E. B. Ashton [New York, Seabury Press, 1973).
19. This is admittedly a mistranslation of the German *Kunstwerk*, a "mistake" that I will account for in Chapter 3.

Chapter 1

1. Susan Buck-Morss briefly relates the photomontage work of John Heartfield to Benjamin's ideas of "natural history" in *The Dialectics of Seeing*, 60f.
2. Maya Deren, "Cinematography: The Creative Uses of Reality," in *The Avant-Garde Film*, ed. P. Adams Sitney. (New York: Anthology Film Archives, 1987), 69.
3. Maud Lavin, *Cut with the Kitchen Knife: The Weimar Photomontages of Hannah Höch* (New Haven, CT: Yale University Press, 1993), 167.
4. Jonathan Z. Smith, *Imagining Religion* (Chicago: University of Chicago Press, 1982), 21.
5. In the introduction to Kimberley C. Patton and Benjamin C. Ray, eds., *A Magic Still Dwells* (Berkeley: University of California Press, 2000), 3–4.
6. Wendy Doniger, *The Implied Spider* (New York: Columbia University Press, 1998), 77.
7. Gold, *Aesthetics and Analysis in Writing on Religion*, 1.
8. Michel Serres, *Angels: A Modern Myth*, trans. Francis Cowper (Paris, New York: Flammarion, 1995), 71.
9. Many of the ideas in the following section stem from issues raised in Susan Buck-Morss, "Aesthetics and Anaesthetics: Walter Benjamin's Artwork Essay Reconsidered," *New Formations*, 20 (1993), 123–43; Terry Eagleton, *The Ideology of the Aesthetic* (Oxford: Basil Blackwell, 1990); and several works by Richard Shusterman, including "The End of Aesthetic Experience," *Journal of Aesthetics and Art Criticism*, 55 (1999): 29–41, "Somaesthetics: A Disciplinary Proposal," *The Journal of Aesthetics and Art Criticism*, 57.3 (Summer 1999): 299–313, and *Performing Live* (Ithaca, NY: Cornell University Press, 2001).
10. The first instance of the use of "aesthetics" in the modern world is found in the penultimate paragraph of Baumgarten's *Reflections on Poetry*, trans. Karl Aschenbrenner and William B. Holther (Berkeley: University of California Press, 1954), 78.
11. Eagleton, *The Ideology of the Aesthetic*, 13. The initial development of the field of aesthetics, Eagleton further states in an excellent phrase, "is thus the first stirrings of a primitive materialism—of the body's long inarticulate rebellion against the tyranny of the theoretical" (ibid.)
12. Ibid.
13. Buck-Morss, "Aesthetics and Anaesthetics," 125.
14. Eagleton, *Ideology of the Aesthetic*, 15, 8.
15. The prominent work here is of course Mary Douglas's *Purity and Danger* (London: Routledge and Kegan Paul, 1966).

16. For more on the cultural relativities of the pure and impure and their relation to the inside-outside dichotomy, see James Aho's intriguing study, *The Orifice as Sacrificial Site* (Hawthorne, NY: Aldine de Gruyter, 2002).

17. Buck-Morss, "Aesthetics and Anesthetics," 127. References to Kant are from *Critique of Judgement*, trans. Werner S. Pluhar (Indianapolis, IN: Hackett, 1987), 133–34.

18. Cf. Edward Farley's *Faith and Beauty*, the first phrase of which reads "This book is about beauty . . . " (1); or simply the title and subtitle of Alejandro García-Rivera's *The Community of the Beautiful*. On the revival of "beauty" in contemporary religious aesthetics, see Grace M. Jantzen, "Beauty for Ashes: Notes on the Displacement of Beauty," *Literature and Theology*, 16.4 (December 2002): 427–49.

19. Noël Carroll, *The Philosophy of Art* (London: Routledge, 1999), 156.

20. Liliane Weissberg, "In Plain Sight," in *Visual Culture and the Holocaust*, ed. Barbie Zelizer. (New Brunswick, NJ: Rutgers University Press, 2001), 13–27.

21. Ian Hunter, "Aesthetics and Cultural Studies," in *Cultural Studies*, eds. Lawrence Grossberg, Cary Nelson, and Paula A. Treichler. (New York: Routledge, 1992), 347. Significantly, Hunter goes on to argue for the relation of aesthetics and ethics: "aesthetics is neither a knowledge, a morality, nor a politics. It is, rather, an ethic: an autonomous set of techniques and practices by which individuals continuously problematize their experience and conduct themselves as the subjects of an aesthetic experience" (358).

22. Carroll, *The Philosophy of Art*, 159.

23. See, among other places, the intriguing ideas about Benjamin and visual culture in James Elkins, "Preface to the book *A Skeptical Introduction to Visual Culture*," *Journal of Visual Culture* 1.1 (April, 2002): 93–99; the constant references to Benjamin in *The Visual Culture Reader*, ed. Nicholas Mirzoeff, 2d ed. (New York: Routledge, 2002); and Christopher Pinney, "Photographic Portraiture in Central India in the 1980s and 1990s," in *The Material Culture Reader* ed. Victor Buchli, (Oxford: Berg Publishers, 2002).

24. Hegel, *Introductory Lectures on Aesthetics*, trans. Bernard Bosanquet (London: Penguin, 1993), 43. Anthony Synnot comments on Hegel's sensorium: "The evolution of humanity, for Hegel, was the shift in the primacy of the sensorium from mouth to eye, reflecting the importance of mind over body again" (*The Body Social* [London and New York: Routledge, 1993], 142).

25. Hélène Cixous (with Catherine Clément), *The Newly Born Woman*, trans. Betsy Wing (Minneapolis: University of Minnesota Press, 1986), 145.

26. Ibid.

27. Nicholas Davey, "The Hermeneutics of Seeing," in *Interpreting Visual Culture*, eds. Ian Heywood and Barry Sandywell, (London: Routledge, 1999), 8. Davey's use of the word "confusion" here is linked to Baumgarten's working out of philosophical categories inherited from Descartes (and others) via Leibniz concerning "clear," "distinct," and "confused" knowledges. It is beyond the interests of this book to extrapolate on this, but in a nutshell, Baumgarten's "aesthetics" was, among other things, an attempt to make the confused realm of sense perception more distinct. By creating categories for the judgment of art, the rational observer can delve into ever deeper realms of life.

28. See Levinas, *Totality and Infinity*, trans. Alphonso Lingis (Pittsburgh: Duquesne University Press, 1969). Levinas notes the importance of sensibility here, but he quickly moves beyond it to show the import of "eros," which I believe could be shown to be a particular crossing of the aesthetic (as sense perception) and the ethical. See in particular Section IV, "Beyond the Face," in *Totality and Infinity*, 254–85.

29. See Luce Irigaray's rejoinder to Levinas in "The Fecundity of the Caress," in *An Ethics of Sexual Difference*, trans. Carolyn Burke and Gillian C. Gill (Ithaca, NY: Cornell University Press, 1993), 185–217.

30. See, for example, Margaret Livingstone, *Vision and Art* (New York: Harry Abrams, 2002); Semir Zeki, *Inner Vision* (New York: Oxford University Press, 1999); and Robert Solso, *Cognition and the Visual Arts* (Cambridge, MA: MIT Press, 1996).

31. On this relation, see George Perrigo Conger, *Theories of Macrocosms and Microcosms in the History of Philosophy* (New York: Russell & Russell, 1967).

32. Classen, *The Color of Angels*, 9. See also the articles in David Howes, ed. *Varieties of Sensual Experience*, edited by David Howes . The works of Classen and Howes are important, I believe, as a necessary corrective to the present-day emphasis on visuality and the image.

Nonetheless, at some level what must be accounted for is the neurophysiological fact that over half of all neurons dealing with sense reception in the human body are connected to the visual sense. There is thus something deep-seated in our biological being that makes sight a prominent (if not the prominent) sense.

33. Catherine Keller's recent *Face of the Deep: A Theology of Becoming* (London: Routledge, 2003) examines the patriarchal roots of a creation "out of nothing." Keller instead posits a *creatio ex profundis* in which the heterogeneity that stands at the heart of all creation has a place to flourish. Keller's book was released too late to enable more engagement with it in my work here, but I believe there may be some strong relations made.

34. For more on these references see Richard Wolin, *Walter Benjamin: An Aesthetic of Redemption* (Berkeley: University of California Press, 1994), 29–77; John McCole, *Walter Benjamin and the Antinomies of Tradition* (Ithaca, NY: Cornell University Press, 1993), 35–70; Vincent Pecora, "Benjamin, Kracauer and Redemptive History," *Genre* 35 (2002): 66–68; and James McBride, "Marooned in the Realm of the Profane: Walter Benjamin's Synthesis of Kabbalah and Communism," *Journal of the American Academy of Religion* 57.2 (Summer, 1987): 241–66.

35. Cf. Marc-Alain Ouaknin, *The Mysteries of the Kabbalah*, trans. Josephine Bacon (New York: Abbeville, 2000), 195.

36. Shimon Shokek, *Kabbalah and the Art of Being* (London: Routledge, 2001), 43.

37. Ouaknin, *Mysteries*, 196.

38. From the *Zohar*, I, 134a. Quoted in Sanford L. Drob, *Symbols of the Kabbalah* (Northvale, NJ: Jason Aronson, 2000), 167–68.

39. Shokek, *Kabbalah*, 44.

40. Ouaknin, *Mysteries*, 200.

41. Ibid., 205.

42. Tomoko Masuzawa, *In Search of Dreamtime*, 15.

43. Hélène Cixous, "Castration or Decapitation?" in ed. Russell Ferguson et al., trans. Annette Kuhn, *Out There: Marginalization and Contemporary Culture*, (New York: New Museum of Contemporary Art, 1990), 354.

44. Ouaknin, *Mysteries*, 221.

45. Lisa Saltzman, *Anselm Kiefer and Art After Auschwitz* (Cambridge: Cambridge University Press, 1999), 36.

46. In a similar vein, Sanford L. Drob relates Lurianic Kabbalah to the notions of deconstruction of Jacques Derrida: "Symbolized in the Breaking of the Vessels, this deconstruction provides us with a caution against being too satisfied with any of the interpretations of constructions we place upon the Kabbalah specifically, or upon the world in general. Indeed it is only by constructing, deconstructing, and then reconstructing our perspectives upon God, the world, and ourselves that we can hope to achieve anything near the breadth of view necessary for a valuable interpretation" (*Symbols of the Kabbalah*, 37).

Chapter 2

1. Harold Bloom, *The Anxiety of Influence* (London: Oxford University Press, 1973), 94–95.

2. See Clifford Geertz "Thick Description: Toward an Interpretive Theory of Culture," *The Interpretation of Cultures* (New York: Basic Books, 1973), 5–10.

3. Sayre Greenfield, *The Ends of Allegory* (Newark: University of Delaware Press, 1988), 18.

4. Angus Fletcher, *Allegory* (Ithaca:, NY: Cornell University Press, 1964), 2–3.

5. Scholem claimed of the *lament-play* that "Marxist categories do not figure in this work" (*Walter Benjamin* [Philadelphia: Jewish Publication Society of America, 1981], 123).

6. Rainer Nägele, *Theater, Theory, Speculation* (Baltimore: Johns Hopkins University Press, 1991), 38.

7. Howard Caygill, "Benjamin, Heidegger and Tradition," in *Walter Benjamin's Philosophy: Destruction and Experience*, eds., Andrew Benjamin and Peter Osborne (New York: Routledge, 1994), 19.

8. Ibid., 20.

9. Benjamin considered *Hamlet* a *Trauerspiel* because Hamlet "wants to die by some accident, and as the fateful stage properties gather around him, as around their lord and master, the drama of fate flares up in the conclusion of this *Trauerspiel*, as something that is contained, but of course overcome, in it" (*OGTD*, 137).

10. Taken from his correspondence with Gershom Scholem in 1918. *The Correspondence of Walter Benjamin, 1920–1940.* eds. Gershom Scholem and Theodor W. Adorno, trans. Manfred R. Jacobson and Evelyn M. Jacobson (Chicago: University of Chicago Press, 1994), 120.

11. Claus Westermann, *Lamentations: Issues and Interpretation* (Minneapolis: Augsburg Fortress, 1994), 81.

12. In a personal letter to the author, fall 1998. These ideas are taken up in Linafelt's *Surviving Lamentations: Catastrophe, Lament, and Protest in the Afterlife of a Biblical Book* (Chicago: University of Chicago Press, 2000). See also Carleen Mandolfo's idea of a lament as a "grievance psalm" in *God in the Dock* (London: Sheffield Academic Press, 2001), 1.

13. This change in language was preserved by Gershom Scholem and is related by Susan Buck-Morss in *The Dialectics of Seeing,* 14.

14. For further views on the religious-political interrelations of revolutionary activity, see "From Messianism to Materialism," in Richard Wolin's *Walter Benjamin,* 107–37.

15. From "The Role of Language in *Trauerspiel* and Tragedy" (1916). In "*Trauerspiel* and Tragedy," another sketch from 1916 unpublished in his lifetime, Benjamin concludes "just as tragedy marks the transition from historical to dramatic time, the mourning play represents the transition from dramatic time to musical time" (*SW I,* 57).

16. Benjamin's first dissertation, "Der Begriff der Kunstkritik in der deutschen Romantik" ("The Concept of Art Criticism in German Romanticism") reasserts the critical work of the early Romantics, particularly Novalis (1772–1801) and Friedrich Schlegel (1772–1829) as a potent basis from which to reconstruct a modern criticism. He was interested in the early romantics—over and against the later romantics, who Benjamin feels perverted the original intentions of romanticism—because of their emphasis on mystical insight and intuition as a response to enlightenment rationality. Novalis, among others, insisted on the role of art as still containing emanations of a pure, original language (*Ursprache*). Such notions fit well with Benjamin's interests in Jewish mysticism. The later romantics, however, messed it all up as they insisted on the singular artistic genius who would stand up in a fallen world and pretend to reclaim the primal word, and often turned "nature" into a mythical deity worthy of worship. While retaining the mystical possibilities of romanticism, the latter excesses of Romanticism were anathema to Benjamin.

17. Philip Rollinson notes how the ancient writers Demetrius, Philo, and Plutarch all use the term "allegory" and "symbol/ic" interchangeably. See *Classical Theories of Allegory and Christian Allegory* (Pittsburgh: Duquesne University Press, 1981), 5–9. This interchangeability essentially continued until the Romantics began to make a controversy out of the difference between the two terms. Goethe, it is generally acknowledged, made the first real split between the terms, consigning allegory as the "bad" form of poetry and symbol as the "good" form of poetry (cf., among other places, Fletcher, *Allegory,* 13–19.)

18. Martin Heidegger, "The Origin of the Work of Art," trans. Albert Hofstader, in *Basic Writings,* ed. David Farrell Krell (New York: HarperCollins, 1993), 145–46.

19. Rainer Rochlitz, *The Disenchantment of Art* (New York: Guilford Press, 1996), 103.

20. Chidester, *Word and Light,* 1.

21. Mary LeCron Foster, "Symbolism: The Foundation of Culture," in *Companion Encyclopedia of Anthropology,* ed. Tim Ingold (London: Routledge, 1994), 366.

22. On a history of allegory and allegorical interpretation I refer to the following: Fletcher's new-critical perspective in *Allegory;* Philip Rollinson's historical study, *Classical Theories of Allegory and Christian Culture;* Theresa M. Kelley's English literature perspective, *Reinventing Allegory* (Cambridge: Cambridge University Press, 1997); and Deborah Madsen's "postmodernist" version, *Rereading Allegory* (New York: St. Martin's Press, 1994).

23. Ferdinand Saussure, *Course in General Linguistics,* eds. Charles Bally and Albert Sechehaye, trans. Wade Baskin (New York: Philosophical Library, 1959), 67.

24. Ibid., 69.

25. Ibid., 68.

26. Julia Kristeva, "From Symbol to Sign," trans. Seán Hand, in *The Kristeva Reader,* ed. Toril Moi (New York: Columbia University Press, 1986), 63–64. This essay was originally written as part of her thesis in linguistics, which in 1970 became her first published book in French under the title, *Le Texte du Roman.*

27. Ibid., 64, 67.

28. Ibid., 66. Inner quote of "an old man . . . " from a fourteenth-century French text.
29. Joel Fineman, "The Structure of Allegorical Desire," *October* 12 (Spring 1980): 50.
30. Kristeva, "Symbol," 70, 72.
31. Ibid., 70–71.
32. Saussure, *Course*, 123.
33. Roman Jakobson, "Closing Statement: Linguistics and Poetics," in *Style in Language*, ed. Thomas A. Sebeok, 358. Quoted in Terence Hawkes, *Structuralism and Semiotics* (Berkeley: University of California Press, 1977), 77.
34. "Closing Statement," 370. Quoted in Hawkes, *Structuralism*, 79.
35. "Closing Statement," 377. Quoted in Hawkes, *Structuralism*, 81.
36. Roman Jakobson and Morris Halle, *Fundamentals of Language* (The Hague: Mouton, 1971 [1956]), 92. The tropes of metaphor and metonymy are taken up in film studies, among other places, in Part IV of Christian Metz's *The Imaginary Signifier* (Bloomington: Indiana University Press, 1982).
37. Kaja Silverman, *The Subject of Semiotics* (Oxford: Oxford University Press, 1983), 89.
38. Jakobson and Halle, *Fundamentals of Language*, 92.
39. Buck-Morss, *The Dialectics of Seeing*, 173.
40. Jean Baudrillard, *The Transparency of Evil: Essays on Extreme Phenomena*, trans. James Benedict (London and New York: Verso, 1993), 7–8.
41. As far as I have seen, only Christine Buci-Glucksmann has thought through the gender of Benjamin's (and Baudelaire's) allegory, though several contemporary feminist writers have attempted to show other dimensions of Benjamin's writing in relation to feminism. Cf. Christine Buci-Lucksmann, *Baroque Reason* (London and Thousand Oaks, CA.: Sage, 1994); Sigrid Weigel, *Body- and Image-Space* (London: Routledge, 1996); and Janet Wolff, "The Feminine in Modern Art," *Theory, Culture, Society* 17.6 (2000).
42. Drucilla Cornell, *Beyond Accommodation* (Lanham, MD: Rowman & Littlefield, 1999), 101.
43. Lesley Northrup, *Ritualizing Women*, (Cleveland: Pilgrim Press, 1997), 54.
44. Ibid., 61.
45. Cornell, *Beyond Accommodation*, 62. While Cornell litters her texts with the word "allegory," she, somewhat frustratingly, never does anything to explain what she means by it.
46. Ibid., 167. She is here evaluating Domna C. Stanton's article "Difference on Trial: A Critique of the Maternal Metaphor in Cixous, Irigaray, and Kristeva," in *The Poetics of Gender*, ed. Nancy K. Miller, (New York: Columbia University Press, 1986).
47. Luce Irigaray, *This Sex Which Is Not One* (Ithaca, NY: Cornell University Press, 1985), 213.
48. Cornell, *Beyond Accommodation*, 169.
49. Ibid., 178.
50. Cf. Sallie McFague, *Models of God* (Philadelphia: Fortress, 1987) and *Metaphorical Theology* (Philadelphia: Fortress, 1985).
51. Rebecca Chopp, *The Power to Speak*, (New York: Crossroad, 1989), 115.
52. Regina Schwartz, *The Curse of Cain* (Chicago: University of Chicago Press, 1997), 176.
53. Kristeva, "Symbol," in *The Kristeva Reader*, 72.
54. Maurice Blanchot, *The Work of Fire*, trans. Charlotte Mandell (Stanford: Stanford University Press, 1995), 327
55. Eagleton, *Ideology of the Aesthetic*, 335.
56. Rochlitz, *The Disenchantment of Art*, 8.
57. Gay Clifford, *The Transformations of Allegory* (London: Routledge and Kegan Paul, 1974), 71. For more on Benjamin and the relation of word and image, see Azade Seyhan, "Visual Citations: Walter Benjamin's Dialectic of Text and Image," in *Languages of Visuality*, ed. Beate Allert (Detroit: Wayne State University Press, 1996), 229–41.
58. Michel Foucault, *The Order of Things*, trans. Alan Sheridan (New York: Random House, 1970), 9. See also Foucault, *This Is Not a Pipe*, trans. James Harkness (Berkeley: University of California Press, 1982).
59. John Welchman, in John Welchman and Judi Freeman, *Dada and Surrealist Word-Image* (Los Angeles: Los Angeles County Museum of Art [Cambridge, MA: MIT Press, 1989], 69.
60. Clement Greenberg, "Modernist Painting," in *The Collected Essays and Criticism*, vol. 4 (Chicago: University of Chicago Press, 1993), 86. In contrast to Greenberg's purity of media, the force of intermediality is similar to that of "intertextuality" brought forth by Mikhail Bakhtin and taken up by Julia Kristeva, who suggests that intertextuality is "the

passage from one sign system to another" that involves the "destruction of the old position and the formation of a new one" (Kristeva, *Revolution in Poetic Language*, trans. Léon Roudiez [New York: Columbia University Press, 1984], 59).

61. Because of its mutating force, allegory became a prime suspect for creative activity in the postmodern arts. Although the quest for purity and the fetishization of the singular work of art in the modern age banished allegory, it was only a banishment, as Craig Owens argues, "in theory," for an allegorical way of seeing how modernism supplies us with many examples of allegory in practice. Owens offers a two-part essay entitled "The Allegorical Impulse: Toward a Theory of Postmodernism" (*Beyond Recognition* [Berkeley: University of California Press, 1992]) in which he retraces, in Benjaminian fashion, the roots of the postmodern within the modern. Along the way he uncovers allegorical works of art throughout the modern and into the postmodern, stopping to comment on the allegorical works of Duchamp, Laurie Anderson, Robert Smithson, and Sherrie Levine, among others.

62. Quoted in Susan A. Handelman, *Fragments of Redemption* (Bloomington: Indiana University Press, 1991), 137.

63. Quoted in Gershom Scholem, *Origins of the Kabbalah*, ed. R.J. Zwi Werblowsky, trans. Allan Arkush (New York: The Jewish Publication Society Princeton, NJ: Princeton University Press, 1987), 25–26.

64. Johanna Drucker, *The Alphabetic Labyrinth* (New York: Thames & Hudson, 1995), 141. See the section on "The Kabbalah," 129–58. See also Marc-Alain Ouaknin, *Mysteries of the Kabbalah*.

65. James McBride, "Marooned in the Realm of the Profane," 247.

66. The Arabic phrase, *ahl al-kitab*, more literally means "people of an earlier revelation" (see especially Sura 3) and refers to Jews, Christians, and Zoroastrians, particularly those monotheistic traditions that place some emphasis on a particular sacred text.

67. Walter Ong, *Orality and Literacy* (London: Routledge, 1982), 132. Certainly, Christian fundamentalism would have been impossible without the mass-produced, printed bible, readily accessible to believers.

68. Ibid., 122.

69. In recent years, popular books such as Leonard Shlain's *The Alphabet Versus the Goddess: The Conflict Between the Word and the Image* (New York: Viking, 1998) and Mitchell Stephens's *The Rise of the Image, The Fall of the Word* (New York: Oxford University Press, 1998) have worked with idea that the image and word are in battle. In distinction, there are a few books that explore the nature of the alphabet, with many references to its visuality. See Drucker's *The Alphabetic Labyrinth*; John Man's *Alpha Beta: How 26 Letters Shaped the Western World* (New York: John Wiley, 2000); and Marc-Alain Ouaknin's *Mysteries of the Alphabet*.

70. Howard Caygill, *Walter Benjamin: The Colour of Experience* (London: Routledge, 1998), 59.

71. Kristeva, *Revolution*, 70.

72. Beatrice Hanssen's *Walter Benjamin's Other History* (Berkeley: University of California Press, 1998) examines the shifting way "natural history" is used throughout the *Trauerspiel* book. There are, first of all, three different ways of spelling it: *natürliche Geschichte*, *Naturgeschichte*, and sometimes *Natur-Geschichte*. The first was used primarily in the prologue and had to do with the origins of the artwork, while the last two were used in the main body. My use of "natural history" corresponds primarily to the last two uses, and for my purposes, primarily entail, the secularization and spatialization of history.

73. Benjamin's well-known text "The Author as Producer" is conjured here, and the idea of the "producer" displays his Marxist outlook. In terms of literary production, the idea of an "editor" I feel comes close to what he is working toward.

74. Mircea Eliade, *The Sacred and the Profane*, trans. Willard R. Trask (San Diego, CA: Harcourt, Brace, and Co., 1959), 96.

75. Ibid., 97–98.

76. Relatedly, and in connection with earlier concerns, Lesley Northrup has recast Eliade's verticality in feminist "horizontal" terms. See especially the chapter "Ritualizing Space and Time" in *Ritualizing Women*.

77. Hanssen, *Walter Benjamin's Other History*, 76.

78. See particularly Richard Wolin's reading of it in *Walter Benjamin: An Aesthetic of Redemption*. Also, Susan Handelman's *Fragments of Redemption* tends toward the ultimate redemption paradigm.
79. Hanssen, *Walter Benjamin's Other History*, 102.
80. Rochlitz, *The Disenchantment of Art*, 111.
81. Buck-Morss, *The Dialectics of Seeing*, 175.
82. Gershom Sholem, *On Jews and Judaism in Crisis* (New York: Schocken Books, 1976), 193.
83. Wolin, *Walter Benjamin*, 73.
84. Scholem, *Walter Benjamin*, 209.
85. Ibid.
86. For more on this, see Roland Boer, "The Bowels of History, or The Perpetuation of Biblical Myth in Walter Benjamin," *Journal of Narrative Theory* 32.3 (2002): 370–89.
87. For surveys of the interpretation of the Song of Songs, see Ann Matter, *The Voice of My Beloved* (Philadelphia: University of Pennsylvania Press, 1990) and Roland Murphy, *The Song of Songs* (Minneapolis: Augsbury Fortress, 1990).
88. Susan A. Handelman, *The Slayers of Moses* (Albany: State University of New York Press, 1982), 75. In her later work *Fragments of Redemption*, Handelman does in fact make a relation to Benjamin's ideas of fragments, and the use of memory is quite similar to rabbinic midrash (cf. 149–53).
89. Kyle Keefer and Tod Linafelt, "The End of Desire: Theologies of Eros in the Song of Songs and *Breaking the Waves*," in *Imag(in)ing Otherness: Filmic Visions of Living Together*, eds. S. Brent Plate and David Jasper (Atlanta: Scholars Press, 1999), 55. Keefer and Linafelt utilize texts by Denys Turner (*Eros and Allegory: Medieval Exegesis of the Song of Songs* [Kalamazoo, MI: Cistercian Publications, 1995]) and Howard Eilberg-Schwartz (*God's Phallus and Other Problems for Men and Monotheism* [Boston: Beacon Press, 1994]).
90. A Benjaminian understanding of allegory would complement other religious literary approaches such as Jill Robbins rereadings in *Prodigal Son/Elder Brother* (Chicago: University of Chicago Press, 1991). In ways amenable to Benjamin's project, Robbins has taken the importance of "otherness" and a midrashic mode of commentary into the relations between Christianity and Judaism, arguing against figural readings in which the Christian reading essentially trumps Jewish mythologizing.
91. See Weigel "The 'Other' in Allegory," in *Body- and Image-Space*, 95–105.
92. Hanssen, *Walter Benjamin's Other History*, 162.
93. Timothy Beal makes the case that this interpretive work amounts to a "colonization" of the Bible, that Christian interpreters have colonized the Jewish elements of the scriptures, rewriting them as their own. Allegory, in Benjamin's terms, proceeds, as will be seen, without a sense of possession (*The Book of Hiding* [New York: Routledge, 1997]).
94. Fineman, "The Structure of Allegorical Desire," 59–60. For an interesting approach to early Christian history and an application of Lacan's and Jakobson's theories of metaphor and metonymy, see Fineman's "Gnosis and the Piety of Metaphor: The Gospel of Truth," in *The Rediscovery of Gnosticism*, volume 1, ed. Bentley Layton (Leiden: E.J. Brill, 1990), 289–318.
95. I am indebted to Michael Taussig's work on issues of transgression and desecration in relation to Benjamin, seen in both his *Mimesis and Alterity: A Particular History of the Senses* (New York: Routledge, 1993) and *Defacement: Public Secrecy and the Labor of the Negative* (Stanford: Stanford University Press, 1999).
96. Winfried Menninghaus, "Walter Benjamin's Theory of Myth," in *On Walter Benjamin*, ed. Gary Smith. (Cambridge, MA: MIT Press. 1988), 299.
97. Joseph Mali, "The Reconciliation of Myth: Benjamin's Homage to Bachofen," *Journal of the History of Ideas* 60.1 (1999): 174.

Chapter 3

1. *Gesammelte Schriften* I (Frankfurt: Suhrkamp Verlag, 1974), 1165.
2. Quoted in Dalia Judovitz, *Unpacking Duchamp* (Berkeley: University of California Press, 1995), 124. I am indebted to Judovitz's book for more of the "full story" on Duchamp's fountain; see 124–35.
3. Ibid., 128.

4. Art historian Matthew Biro explicitly relates the significance of Duchamp's readymades to Benjamin, and especially the destruction of the aura: "As a form, the readymade removed the artist's touch from the work of art, in a sense denying both the transformative creative power of the artist as well as art's essentially human and subjective origins. Finally, by being mass-produced, the readymade denied art's originality. As such, Duchamp's readymades may be understood as the 'first' works of art that deliberately attempt to eschew 'aura'" (Matthew Biro, *Anselm Kiefer and the Philosophy of Martin Heidegger* [Cambridge: Cambridge University Press, 1998], 242). Biro further notes how Anselm Kiefer was himself intrigued by Duchamp's work of art and quotes Kiefer as follows: "What fascinates me about Duchamp is the idea of tearing down the wall between the art object and reality" (quoted in Biro, *Anselm Kiefer*, 304 n. 111).

5. Clive Bell, *Art* (London: Chatto & Windus, 1914), 7.

6. Benjamin himself played with the difference between *arbeit* and *werk* in reference to what in English has become known as the *Arcades Project*. In German this project was referred to by the editors of Benjamin's collected works as "Passagen-Werk," while Benjamin made clear in notes on the project that he thought of it as "Passagen-arbeit." See Richard Wolin, *Walter Benjamin*, xl.

7. Betsy Flèche, "The Art of Survival: The Translation of Walter Benjamin," *SubStance* 28.2 (1999): 105.

8. "The Work of Art" is included in such diverse collections as *Film Theory and Criticism*. 4th ed., eds. Gerald Mast, Marshall Cohen, and Leo Braudy (New York: Oxford University Press, 1992); *Art in Theory, 1900–1990*, eds. Charles Harrison and Paul Wood (Oxford, U.K. and Cambridge, Ma.: Basil Blackwell, 1992); and *Aesthetics: Classic Readings from the Western Tradition*, 2nd ed., ed. Dabney Townsend (Belmont, CA: Wadsworth, 2001). In addition, it is referred to innumerable times throughout contemporary film, literary, and visual studies.

9. Editors' notes in *SW III*, 122.

10. Editors' notes in *SW IV*, 270.

11. Rudolf Otto, *The Idea of the Holy*, trans. John Harvey (London: Oxford University Press, 1958), 31.

12. Otto, *The Idea of the Holy*, 31.

13. Geertz, "Religion as a Cultural System," in *The Interpretation of Cultures*, 90; emphasis added.

14. Ibid., 109, 112.

15. Ouaknin, *Mysteries of the Kabbalah*, 198.

16. Samuel Weber, *Mass Mediauras* (Sydney: Power Publications, 1996), 85.

17. Robert S. Nelson suggests how art history and its lectures were transformed by the technological reproduction of slides, bringing them into the space of the lecture: "With photography and especially with the slide lecture's ability to fuse words and images, the artwork is present in the discursive space—hence the use of deictics—and it requires less verbal evocation or description. As Wölfflin put it after rhetorical fashion had changed, words no longer overwhelmed art" ("The Slide Lecture, or the Work of Art History in the Age of Mechanical Reproduction," *Critical Inquiry* 26.3 (Spring 2000): 432.

18. Joel Snyder, "Benjamin on Reproducibility and Aura," in *Benjamin*, ed. Gary C. Smith (Chicago: University of Chicago Press, 1989), 169.

19. Greenberg, "Modernist Painting" *Collected Essays, Vol. 4* (Chicago, IL: University of Chicago Press, 1993), 86.

20. Ibid., 930.

21. Rochlitz, *The Disenchantment of Art*, 158.

22. Ibid., 8.

23. *Hegel on the Arts*, 37–8.

24. For more on the relation of religion and the museum, see Carol Duncan, *Civilizing Rituals: Inside Public Art Museums* (London: Routledge, 1995) and Crispin Paine, *Godly Things: Museums, Objects, and Religion* (London: Leicester University Press, 2000). On the way museums as "collections" operate in the construction of knowledge, see Eilean Hooper-Greenhill, *Museums and the Shaping of Knowledge* (London: Routledge, 1992) and Didier Maleuvre, *Museum Memories: History, Technology, Art* (Stanford: Stanford University Press, 1999).

25. Quoted in Douglas Crimp and Louis Lawler, *On the Museum's Ruins* (Cambridge, MA: MIT Press, 1993), 294.
26. "Valéry Proust Museum," quoted in Crimp and Lawler, *On the Museum's Ruins*, 44.
27. Crimp and Lawler, *On the Museum's Ruins*, 295.
28. Ibid., 302.
29. Betsy Flèche, "The Art of Survival: The Translation of Walter Benjamin," *SubStance* 28.2 (1999): 99.
30. Richard Cohen, *Jewish Icons* (Berkeley: University of California Press, 1998), 201.
31. Cohen, *Jewish Icons*, 202–3.
32. Cf. Margaret Miles on Christian icons in the sixth century: "An increment of viewer engagement, and thus of potential for worship of the icon itself, was inaugurated by the frontal presentation of holy figures. In frontal presentation, the icons' large eyes held the worshipper's gaze, encouraging devotion to the icon rather than to its prototype" ("Image," in *Critical Terms for Religious Studies*, ed. Mark C. Taylor [Chicago: University of Chicago Press, 1998], 165) and Diana L. Eck, "When Hindus stand on tiptoe and crane their necks to see, through the crowd, the image of Lord Krishna, they wish not only to 'see,' but to be seen. The gaze of the huge eyes of the image meets that of the worshipper, and that exchange of vision lies at the heart of Hindu worship" (*Darshan*, 3rd ed. [New York: Columbia University Press, 1998], 7).
33. Gershom Scholem, "Letter to Benjamin," in *Aesthetics and Politics*, ed. Ernst Bloch. (London: Verso, 1980), 123.
34. Jacques Lacan, "The Mirror Stage," in *Écrits*, trans. Alan Sheridan (New York: W. W. Norton, 1977), 1–2. The version provided here is from the 1949 version of Lacan's text.
35. Ibid, 2.
36. Ibid.
37. See especially the chapter, "The Eye and the Gaze," in Jacques Lacan, *The Four Fundamental Concepts of Psycho-Analysis*, trans. Alan Sheridan, (New York: W. Norton, 1981).
38. Maya Deren, "Notes on Ritual and Ordeal," *Film Culture* 39 (1965): 10. Deren's struggle at the end of her life to film Haitian rituals tested the limits of her abilities as an artist: "I had begun as an artist, as one who would manipulate the elements of a reality into a work of art in the image of my creative integrity; I end by recording, as humbly and accurately as I can, the logics of a reality which had forced me to recognize its integrity, and to abandon my manipulations" (*The Divine Horsemen* [New York: Chelsea House, 1970], 6).
39. See Kristeva, *Revolution in Poetic Language*, .
40. Cf. William G. Doty, *Mythography*, 2d ed. (Tuscaloosa: University of Alabama Press, 2000), 240–44; and John Shelton Lawrence and Robert Jewett's *The Myth of the American Superhero* (Grand Rapids, MI: W. B. Eerdmans, 2002).
41. Cf. many publications, including the early work of Kandinsky himself in *Concerning the Spiritual in Art*, trans. M. T. H. Sadler (New York: Dover, 1977); the work of Protestant theologian Paul Tillich, for example, *On Art and Architecture* (New York: Crossroad, 1987); several of the articles in Diane Apostolos-Cappadona, ed., *Art, Creativity, and the Sacred* (New York: Continuum, 1995); and exhibition catalogs such as *The Spiritual in Art: Abstract Painting, 1890–1985* (New York: Abbeville Press, Los Angeles: Los Angeles County Museum of Art, 1986); and *Negotiating Rapture : The Power of Art to Transform Lives*, eds. Richard Francis, Homi K. Bhabha, and Yve Alain Bois (Chicago: Museum of Contemporary Art, 1996).
42. Rochlitz, *The Disenchantment of Art*, 3.
43. Interestingly, this quotation from Freud is found in the first and third versions of the essay, but not in the second, from which I have been quoting. This quotation is from the third, "unfinished" version.
44. Snyder, "Benjamin on Reproducibility and Aura," 170.
45. David Bordwell and Kristin Thompson, *Film Art*, 6th ed. (New York: McGraw Hill, 2001), 216.
46. Douglas, *Purity and Danger*, 64.
47. Jonathan Crary takes up some of Benjamin's ideas about distraction and concentration in *Suspensions of Perception* (Cambridge, MA: MIT Press, 1999), setting Benjamin's writings on distraction alongside those of Adorno, Georg Simmel, Siegfried Kracauer, and others. Contra Benjamin in "the Work of Art," Crary argues that "attention and distraction cannot

be thought outside of a continuum in which the two ceaselessly flow into one another, as part of a social field in which the same imperatives and forces incite one and the other" (51).

48. Benjamin, *Illuminations*, trans. Harry Zohn (New York: Harcourt, Brace and World, 1968), 243.

49. Howard Eiland, "Reception in Distraction," *boundary 2* 30.1 (2003): 56, n.10.

50. There is also more in this comparison of contemplation-dissemination that we have seen before. In the midst of his dealings with allegory, Benjamin provides the example of a lament-play by Lope de Vega, *The Confused Court*. There he mentions that the "court" [*Hof*] "is subject to the law of 'dispersal' [*Zerstreuung*] and 'collectedness' [*Sammlung*]. Things are assembled according to their significance; indifference to their existence [*Dasein*] allowed them to be dispersed again" (*OGTD*, 188). First of all, *Hof* ("court") is a rough synonym in German to "aura," and that aura is here made up of another two-part process: *Zerstreuung* and *Sammlung*. (besides its translation as "farm," "hotel," or "court," *Hof* is a "halo" or a "corona" around the sun or the moon.) Further such relations are made by Samuel Weber in *Mass Mediauras*, 93.
Noting the variances of meaning surrounding the term *Zerstreuung* in Benjamin's corpus, Howard Eiland, in "Reception in Distraction," states: "The opposition now would seem to be between mere distraction and, shall we say, productive distraction—between distraction as a skewing of attention, or as abandonment to diversion, and distraction as a spur to new ways of perceiving" (60).

51. Sigmund Freud, *The Ego and the Id*, in *The Standard Edition*, vol. XIX, trans. James Strachey (London: Hogarth Press, 1961), 19.

52. Ibid., 26.

53. Ibid., n.1.

54. Susan Buck-Morss, "Aesthetics and Anaesthetics", 131.

55. Ibid., 124.

56. For more on this, see Susan Buck-Morss's *Dreamworld and Catastrophe* (Cambridge, Ma.: MIT Press, 2000).

57. On the orientalizing approaches, see the introduction to Karen Pechilis Prentiss, *The Embodiment of Bhakti* (Oxford: Oxford University Press, 1999).

58. Philip Lutgendorf, *The Life of a Text* (Berkeley: University of California Press, 1991), 56.

59. Prentiss, *Embodiment of Bhakti*, 5.

60. Nancy M. Martin, "North Indian Hindi Devotional Literature," in *The Blackwell Companion to Hinduism*, ed. Gavin Flood (Oxford: Basil Blackwell, 2003), 183.

61. Lawrence Babb, in the introduction to *Media and the Transformation of Religion in South Asia*, eds. Lawrence A. Babb and Susan S. Wadley (Philadelphia: University of Pennsylvania Press, 1995), 2, 4.

62. Contrary to Eurocentric history, the printing press was originally developed in China. The first printed book known to exist is a copy of the Diamond Sutra, dated at 868 CE. Meanwhile, the first printing press with movable type was developed in eleventh-century China. Western scholars, in their desire for origins and ontological primacy, will suggest that Gutenberg was the first to use *metal* typecasts, while the Chinese used only clay.

63. Elizabeth Eisenstein, *The Printing Revolution in Early Modern Europe* (Cambridge: Cambridge University Press, 1983), 152, 153.

64. Scholem, "Letter to Benjamin," in *Aesthetics and Politics*, 124.

65. Miriam Hansen, "Benjamin, Cinema and Experience: 'The Blue Flower' in the Land of Technology," *New German Critique* 40 (Winter 1987): 186.

66. The quotation is from Anita Guha, the actress who played Santoshi Ma, quoted in Lutgendorf, "*Jai Santoshi Maa* Revisited," in *Representing Religion in World Cinema: Filmmaking, Mythmaking, Culture Making* ed. S. Brent Plate (New York: Palgrave Macmillan, 2003), 19–42.

67. Fundamentalism, in this regard, may be seen as inherently "postmodern" in the way it inverts the relation between object (Christ) and reproduction of object (Bible), and would be of interest to Jean Baudrillard's conception of the simulacra.

68. Michael Taussig, "Transgression," in *Critical Terms for Religious Studies*, ed. Mark C. Taylor (Chicago: University of Chicago Press, 1998), 349.

69. Taussig, *Defacement*, 4, emphasis added.

Chapter 4

1. Herbert Muschamp, "Things Generally Wrong in the Universe," *New York Times,* May 30, 1993, Arts and Leisure section, 30.
2. There are many ways in which the themes of sacrifice that I am spelling out here parallel those of Girard, but there are, I believe, strong divergences from Girard's theories. In *Things Hidden Since the Foundation of the World* (Stanford: Stanford University Press, 1978) and *The Scapegoat* (Baltimore: Johns Hopkins University Press, 1986).
3. Cf. Maurice Blanchot, *The Unavowable Community,* trans. Pierre Joris (Tarrytown, NY: Station Hill Press, 1988); and Jean-Luc Nancy, *The Inoperative Community,* trans. Lisa Garbas et al. (Minneapolis: University of Minnesota Press, 1991).
4. See Victor Turner, "Liminality and Communitas," in *The Ritual Process* (New York: Aldine de Gruyter, 1995), 94–130.
5. Wolin, *Walter Benjamin,* 132.
6. Kristeva, "Women's Time," in *The Kristeva Reader,* 210. trans. Alice Jardine and Harry Blake.
7. Jacques Derrida, *Dissemination,* trans. Barbara Johnson (Chicago: University of Chicago Press, 1981), 133.
8. Indeed, the many notebooks of Benjamin's unfinished *Arcades Project* were left in Bataille's care at the Bibliothèque Nationale. For more on the College of Sociology, see Denis Hollier's edited *The College of Sociology, 1937–1939* (Minneapolis: University of Minnesota Press, 1988).
9. Zola, "Les Squares," in *Contes et nouvelles,* ed. Roger Ripoll (Paris: Gallimard, 1976). Discussed in Denis Hollier, *Against Architecture: The Writings of Georges Bataille,* trans. Betsy Wing (Cambridge, MA: MIT Press, 1989).
10. Bataille, *Oeuvres complètes, vol. 13,* ed. Henri Mitterand, ed. (Paris: Cercle du Livre Précieux, 1968), 194. Quoted in Hollier, *Against Architecture,* xvii.
11. Hollier, *Against Architecture,* xxii. For a fictionalized account of Zola's views of a modern Paris, see his novel, *The Belly of Paris,* trans. Ernest Alfred Vizetelly (Los Angeles: Sun and Moon Press, 1996).
12. Quotations from "Abattoir" and "Musée" in Denis Hollier, *Against Architecture,* xii–xiii.
13. Ibid., xiii.
14. Georges Bataille, *Erotism: Death & Sensuality,* trans. Mary Dalwood (San Francisco: City Lights, 1986), 89.
15. Ibid., 92.
16. Part of this first section appeared in a similar form as part of my article "Seeing the Body of Death: Sacrifice and Giving in Rembrandts' *The Slaughtered Ox,*" *Soundings* 85.3–4 (Fall/Winter 2002): 235–260.
17. On the relation of the *Arcades Project* to Talmudic dimensions, see Henry Sussman, "Between the Registers: The Allegory of Space in Walter Benjamin's *Arcades Project*" *boundary 2* 30.1 (2003): 169–90.
18. Maurice Blanchot, *The Infinite Conversation,* trans. Susan Hanson (Minneapolis: University of Minnesota Press, 1993), xii.
19. Anna Stüssi, "Erinnerung an die Zukunft," *Paelaestra,* 266 (1977), 59. Quoted in Graeme Gilloch, *Myth and Metropolis* (London: Polity Press, 1996), 76.
20. Gilloch, *Myth and Metropolis,* 77.
21. See Janet Wolff's writings, especially "The Invisible Flâneuse: Women and the Literature of Modernity," *Theory, Culture & Society* 2.3 (1985): 37–46.
22. Yosef Hayim Yerushalmi, *Zakhor: Jewish History and Jewish Memory* (Seattle: University of Washington Press, 1996), 110.
23. Ibid., 15.
24. Rainer Rochlitz, *The Disenchantment of Art ,* 210.
25. Arthur Danto, "The Vietnam Veterans Memorial," *The Nation,* Aug. 31,1986: 152. Quoted in James E. Young, *The Texture of Memory* (New Haven, CT: Yale University Press, 1993), 3. Young's work continues to be vital along these lines, though his difference between monuments and memorials is somewhat simpler. Memorials are the generic sites, days, books, and sculptures, whereas monuments are the plastic objects within the sites: "A memorial may be a day, a conference, or a space, but it need not be a monument. A monument, on the other hand, is always a kind of memorial" (ibid., 4).

Note also many other recent publications on the topic such as Robert S. Nelson and Margaret Olin, eds., *Monuments and Memory, Made and Unmade* (Chicago: University of Chicago Press, 2003); Jeffrey K. Olick, ed., *States of Memory: Continuities, Conflicts, and Transformations in National Retrospection* (Durham, NC: Duke University Press, 2003); and John Gillis, ed., *Commemorations: The Politics of National Identity* (Princeton, NJ: Princeton University Press, 1994).

26. Marita Sturken, "The Wall, the Screen, and the Image: The Vietnam Veterans Memorial," *Representations* 35 (Summer 1991): 120.

27. Yerushalmi, *Zakhor*, 44. There may also be something in Yerushalmi's account that strikes a difference between the monument and memorial as being the difference between Greek and Jew. Although not discussing monuments and memorials per se, he does suggest, "If Herodotus was the father of history, the fathers of meaning in history were the Jews" (8). It is little coincidence therefore that the Washington Monument adopts a Greek style.

28. Quoted in Gilloch, *Myth and Metropolis*, 73.

29. Gilloch, *Myth and Metropolis*, 73.

30. John McCole, *Walter Benjamin and the Antinomies of Tradition*, 261.

31. Ibid., 262–63.

32. As if the relation between the senses and memory needed scientific proof, three Swedish scholars recently discovered that tinnitus (ringing in the ears) impairs the ability to remember details of the past. In an experiment, cue words were read to members of one group not suffering from tinnitus and one group that was, and the subjects were asked what autobiographical memories were triggered by various words. Those with tinnitus remembered events but were unable to recall much detail surrounding the events; those without tinnitus could go into great detail about the past. Gerhard Andersson, Christian Ingerholt, Markus Jansson, *Psychology & Health*, 18.5 (Oct. 2003): 667.

33. Fredric Jameson, *Signatures of the Visible* (New York: Routledge, 1990), 1–2.

34. C. Nadia Seremetakis, "Memory of the Senses," in *The Senses Still: Perception and Memory as Material Culture in Modernity,* ed. C. Nadia Seremetakis (Chicago: University of Chicago Press, 1996), 5–6.

35. Ibid., 9.

36. Pierre Nora, "Between Memory and History: *Les Lieux de Mémoire*," trans. Marc Rousebush, *Representations* 26 (1989): 13.

37. Danièle Hervieu-Léger, *Religion as a Chain of Memory*, trans. Simon Lee. (New Brunswick, NJ: Rutgers University Press, 2000); Smith, *Imagining Religion,* 20.

38. Tyrus Miller, "Mimesis, Mimicry, and Critical Theory in Exile: Walter Benjamin's Approach to the Collège de Sociologie," in *Borders, Exile, Diasporas*, eds. Elazar Barkan and Marie Denis Shelton (Stanford: Stanford University Press, 1998).

39. Pierre Klossowski, "Between Marx and Fourier," in *On Walter Benjamin*, ed. Gary C. Smith trans. Susan Z. Bernstein, (Chicago: University of Chicago Press, 1988), 369.

40. Terry Eagleton, The *Ideology of the Aesthetic*, 28.

41. Blanchot, *The Unavowable Community*, 25.

Bibliography

Abbas, M.A. *Walter Benjamin's Collector: The Fate of Modern Experience*. Milwaukee, WI: University of Wisconsin–Milwaukee Center for Twentieth Century Studies, 1986.

Adorno, Theodor. *Negative Dialectics*. Translated by E.B. Ashton. New York: Seabury Press, 1973.

Adorno, Theodor W., Henri Lonitz, and Walter Benjamin. *The Complete Correspondence, 1928–1940*. Cambridge: Polity Press, 1999.

Aho, James. *The Orifice as Sacrificial Site: Culture, Organization, and the Body*. Hawthorne, NY: Aldine de Gruyter, 2002.

Alter, Robert. *Necessary Angels: Tradition and Modernity in Kafka, Benjamin, and Scholem*. Cambridge, MA: Harvard University Press, 1991.

American Heritage Dictionary. 3d ed. Boston: Houghton Mifflin, 1992.

Andersson, Gerhard, Christian Ingerholt, and Markus Jannson. "Autobiographical Memory in Patients with Tinnitus." *Psychology and Health* 18, no. 5 (October 2003): 667–75.

Apostolos-Cappadona, Diane. *Art, Creativity, and the Sacred: An Anthology in Religion and Art*. New York: Crossroad, 1995.

Attridge, Derek. "Innovation, Literature, Ethics: Relating to the Other." *PMLA* 114, no. 1 (1999): 21–31.

Babb, Lawrence A., and Susan S. Wadley, eds. *Media and the Transformation of Religion in South Asia*. Philadelphia: University of Pennsylvania Press, 1995.

Balthasar, Hans Urs von. *The Glory of the Lord: A Theological Aesthetics*. San Francisco and New York: Ignatius Press; Crossroad, 1983–1991.

Bataille, Georges. *Erotism: Death and Sensuality*. Translated by Mary Dalwood. San Francisco: City Lights, 1986.

———. *Inner Experience*. Translated by Leslie Anne Boldt. Albany: State University of New York, 1988.

Baudrillard, Jean. *The Transparency of Evil: Essays on Extreme Phenomena*. London and New York: Verso, 1993.

Baumgarten, Alexander. *Reflections on Poetry*. Translated by Karl Aschenbrenner and William B. Holther. Berkeley: University of California Press, 1954.

Beal, Timothy. *The Book of Hiding*. New York: Routledge, 1997.

———. *Religion and Its Monsters*. New York: Routledge, 2002.

Begbie, Jeremy. *Voicing Creation's Praise: Towards a Theology of the Arts*. Edinburgh: T. & T. Clark, 1991.

Bell, Clive. *Art*. London: Chatto & Windus, 1914.

Benjamin, Andrew E., and Peter Osborne. *Walter Benjamin's Philosophy: Destruction and Experience*. London: Routledge, 1994.

Benjamin, Walter. *The Correspondence of Walter Benjamin*. Edited by Gershom Scholem and Theodor W. Adorno. Translated by Manfred R. Jacobson and Evelyn M. Jacobson. Chicago: University of Chicago Press, 1994.

———. *Illuminations*. 1st ed. Translated by Harry Zohn. New York: Harcourt Brace & World, 1968.

———. *The Origin of German Tragic Drama*. Translated by John Osborne. London: Verso, 1977.

Benjamin, Walter. Marcus Paul Bullock, and Michael William Jennings. *Selected Writings.* Cambridge, MA: Belknap Press of Harvard University Press, 1996.

Benjamin, Walter. and Peter Demetz. *Reflections: Essays, Aphorisms, Autobiographical Writings.* New York: Harcourt Brace Jovanovich, 1978.

Benjamin, Walter. Gershom Scholem, and Theodor Adorno. *The Correspondence of Walter Benjamin and Gershom Scholem, 1932–1940.* New York: Schocken Books, 1989.

Benjamin, Walter. and Rolf Tiedemann. *The Arcades Project.* Cambridge, MA: Belknap Press of Harvard University Press, 1999.

Bernd, Witte. *Walter Benjamin: An Intellectual Biography.* Detroit: Wayne Statch University Press, 1991.

Bhatt, Govardhan P. *The Basic Ways of Knowing: An In-Depth Study of Kumarila's Contribution to Indian Epistemology.* 2d ed. Delhi: Motilal Banarsidass, 1989.

Biro, Matthew. *Anselm Kiefer and the Philosophy of Martin Heidegger.* Cambridge: Cambridge University Press, 1998.

Blanchot, Maurice. *The Infinite Conversation.* Translated by Susan Hanson. Minneapolis: University of Minnesota Press, 1993.

———. *The Unavowable Community.* Translated by Pierre Joris. Tarrytown, NY: Station Hill Press, 1988.

———. *The Work of Fire.* Translated by Charlotte Mandell. Stanford: Stanford University Press, 1995.

Bloch, Ernst. *Aesthetics and Politics.* London: NLB, 1977.

Bloom, Harold. *The Anxiety of Influence.* London: Oxford University Press, 1973.

Boer, Roland. "The Bowels of History, or the Perpetuation of Biblical Myth in Walter Benjamin." *Journal of Narrative Theory* 32, no. 3 (2002): 370–89.

Bordwell, David, and Kristin Thompson. *Film Art.* 6th ed. New York: McGraw-Hill, 2001.

Britt, Brian M. *Walter Benjamin and the Bible.* New York: Continuum, 1996.

Brodersen, Momme, and Martina Dervis. *Walter Benjamin: A Biography.* Translated by Malcolm R. Green and Ingrida Ligers. London: Verso, 1996.

Buci-Glucksmann, Christine. *Baroque Reason: The Aesthetics of Modernity.* London/Thousand Oaks, CA: Sage, 1994.

Buck-Morss, Susan. "Aesthetics and Anaesthetics: Walter Benjamin's Artwork Essay Reconsidered." *New Formations* 20 (1993).

———. *Dreamworld and Catastrophe: The Passing of Mass Utopia in East and West.* Cambridge, MA: MIT Press, 2000.

———. *The Origin of Negative Dialectics: Theodor W. Adorno, Walter Benjamin and the Frankfurt Institute.* New York: Free Press, 1997.

Buck-Morss, Susan, and Walter Benjamin. *The Dialectics of Seeing: Walter Benjamin and the Arcades Project.* Cambridge, MA: MIT Press, 1989.

Cadava, Eduardo. *Words of Light: Theses on the Photography of History.* Princeton, NJ: Princeton University Press, 1997.

Carroll, Noël. *The Philosophy of Art.* London: Routledge, 1999.

Caygill, Howard. "Benjamin, Heidegger, and Tradition." In *Walter Benjamin's Philosophy: Destruction and Experience,* edited by Andrew Benjamin and Peter Osborne. New York: Routledge, 1994. 1–31.

———. *Introducing Walter Benjamin.* New York: Totem Books, 1998.

———. *Walter Benjamin: The Colour of Experience.* London: Routledge, 1998.

Caygill, Howard, Alex Coles, and Richard Appignanesi. *Introducing Walter Benjamin.* Duxford: Icon, 2000.

Certeau, Michel de. *The Practice of Everyday Life.* Berkeley: University of California Press, 1984.

César, Jasiel. *Walter Benjamin on Experience and History: Profane Illumination.* San Francisco: Mellen Research University Press, 1992.

Chidester, David. *Word and Light: Seeing, Hearing, and Religious Discourse.* Urbana: University of Illinois Press, 1992.

Chopp, Rebecca. *The Power to Speak.* New York: Crossroad, 1989.

Cixous, Hélène. "Castration or Decapitation?" In *Out There: Marginalization and Contemporary Culture,* edited by Russell Ferguson et al., translated by Annette Kuhn. New York: New Museum of Contemporary Art, 1990. 345–56.

Cixous, Hélène, and Catherine Clément. *The Newly Born Woman.* Translated by Betsy Wing. Minneapolis: University of Minnesota Press, 1986.

Classen, Constance. *The Color of Angels: Cosmology, Gender, and the Aesthetic Imagination*. New York: Routledge, 1998.

———. *Worlds of Sense: Exploring the Senses in History and Across Cultures*. New York: Routledge, 1993.

Clifford, Gay. *The Transformations of Allegory*. London: Routledge and Kegan Paul, 1974.

Clifford, Geertz. "Religion as a Cultural System." In *The Interpretation of Cultures*. New York: Basic Books, 1983. 87–125.

Cohen, Margaret. *Profane Illumination: Walter Benjamin and the Paris of Surrealist Revolution*. Berkeley: University of California Press, 1993.

Cohen, Richard. *Jewish Icons: Art and Society in Modern Europe*. Berkeley: University of California Press, 1998.

Coles, Alex. *The Optic of Walter Benjamin*. London: Black Dog Publishing, 1999.

Conger, George Perrigo. *Theories of Macrocosms and Microcosms in the History of Philosophy*. New York: Russell & Russell, 1967.

Cornell, Drucilla. *The Philosophy of the Limit*. New York: Routledge, 1992.

———. *Beyond Accommodation*. Lanham, MA: Rowman & Littlefield, 1999.

Crary, Jonathan. *Techniques of the Observer: On Vision and Modernity in the Nineteenth Century*. Cambridge, MA: MIT Press, 1990.

———, and NetLibrary Inc. *Suspensions of Perception: Attention, Spectacle, and Modern Culture*. Cambridge, MA: MIT Press, 1999.

Crimp, Douglas, and Louise Lawler. *On the Museum's Ruins*. Cambridge, MA: MIT Press, 1993.

Davey, Nicholas. "The Hermeneutics of Seeing." In *Interpreting Visual Culture*, edited by Ian Heywood and Barry Sandywell. London: Routledge, 1999.

Deren, Maya. "Cinematography: The Creative Uses of Reality." In *The Avant-Garde Film*, edited by P. Adams Sitney. New York: Anthology Film Archives, 1978, 60–73.

———. *The Divine Horsemen*. New York: Chelsea Hoouse, 1970.

———. "Notes on Ritual and Ordeal." *Film Culture* 39 (1965): 10.

Derrida, Jacques. *Dissemination*. Translated by Barbara Johnson. Chicago: University of Chicago Press, 1981.

———. "Psyche: Inventions of the Other." In *Reading De Man Reading*, edited by Lindsay Waters and Wlad Godzich. Minneapolis: University of Minnesota Press, 1989, 25–65.

Desjarlais, Robert R. *Sensory Biographies: Lives and Deaths Among Nepal's Yolmo Buddhists*. Berkeley: University of California Press, 2003.

Doniger, Wendy. *The Implied Spider: Politics and Theology in Myth*. New York: Columbia University Press, 1998.

Doty, William G. *Mythography: The Study of Myths and Rituals*. 2d ed. Tuscaloosa: University of Alabama Press, 2000.

Douglas, Mary. *Purity and Danger*. London: Routlege and Kegan Paul, 1966.

Drob, Sanford L. *Symbols of the Kabbalah: Philosophical and Psychological Perspectives*. Northvale, NJ: Jason Aronson, 2000.

Drucker, Johanna. *The Alphabetic Labyrinth*. New York: Thames & Hudson, 1995.

Duncan, Carol. *Civilizing Rituals: Inside Public Art Museums*. London: Routledge, 1995.

Eagleton, Terry. *The Ideology of the Aesthetic*. Oxford: Basil Blackwell, 1990.

———. *Walter Benjamin, or, Towards a Revolutionary Criticism*. London: Verso, 1981.

Eck, Diana L. *Darshan, Seeing the Divine Image in India*. 3d ed. New York: Columbia University Press, 1998.

Eiland, Howard. "Reception in Distraction." *boundary 2* 30, no. 1 (2003): 51–66.

Eilberg-Schwartz, Howard. *God's Phallus and Other Problems for Men and Monotheism*. Boston: Beacon Press, 1994.

Eisenstein, Elizabeth. *The Printing Revolution in Early Modern Europe*. Cambridge: Cambridge University Press, 1983.

Eliade, Mircea. *The Sacred and the Profane*. Translated by Willard R. Trask. San Diego, CA: Harcourt, Brace, 1959.

Elkins, James. "Preface to the Book *A Skeptical Introduction to Visual Culture*." *Journal of Visual Culture* 1, no. 1 (April 2002): 93–99.

Farley, Edward. *Faith and Beauty*. Burlington, VT: Ashgate, 2001.

Ferris, David S. *Walter Benjamin: Theoretical Questions*. Stanford: Stanford University Press, 1996.

Fineman, Joel. *The Rediscovery of Gnosticism.* Vol. 1. Edited by Bentley Layton. Leiden: E.J. Brill, 1990.

————. "The Structure of Allegorical Desire." *October* 12 (1980).

Fitzgerald, Timothy. "Experience." In *Guide to the Study of Religion,* edited by Willi Braun and Russell T. McCutcheon, London: Cassell, 2000, 125–39.

Flèche, Betsy. "The Art of Survival: The Translation of Walter Benjamin." *SubStance* 28, no. 2 (1999): 95–109.

Fletcher, Angus. *Allegory: The Theory of a Symbolic Mode.* Ithaca, NY: Cornell University Press, 1964.

Foster, Mary LeCron. "Symbolism: The Foundation of Culture." In *Companion Encyclopedia of Anthropology,* edited by Tim Ingold. London: Routledge, 1994, 366–95.

Foucault, Michel. *The Order of Things.* Translated by Alan Sheridan. New York: Random House, 1970.

————. *This Is Not a Pipe.* Translated by James Harkness. Berkeley: University of California Press, 1982.

Francis, Richard, Homi K. Bhabha, and Yve Alain Bois, eds. *Negotiating Rapture: The Power of Art to Transform Lives.* Chicago: Museum of Contemporary Art, 1996.

Freeman, Judi, and John C. Welchman. *The Dada & Surrealist Word-Image.* Los Angeles: Los Angeles County Museum of Art/Cambridge, MA: MIT Press, 1989.

Freud, Sigmund. *The Ego and the Id.* Translated by James Strachey. Vol. XIX of the Standard Edition. London: Hogarth Press, 1961.

Frisby, David. *Fragments of Modernity: Theories of Modernity in the Work of Simmel, Kracauer, and Benjamin.* 1st MIT Press ed. Cambridge, MA: MIT Press, 1986.

García-Rivera, Alejandro. *The Community of the Beautiful: A Theological Aesthetics.* Collegeville, MN: Liturgical Press, 1999.

Geaney, Jane. *On the Epistemology of the Senses in Early Chinese Thought.* Honolulu: University of Hawaii Press, 2002.

Geertz, Clifford. *The Interpretation of Cultures.* New York: Basic Books, 1973.

Geurts, Kathryn Linn. *Culture and the Senses: Bodily Ways of Knowing in an African Community.* Berkeley: University of California Press, 2002.

Gillis, John, ed. *Commemorations: The Politics of National Identity.* Princeton, NJ: Princeton University Press, 1994.

Gilloch, Graeme. *Myth and Metropolis: Walter Benjamin and the City.* Cambridge, UK: Polity Press in association with Blackwell Publishers, 1996.

————. *Walter Benjamin: Critical Constellations.* London: Polity Press, 2002.

Girard, René. *The Scapegoat.* Baltimore: Johns Hopkins University Press, 1986.

————. *Things Hidden Since the Foundation of the World.* Stanford: Stanford University Press, 1978.

Gold, Daniel. *Aesthetics and Analysis in Writing on Religion: Modern Fascinations.* Berkeley: University of California Press, 2003.

Greenberg, Clement. "Modernist Painting." In *The Collected Essays and Criticism.* Vol. 4. Chicago: University of Chicago Press, 1993.

Greenfield, Sayre. *The Ends of Allegory.* Newark: University of Delaware Press, 1988.

Grimes, Ronald L. *Deeply into the Bone: Re-Inventing Rites of Passage.* Berkeley: University of California Press, 2000.

Handelman, Susan A. *Fragments of Redemption: Jewish Thought and Literary Theory in Benjamin, Scholem, and Levinas.* Bloomington: Indiana University Press, 1991.

————. *The Slayers of Moses: The Emergence of Rabbinic Interpretation in Modern Literary Theory.* Albany: State University of New York Press, 1982.

Hansen, Miriam W. "Benjamin, Cinema and Experience: 'The Blue Flower in the Land of Technology.'" *New German Critique* 40 (1987): 179–224.

Hanssen, Beatrice. *Walter Benjamin's Other History: Of Stones, Animals, Human Beings, and Angels.* Berkeley: University of California Press, 1998.

Hanssen, Beatrice, and Andrew E. Benjamin, eds. *Walter Benjamin and Romanticism, Walter Benjamin Studies Series.* New York: Continuum, 2002.

Hawkes, Terence. *Structuralism and Semiotics.* Berkeley: University of California Press, 1977.

Hegel, Georg Wilhelm Friedrich. *Hegel on the Arts.* Translated by Henry Paolucci. New York: Frederick Ungar, 1979.

———. *Introductory Lectures on Aesthetics.* Translated by Bernard Bosanquet. London: Penguin, 1993.

Heidegger, Martin. *Basic Writings.* Edited by David Farrell Krell. Translated by Albert Hofstader. New York: HarperCollins, 1993.

Hervieu-Léger, Danièle. *Religion as a Chain of Memory.* Translated by Simon Lee. New Brunswick, NJ: Rutgers University Press, 2000.

Hewitt, Marsha. *Critical Theory of Religion: A Feminist Analysis.* Minneapolis: Augsburg Fortress Press, 1995.

Hoffman, Donald D. *Visual Intelligence: How We Create What We See.* New York: W.W. Norton, 1998.

Hollier, Denis. *Against Architecture: The Writings of Georges Bataille.* Translated by Betsy Wing. Cambridge, MA: MIT Press, 1989.

Hollier, Denis, ed. *The College of Sociology, 1937–1939.* Minneapolis: University of Minnesota Press, 1988.

Hooper-Greenhill, Eilean. *Museums and the Shaping of Knowledge.* London: Routledge, 1992.

Howes, David, ed. *Varieties of Sensory Experience: A Sourcebook in the Anthropology of the Senses.* Toronto: University of Toronto Press, 1991.

Humphrey, Nicholas. *A History of the Mind.* New York: Simon & Schuster, 1992.

Hunter, Ian. "Aesthetics and Cultural Studies." In *Cultural Studies,* edited by Lawrence Grossberg, Cary Nelson, and Paula A. Treichler. New York: Routledge, 1992.

Irigaray, Luce. "The Fecundity of the Caress." In *An Ethics of Sexual Difference.* Translated by Carolyn Burke and Gillian C. Gill. Ithaca, NY: Cornell University Press, 1993.

———. *This Sex Which Is Not One.* Ithaca, NY: Cornell University Press, 1985.

Jacobs, Carol. *In the Language of Walter Benjamin.* Baltimore: Johns Hopkins University Press, 1999.

Jakobson, Roman, and Morris Halle. *Fundamentals of Language.* The Hague: Mouton, 1971.

Jantzen, Grace M. "Beauty for Ashes: Notes on the Displacement of Beauty." *Literature and Theology* 16, no. 4 (2002): 427–49.

Jennings, Michael William. *Dialectical Images: Walter Benjamin's Theory of Literary Criticism.* Ithaca, NY: Cornell University Press, 1987.

Judovitz, Dalia. *Unpacking Duchamp.* Berkeley: University of California Press, 1995.

Kafka, Franz. *Parables and Paradoxes.* New York: Schocken Books, 1961.

Kandinsky, Wassily. *Concerning the Spiritual in Art.* Translated by M.T.H. Sadler. New York: Dover, 1977.

Kant, Immanuel. Translated by Werner S. Pluhar. *Critique of Judgement.* Indianapolis, IN: Hackett, 1987.

Keefer, Kyle, and Tod Linafelt. "The End of Desire: Theologies of Eros in the Song of Songs and *Breaking the Waves.*" In *Imag(in)ing Otherness: Filmic Visions of Living Together,* edited by S. Brent Plate and David Jasper. Atlanta: American Academy of Religion/New York: Oxford University Press, 1999, 49–60.

Keller, Catherine. *Face of the Deep: A Theology of Becoming.* London: Routledge, 2003.

Kelley, Theresa M. *Reinventing Allegory.* Cambridge, MA: Cambridge University Press, 1997.

Klossowski, Pierre. "Between Marx and Fourier." In *On Walter Benjamin,* edited by Gary C. Smith, translated by Susan Z. Bernstein. Cambridge, MA: MIT Press, 1988, 367–70.

Koepnick, Lutz P. *Walter Benjamin and the Aesthetics of Power.* Lincoln: University of Nebraska, 1999.

Kohlenbach, Margarete. *Walter Benjamin: Self-Reference and Religiosity.* New York: Palgrave Macmillan, 2002.

Kristeva, Julia. *The Kristeva Reader.* Edited by Toril Moi. Translated by Seán Hand. New York: Columbia University Press, 1986.

———. *Revolution in Poetic Language.* Translated by Léon Roudiez. New York: Columbia University Press, 1984.

Lacan, Jacques. *The Four Fundamental Concepts of Psycho-Analysis.* Translated by Alan Sheridan. New York: W.W. Norton, 1981.

———. "The Mirror Stage." In *Écrits: A Selection.* Translated by Alan Sheridan. New York: W.W. Norton, 1997.

Lavin, Maud. *Cut with the Kitchen Knife: The Weimar Photomontages of Hannah Höch.* New Haven, CT: Yale University Press, 1993.

Lawrence, John Shelton, and Robert Jewett. *The Myth of the American Superhero.* Grand Rapids, MI: W.B. Eerdmans, 2002.

Lessing, Gotthold Ephraim. *Laocoön.* New York: Farrar, Straus, & Giroux, 1969.

Levinas, Emmanuel. *Totality and Infinity.* Translated by Alphonso Lingis. Pittsburgh: Duquesne University Press, 1969.

Linafelt, Tod. *Surviving Lamentations: Catastrophe, Lament, and Protest in the Afterlife of a Biblical Book.* Chicago: University of Chicago Press, 2000.

Lindberg, David C. *Theories of Vision from al-Kindi to Kepler.* Chicago: University of Chicago Press, 1976.

Livingstone, Margaret. *Vision and Art: The Biology of Seeing.* New York: Harry Abrams, 2002.

Lutgendorf, Philip. *The Life of a Text: Performing the Ramcaritmanas of Tulsidas.* Berkeley: University of California Press, 1991.

Lyotard, Jean François. *The Postmodern Condition: A Report on Knowledge.* Minneapolis: University of Minnesota Press, 1984.

Madsen, Deborah. *Rereading Allegory.* New York: St. Martin's Press, 1994.

Maleuvre, Didier. *Museum Memories: History, Technology, Art.* Stanford: Stanford University Press, 1999.

Mali, Joseph. "The Reconciliation of Myth: Benjamin's Homage to Bachofen." *Journal of the History of Ideas* 60, no. 1 (1999): 165–87.

Man, John. *Alpha Beta: How 26 Letters Shaped the Western World.* New York: John Wiley, 2000.

Marcus, Laura, and Lynda Nead, eds. *The Actuality of Walter Benjamin.* London: Lawrence and Wishart, 1998.

Martin, Nancy M. "North Indian Hindi Devotional Literature." In *The Blackwell Companion to Hinduism,* edited by Gavin Flood, Oxford: Basil Blackwell, 2003, 182–98.

Masuzawa, Tomoko. *In Search of Dreamtime: The Quest for the Origin of Religion.* Chicago: University of Chicago Press, 1993.

Matter, Ann. *The Voice of My Beloved.* Philadelphia: University of Pennsylvania Press, 1990.

McBride, James. "Marooned in the Realm of the Profane: Walter Benjamin's Synthesis of Kabbalah and Communism." *Journal of the American Academy of Religion* 57, no. 2 (1987): 241–66.

McCole, John. *Walter Benjamin and the Antinomies of Tradition.* Ithaca, NY: Cornell University Press, 1993.

McFague, Sallie. *Metaphorical Theology.* Philadelphia: Fortress, 1985.

———. *Models of God.* Philadelphia: Fortress, 1987.

Menninghaus, Winfried. "Walter Benjamin's Theory of Myth." In *On Walter Benjamin,* edited by Gary C. Smith, translated by Susan Z. Bernstein. Cambridge, MA: MIT Press, 1988.

Metz, Christian. *The Imaginary Signifier: Psychoanalysis and the Cinema.* Bloomington: Indiana University Press, 1982.

Miles, Margaret. "Image." In *Critical Terms for Religious Studies,* edited by Mark C. Taylor. Chicago: University of Chicago Press, 1998, 160–72.

Miller, Nancy K., ed. *The Poetics of Gender.* New York: Columbia University Press, 1986.

Miller, Tyrus. "Mimesis, Mimicry, and Critical Theory in Exile: Walter Benjamin's Approach to the Collège de Sociologie." In *Borders, Exile, Diaspora.* Edited by Elazar Barkan and Marie Denis Shelton. Stanford: Stanford University Press, 1998.

Mirzoeff, Nicholas. *The Visual Culture Reader.* 2d ed. New York: Routledge, 2002.

Missac, Pierre, and Shierry Weber Nicholsen. *Walter Benjamin's Passages.* Cambridge, MA: MIT Press, 1995.

Murphy, Roland. *The Song of Songs.* Minneapolis: Augsburg Fortress, 1990.

Muschamp, Herbert. "Things Generally Wrong in the Universe." *New York Times,* May 30, 1993. Arts and Leisures section, 30.

Nägele, Rainer. *Theater, Theory, Speculation: Walter Benjamin and the Scenes of Modernity.* Baltimore: Johns Hopkins University Press, 1991.

Nancy, Jean-Luc. *The Inoperative Community.* Translated by Lisa Garbus, Michael Holland, Peter Connor, and Simona Sawhney. Minneapolis: University of Minnesota Press, 1991.

Nelson, Robert S. "The Slide Lecture, or the Work of Art History in the Age of Mechanical Reproduction." *Critical Inquiry* 26, no. 3 (Spring 2000): 414–34.

Nelson, Robert S., and Margaret Olin, eds. *Monuments and Memory, Made and Unmade.* Chicago: University of Chicago Press, 2003.

Nora, Pierre. "Between Memory and History: *Les Lieux de Mémoire.*" Translated by Marc Rousebush. *Representations,* 26 (1989): 13.

Northrup, Lesley. *Ritualizing Women.* Cleveland: Pilgrim Press, 1997.

Olick, Jeffrey K., ed. *States of Memory: Continuities, Conflicts, and Transformations of National Retrospection.* Durham, NC: Duke University Press, 2003.

Ong, Walter. *Orality and Literacy.* London: Routledge, 1982.

———. *The Presence of the Word.* Minneapolis: University of Minnesota Press, 1981.

Otto, Rudolf. *The Idea of the Holy.* Translated by John Harvey. London: Oxford University Press, 1958.

Ouaknin, Marc-Alain. *Mysteries of the Alphabet.* Translated by Josephine Bacon. New York: Abbeville Press, 1999.

———. *The Mysteries of the Kabbalah.* Translated by Josephine Bacon. New York: Abbeville Press, 2000.

Owens, Craig. *Beyond Recognition: Representation, Power, and Culture.* Berkeley: University of California Press, 1992.

Paden, William. *Religious Worlds: The Comparative Study of Religion.* Boston: Beacon Press, 1994.

Paine, Crispin. *Godly Things: Museums, Objects, and Religion.* London: Leicester University Press, 2000.

Patt, Lise, and the Institute of Cultural Inquiry. *Benjamin's Blind Spot: Walter Benjamin and the Premature Death of Aura: With the Manual of Lost Ideas.* Santa Monica, CA: Institute of Cultural Inquiry, 2001.

Patton, Kimberley C., and Benjamin C. Ray, eds. *A Magic Still Dwells.* Berkeley: University of California Press, 2000.

Pecora, Vincent. "Benjamin, Kracauer and Redemptive History." *Genre,* 35 (2002): 55–87.

Pensky, Max. *Melancholy Dialectics: Walter Benjamin and the Play of Mourning.* Amherst: University of Massachusetts Press, 1993.

Pinney, Christopher. "Photographic Portraiture in Central India in the 1980s and 1990s." In *The Material Culture Reader,* edited by Victor Buchli. Oxford: Berg Publishers, 2002, 81–103.

Plate, S. Brent "Seeing the Body of Death: Sacrifice and Giving in Rembrandt's *The Slaughtered Ox.*" *Soundings* 85, no. 3–4 (Fall/Winter 2002): 235–60.

———, ed. *Religion, Art, and Visual Culture: A Cross-Cultural Reader.* New York: Palgrave Macmillan, 2002.

———, ed. *Representing Religion in World Cinema: Filmmaking, Mythmaking, Culture Making.* New York: Palgrave Macmillan, 2003.

Plate, S. Brent, and David Jasper, eds. *Imag(in)ing Otherness: Filmic Versions of Living Together.* Atlanta: Scholars Press, 1999.

Prentiss, Karen Pechilis. *The Embodiment of Bhakti.* Oxford: Oxford University Press, 1999.

Proudfoot, Wayne. *Religious Experience.* Berkeley: University of California Press, 1985.

Renfrew, Colin. *Figuring It Out: What Are We? Where Do We Come From? The Parallel Visions of Artists and Archaeologists.* London: Thames & Hudson, 2003.

Richter, Gerhard. *Benjamin's Ghosts: Interventions in Contemporary Literary and Cultural Theory.* Stanford: Stanford University Press, 2002.

———. *Walter Benjamin and the Corpus of Autobiography.* Detroit: Wayne State University Press, 2000.

Ricoeur, Paul. *The Symbolism of Evil.* Translated by Emerson Buchanan. Boston: Beacon Press, 1967.

Robbins, Jill. *Prodigal Son/Elder Brother: Interpretation and Alterity in Augustine, Petrarch, Kafka, and Levinas.* Chicago: University of Chicago Press, 1991.

Rochlitz, Rainer. *The Disenchantment of Art: The Philosophy of Walter Benjamin.* New York: Guilford Press, 1996.

Rollinson, Philip. *Classical Theories of Allegory and Christian Culture.* Pittsburgh: Duquesne University Press, 1981.

Saltzman, Lisa. *Anselm Kiefer and Art After Auschwitz.* Cambridge, MA: Cambridge University Press, 1999.

Saussure, Ferdinand. *Course in General Linguistics.* Edited by Charles Bally and Albert Sechehaye. Translated by Wade Baskin. New York: Philosophical Library, 1959.

Scholem, Gershom. "Letter to Benjamin." In *Aesthetics and Politics,* edited by Ernst Bloch. London: Verso, 1980.

———. *On Jews and Judaism in Crisis: Selected Essays.* New York: Schocken Books, 1976.

———. *Origins of the Kabbalah.* Edited by R.J. Zwi Werblowski. Translated by Allan Arkush. New York: The Jewish Publication Society/Princeton, NJ: Princeton University Press, 1987.

———. *Walter Benjamin: The Story of a Friendship.* Philadelphia: Jewish Publication Society of America, 1981.

Schwartz, Regina. *The Curse of Cain.* Chicago: University of Chicago Press, 1997.

Seremetakis, C. Nadia. "Memory of the Senses." In *The Senses Still: Perception and Memory As Material Culture in Modernity,* edited by C. Nadia Seremtakis. Chicago: University of Chicago Press, 1996.

Serres, Michel. *Angels: A Modern Myth.* Translated by Francis Cowper. Paris/New York: Flammarion, 1995.

———. *Les Cinq Sens,* Paris: B. Grasset, 1985.

Seyhan, Azade. "Visual Citations: Walter Benjamin's Dialectic of Text and Image." In *Languages of Visuality,* edited by Beate Allert. Detroit: Wayne State University Press, 1996, 229–41.

Sharf, Robert. "Experience." In *Critical Terms for Religious Studies,* edited by Mark C. Taylor. Chicago: University of Chicago Press, 1998, 94–116.

Shlain, Leonard. *The Alphabet Versus the Goddess: The Conflict Between the Word and the Image.* New York: Viking Press, 1998.

Shokek, Shimon. *Kabbalah and the Art of Being.* London: Routledge, 2001.

Shusterman, Richard. "The End of Aesthetic Experience." *Journal of Aesthetics and Art Criticism* 55 (1999): 29–41.

———. *Performing Live.* Ithaca, NY: Cornell University Press, 2001.

———. "Somaesthetics: A Disciplinary Proposal." *Journal of Aesthetics and Art Criticism,* 57, no. 3 (1999): 299–313.

Silverman, Kaja. *The Subject of Semiotics.* Oxford: Oxford University Press, 1983.

———. *The Threshold of the Invisible World.* New York: Routledge, 1996.

Smart, Ninian. *Worldviews: Crosscultural Explorations of Human Beliefs.* 3d ed. Upper Saddle River, NJ: Prentice Hall, 2000.

Smith, Gary C. ed, *Benjamin—Philosophy, History, Aesthetics.* Chicago: University of Chicago Press, 1989.

———. *On Walter Benjamin: Critical Essays and Recollections.* Cambridge, MA: MIT Press, 1988.

Smith, Jonathan Z. *Imagining Religion: From Babylon to Jamestown.* Chicago: University of Chicago Press, 1982.

Snyder, Joel. "Benjamin on Reproducibility and Aura." In *Benjamin: Philosophy, Aesthetics, History,* edited by Gary C. Smith, Chicago: University of Chicago Press, 1989, 158–74.

Solso, Robert. *Cognition and the Visual Arts.* Cambridge, MA: MIT Press, 1996.

Starbuck, Edwin Diller. "The Intimate Senses as Sources of Wisdom." *Journal of Religion* 1, no. 2 (1921): 129–45.

Steinberg, Michael P. *Walter Benjamin and the Demands of History.* Ithaca, NY: Cornell University Press, 1996.

Stephens, Mitchell. *The Rise of the Image, the Fall of the Word.* New York: Oxford University Press, 1998.

Sturken, Marita. "The Wall, the Screen, and the Image: The Vietnam Veterans Memorial." *Representations* 35 (Summer 1991): 118–42.

Sussman, Henry. "Between the Registers: The Allegory of Space in Walter Benjamin's *Arcades Project.*" *boundary 2* 30, no. 1 (2003): 169–90.

Synnot, Anthony. *The Body Social.* London/New York: Routledge, 1993.

Taussig, Michael. *Defacement: Public Secrecy and the Labor of the Negative.* Stanford: Stanford University Press, 1999.

———. *Mimesis and Alterity: A Particular History of the Senses.* New York: Routledge, 1993.

———. "Transgression." In *Critical Terms for Religious Studies,* edited by Mark C. Taylor. Chicago: University of Chicago Press, 1998.

Taylor, Mark C. ed. *Critical Terms for Religious Studies.* Chicago: University of Chicago Press, 1998.

———. *Disfiguring: Art, Architecture, Religion.* Chicago: University of Chicago Press, 1992.

Tillich, Paul. *On Art and Architecture.* New York: Crossroad, 1987.

Turner, Denys. *Eros and Allegory: Medieval Exegesis of the Song of Songs.* Kalamazoo, MI: Cistercian Publications, 1995.

Turner, Victor. *The Ritual Process.* Hawthorne, NY: Aldine de Gruyter, 1995, 94–130.

Vinge, Louise. *The Five Senses: Studies in a Literary Tradition*. Lund: LiberLäromedel, 1975.

Waters, Lindsay, and Wlad Godzich, eds. *Reading De Man Reading*. Minneapolis: University of Minnesota Press, 1988.

Weber, Samuel. *Mass Mediauras*, Sydney: Power Publications, 1996.

Weigel, Sigrid. *Body- and Image-Space: Re-Reading Walter Benjamin*. Translated by Georgina Paul. London ; New York: Routledge, 1996.

Weissberg, Liliane. "In Plain Sight." In *Visual Culture and the Holocaust*, edited by Barbie Zelizer. New Brunswick, NJ: Rutgers University Press, 2001.

Welchman, John, and Judi Freeman. *Dada and Surrealist Word-Image*. Los Angeles: Los Angeles County Museum of Art/Cambridge, MA: MIT Press, 1989.

Westermann, Claus. *Lamentations: Issues and Interpretation*. Minneapolis: Augsburg Fortress, 1994.

Witte, Bernd. *Walter Benjamin: An Intellectual Biography*. Translated by James Rolleston. Detroit: Wayne State University Press, 1991.

Wolff, Janet. "The Feminine in Modern Art." *Theory, Culture, & Society* 17, no. 6 (2000): 33–54.

———. "The Invisible Flâneuse: Women and the Literature of Modernity." *Theory, Culture, & Society* 2, no. 3 (1985): 37–46.

Wolin, Richard. *Walter Benjamin: An Aesthetic of Redemption*. Berkeley: University of California Press, 1994.

Yerushalmi, Yosef Hayim. *Zakhor: Jewish History and Jewish Memory*. Seattle: University of Washington Press, 1996.

Young, James E. *The Texture of Memory*. New Haven, CT: Yale University Press, 1993.

Zeki, Semir. *Inner Vision: An Exploration of Art and the Brain*. New York: Oxford University Press, 1999.

Zola, Émile. *The Belly of Paris*. Translated by Ernest Alfred Vizetelly. Los Angeles: Sun and Moon Press, 1996.

———. "Les Squares." In *Contes et nouvelles,* edited by Roger Ripoll. Paris: Gallimaard, 1976.

Index